The name of M. Nelkon is associated with physics throughout the English-speaking world. Now a full-time author, he was previously Head of Science at William Ellis School, London and an examiner for the London, Cambridge and Welsh Boards. He is the co-author with M. V. Detheridge of *Advanced Physics* in the Pan Study Aids series.

M. V. Detheridge has wide teaching experience, and is currently Deputy Head Teacher at William Ellis School, London. He has been an examiner for the Oxford and Cambridge Board. He is the co-author with M. Nelkon of *Advanced Physics* in the Pan Study Aids series.

Both authors have first-class degrees in physics.

Pan Study Aids for GCSE include:

Accounting

Biology

Chemistry

Commerce

Computer Studies

Economics

English Language

French

Geography 1

Geography 2

German

History 1: World History since 1914

History 2: Britain and Europe since 1700

Human Biology

Mathematics

Physics

Sociology

Study Skills

PHYSICS

M. Nelkon and M. V. Detheridge

A Pan Original

Pan Books   London, Sydney and Auckland

First published 1987 by Pan Books Ltd,
Cavaye Place, London SW10 9PG

9 8 7 6 5 4 3

© M. Nelkon and M. V. Detheridge 1987

ISBN 0 330 29942 5

Text design by Peter Ward
Text illustration by M L Design
Photoset by Parker Typesetting Service, Leicester
Printed and bound in Spain by
Mateu Cromo SA, Madrid

CONTENTS

TO THE STUDENT

This book is a study guide in **Physics** for GCSE. It is not a full textbook but is intended to help you in your final revision for examinations. For greater detail in some sections you are recommended to consult *Principles of Physics*, by M Nelkon (Collins Educational).

The material included in this book covers all the main topics in the syllabuses of the examination boards. Not every topic is included in any particular syllabus. To help you decide which to study there is a **grid** printed after this preface. This grid lists each section of the book, and indicates by means of a dot, whether that section is in each syllabus. Find out which syllabus you are doing, and then you need only study the appropriate sections.

The GCSE national criteria require applications of physics to be discussed. To take account of this, we have included work on world energy resources, domestic electricity, applications of electronics, and nuclear power generation, as well as others.

To help you understand how GCSE papers are organized we have also made a chart which shows the various options open to you and the grades which are possible for any particular choice. For example, you will only be able to get the higher grades if you try the more difficult papers. On the other hand you need to be confident that you can handle these papers if you try them. It will be much harder to get marks on them. Your teacher will advise you on the best papers to take, and it would be wise to heed this advice.

When you read the text you will often come up against a '**Checklist**'. This is a short set of questions based on what has just gone before. Research has shown that it is wise to look back over (review) your work a short time after you have finished it. This is the purpose of the checklists – to give you a focus for that first review. It is also important to review work at intervals after that. An ideal plan would be to look back again – very quickly – the next day, then in a week's time, and then at a longer interval.

You will also find '**Summaries**'. These indicate what you should KNOW, what you should UNDERSTAND, and what you should be able to DO. Look through these carefully and make sure you can achieve as much of this as possible.

More difficult parts of the text are marked by a line in the margin:

These sections can be left out when you first read through the book. Many of these sections will also only be examined on the more difficult papers.

When you are working, make sure that you are in a **comfortable position**, at a **desk or table**. Use paper to make **short notes** on what you read. Make sure that you **jot down answers** to checklists, and that you **try the questions** on each section. Here are some questions to think about concerned with working:

1 Can you really keep your mind on the job lying on a bed, or sprawled in a comfortable arm chair?
2 Do you really need that extra snack, and if you do can you stop it turning into a feast taking ages to prepare and consume?
3 Do you really need to telephone your boy/girl friend to discuss that complicated bit about electricity? Can you really stop the conversation from going on to talk about the week's social activities?

EXAMS

You may meet a variety of types of exam question.

1 MULTIPLE CHOICE

Make sure you pace yourself during the paper. Don't go so quickly that you make silly mistakes, but don't spend so long on one question that you cannot finish the paper. If you can eliminate some alternatives, but are not sure between others, then guess from the ones that you can't eliminate.

2 SHORT ANSWER QUESTIONS

Here you give a short answer in words or do a small calculation. In doing calculations in any sort of written paper make sure you show your working. Write down the formula you are going to use before putting in the numbers. Make sure also that you do what the question asks. It is a good idea to underline words in the question such as 'state', 'explain', 'calculate', 'describe'. It is a waste of time, for example, to explain a law if you were only asked to state it. On the other hand, you cannot expect full marks for an explanation if you have only given a statement.

3 STRUCTURED QUESTIONS

These consist of a series of short answer questions often all related.

4 FREE RESPONSE QUESTIONS

Here you will have to do a more extended piece of writing. It will be much more up to you what you include and what you do not. Always try to be relevant, and make sure you divide your time up sensibly. It is almost always a mistake to spend too long on one question.

PRACTICAL WORK

All courses will contain an element of teacher assessed practical work. How and when this is done will depend a lot on your teacher, and the guidelines given for each syllabus. All schemes of assessment do, however, have some things in common. There are four broad areas and you will have to demonstrate your ability in each of these.

1 MEASUREMENT AND OBSERVATION

Can you make precise observations and accurate readings with a range of equipment used in a physics lab?

2 USE OF APPARATUS

Can you select the most approriate apparatus for a particular job. Can you set apparatus up correctly? Can you follow written instructions which may be given to you? Do you treat apparatus sensibly to prevent damage?

3 DESIGN OF EXPERIMENTS

Can you work out an experiment to measure something, or to test an idea? Can you design your experiment bearing in mind safety procedures?

4 RESULTS AND CONCLUSIONS

Can you set out results clearly using tables, graphs, charts or other methods? Can you make valid conclusions from the results? Can you write a clear report of your work?

STRUCTURE OF THE EXAMINATION

The following tables set out the structure of the examination for each board. Optional papers are shown with a bracket. The open end of the bracket shows which range of grades the paper is designed for. The percentages show the marks allocated to each paper.

LEAG – LONDON & EAST ANGLIAN GROUP

C – G		A – D
30%	Paper 1. 50 Multiple Choice	30%
50%	Paper 2. Short & Structured	
	Paper 3. Structured & Free Response	50%
20%	Teacher-Assessed Practical Work	20%

To the student

MEG – MIDLAND EXAMINING GROUP

C – G		A – G
40%	Paper 1. 40 Multiple Choice	40%
40%	Paper 2. Short & Structured	40%
	Paper 3. More difficult questions.	No weighting. Used to decide if A or B can be given.
20%	Teacher-Assessed Practical Work	20%

SEG – SOUTHERN EXAMINING GROUP

C – G		A – G
28%	Paper 1. 40 Multiple Choice	20%
42%	Paper 2. Short & Structured	25%
	Paper 4. Structured & Free Response	25%
30%	Paper 3. Teacher-Assessed Practical Work	30%

NEA – NORTHERN EXAMINING ASSOCIATION

C – G		A – F
80%	Level P. Structured & Short	
	Level Q. Variety of Questions	80%
20%	Teacher-Assessed Practical Work	20%

The board state that exceptionally it may be possible to get a B grade on Level P, or G on Level Q.

NISEC – NORTHERN IRELAND SCHOOLS EXAMINATION COUNCIL

C – G		A – G
35%	Paper 1. 40 Multiple Choice	17.5%
45%	Paper 2. Structured & Free Response	22.5%
	Paper 3. Short, Free Response + question on practical skills	50%
20%	Teacher-Asssessed Practical Work	10%

WJEC – WELSH JOINT EDUCATION COMMITTEE

C–G		A–E
80%	Paper 1. Variety of Questions	
	Paper 2. Variety of Questions	80%
20%	Practical Work – Teacher Assessment + Practical Test set by the Board.	20%

		LEAG	MEG	NEA	NISEC	SEG	WJEC
1.1	Scalars and Vectors. Speed, Distance, Displacement	●	●	●	●	●	●
1.2	Velocity	●	●	●	●	●	●
1.3	Example on Vectors	●	●	●	●	●	●
1.4	Units of Mass, Length, Time	●	●	●	●	●	●
1.5	Acceleration	●	●	●	●	●	●
1.6	Example on Acceleration	●	●	●	●	●	●
1.7	Maximum Height under Gravity	●	●	●	●	●	●
1.8	Motion Graphs. Displacement–time Graph	●	●	●	●	●	●
1.9	Velocity–time Graphs	●	●	●	●	●	●
1.10	Example on Velocity-time Graph	●	●	●	●	●	●
1.11	Equations of Motion	●	●	●	●	●	●
1.12	Formula for Distance		●		●	●	●
1.13	Equations of Motion – cont.		●		●	●	●
1.14	Examples on Motion		●		●	●	●
1.15	Mass. Inertia	●	●	●	●	●	●
1.16	Forces. The Newton	●	●	●	●	●	●
1.17	Forces at a Distance	●	●	●	●	●	●
1.18	Relation between Force, Mass, Acceleration	●	●	●	●	●	●
1.19	Motion Under Balanced Forces. Terminal Velocity	●	●	●	●	●	●
1.20	How to Use $F = ma$ with Several Forces	●	●	●	●	●	●

	LEAG	MEG	NEA	NISEC	SEG	WJEC
1.21 Work	•	•	•	•	•	•
1.22 Energy	•	•	•	•	•	•
1.23 Kinetic Energy	•	•	•	•	•	•
1.24 Proof of Kinetic Energy Formula	•	•	•	•	•	
1.25 Potential Energy. Gravitational and Elastic (molecular)	•	•	•	•	•	•
1.26 Transfer of Potential and Kinetic Energy	•	•	•	•	•	•
1.27 Energy Transformation. The Principle of Conservation of Energy	•	•	•	•	•	•
1.28 Power	•	•	•	•	•	•
1.29 Efficiency of Machines	•	•	•	•	•	•
1.30 Machines. Force Multipliers	•	•	•	•	•	•
1.31 Gears	•	•	•	•	•	•
1.32 Examples on Work and Efficiency of a Machine	•	•	•	•	•	•
1.33 Action and Reaction – Newton's Law	•		•	•		•
1.34 Force and Momentum						•
1.35 Examples on Momentum						•
1.36 Conservation of Momentum						•
2.1 Meaning and Calculation of a Moment	•	•		•	•	
2.2 Pivoted Objects in Equilibrium. Principle of Moments	•	•		•	•	
2.3 Centre of Gravity	•	•		•	•	
2.4 Stability of Objects. Stable Equilibrium	•	•		•	•	
2.5 Unstable Equilibrium	•	•		•	•	
2.6 Examples on Stable and Unstable Equilibrium	•	•		•	•	
2.7 Equilibrium with Parallel Forces	•	•		•	•	

	LEAG	MEG	NEA	NISEC	SEG	WJEC
3.21 Pressure–Temperature Change at Constant Volume	•		•		•	
3.22 Volume–Temperature Change at Constant Pressure	•		•		•	
3.23 General Gas Law or Equation of State	•		•		•	
3.24 Example on Gas Law	•		•		•	
3.25 Theory of Conduction	•		•	•	•	•
3.26 Good and Bad Conductors	•	•	•	•	•	•
3.27 Heat Insulation	•	•	•	•	•	•
3.28 Convection. Convection Currents	•	•	•		•	•
3.29 Home Hot-Water System	•	•	•		•	•
3.30 Sea and Land Breezes	•	•	•		•	•
3.31 Radiation	•	•	•		•	•
3.32 Emitters and Absorbers of Radiation	•	•	•		•	•
3.33 Nature and Properties of Heat Radiation	•	•	•		•	•
3.34 Thermos Flask	•	•	•		•	•
3.35 Solar Energy Uses	•	•	•		•	•
3.36 Heat Capacity			•	•	•	•
3.37 Specific Heat Capacity			•	•	•	•
3.38 Examples on Heat Transfer and Temperature Change			•	•	•	•
3.39 Specific Heat Capacity Measurement			•	•	•	•
3.40 Latent Heat		•		•	•	•
3.41 Molecular Theory of Latent Heat of Fusion		•		•	•	•
3.42 Specific Latent Heat of Fusion				•	•	•
3.43 Melting of Ice to Water				•	•	•
3.44 Measuring l for Ice				•	•	•
3.45 Melting Point		•		•	•	•

	LEAG	MEG	NEA	NISEC	SEG	WJEC
3.46 Latent Heat of Vaporization (evaporation)		●		●	●	●
3.47 Molecular Theory		●		●	●	●
3.48 Specific Latent Heat of Vaporization				●	●	●
3.49 Condensation: Vapour to Liquid Change				●	●	●
3.50 Difference between Evaporation and Boiling		●		●	●	●
3.51 Cooling due to Evaporation		●		●	●	●
3.52 Kinetic Theory Explanation		●		●	●	●
3.53 Boiling Point and Pressure		●		●	●	●
3.54 Why we Perspire		●		●	●	●
3.55 The Refrigerator		●		●	●	●
3.56 World Energy Resources			●	●	●	
3.57 Non-renewable Energy Sources			●	●	●	
3.58 Renewable Energy Sources			●	●	●	
4.1 Production and Movement of Waves	●	●	●	●	●	●
4.2 Transverse and Longitudinal Waves	●	●	●	●	●	●
4.3 Types of Wave	●	●	●	●	●	●
4.4 Wave Speed	●	●	●	●	●	●
4.5 Frequency and Wavelength	●	●	●	●	●	●
4.6 Wave Properties	●	●	●	●	●	●
4.7 Reflection	●	●	●			●
4.8 Refraction	●	●	●			●
4.9 Diffraction	●	●				●
4.10 Interference	●	●				●
4.11 Production and Propagation of Sound	●	●	●	●	●	●
4.12 Speed of Sound	●	●	●	●	●	●

	LEAG	MEG	NEA	NISEC	SEG	WJEC
7.10 Electromagnetic Induction – Experimental Observations	•	•	•	•	•	•
7.11 Laws of Induction	•	•	•		•	•
7.12 Induced e.m.f. in a Straight Wire	•		•		•	•
7.13 The a.c. Dynamo or Alternator		•	•		•	•
7.14 Tape Recorder Heads			•			
7.15 The Transformer	•	•	•		•	•
7.16 Energy in a Transformer		•	•		•	•
7.17 Energy Loss in a Transformer		•	•		•	•
7.18 How a Transformer Works	•	•	•		•	•
7.19 Generation of Electricity		•	•	•	•	•
7.20 Transmission of Electrical Energy		•	•		•	•
7.21 The National Grid System		•			•	•
8.1 Thermionic Emission	•	•	•	•	•	•
8.2 Structure of a Cathode Ray Tube	•	•	•	•	•	•
8.3 The Y-Plates	•	•	•	•	•	•
8.4 The Time-base	•	•	•	•	•	•
8.5 Television Tubes		•				
8.6 The Semiconductor Diode	•	•	•	•		•
8.7 Half-wave Rectification	•	•			•	
8.8 The Bridge Rectifier	•	•			•	
8.9 The Transistor as a Switch	•		•			•
8.10 The Potential Divider	•	•	•			•
8.11 Potential Divider with a Transistor	•		•			•
8.12 Use of Transistor in Light Alarm Circuit	•		•			•
8.13 Other Alarm Circuits	•		•			•
8.14 Digital Circuits – Logic States		•	•			•
8.15 Gates		•	•	•		•
8.16 Light Emitting Diodes		•	•	•		•

	LEAG	MEG	NEA	NISEC	SEG	WJEC
8.17 Latches		•	•	•		•
8.18 Applications of Gates		•	•	•		•
8.19 Combinations of Gates		•	•	•		•
9.1 Atomic Structure	•	•	•	•	•	•
9.2 Proton and Mass Numbers	•	•	•	•	•	•
9.3 Ions	•	•	•	•	•	•
9.4 Isotopes	•	•	•	•	•	•
9.5 Radioactive Sources	•	•	•	•	•	•
9.6 Radiation Detectors	•	•	•	•	•	•
9.7 Counters and Ratemeters	•	•	•	•	•	•
9.8 Background Radiation		•	•	•		
9.9 Properties of α- and β-particles and γ-rays	•	•	•	•	•	•
9.10 Nature of α- and β-particles and γ-rays		•	•	•	•	•
9.11 Effect of a Magnetic Field		•		•		
9.12 Health Hazards	•	•	•	•	•	•
9.13 Summary of Properties	•	•	•	•	•	•
9.14 The Nuclear Atom		•				
9.15 Nuclear Changes in Radioactive Emission		•	•	•	•	•
9.16 Half-life	•	•	•	•	•	•
9.17 Uses of Radioactive Isotopes		•	•	•		•
9.18 Nuclear Fission – Chain Reactions	•	•	•		•	
9.19 Nuclear Power Reactors	•	•	•		•	
9.20 Problems of Nuclear Power Generation	•	•	•			
9.21 Nuclear Waste	•	•	•			
9.22 Nuclear Fusion		•	•			

MECHANICS

CONTENTS

MOTION

In this chapter we deal with topics connected with **motion**, such as speed, velocity and acceleration. Engineers who design racing cars and aeroplanes always make tests on their speed and acceleration. Electronic engineers who design cathode-ray tubes used in radar, for example, have to deal with the velocity and acceleration of electrons in the tubes. Unlike cars or aeroplanes, electrons are very small particles having a mass about 1/2000th of a hydrogen atom.

1.1 SCALARS AND VECTORS. SPEED, DISTANCE, DISPLACEMENT

A top-class Olympic sprinter may run 100 metres in 10.0 seconds. In this case

$$\text{average speed} = \frac{\text{distance}}{\text{time}} = \frac{100\,\text{m}}{10.0\,\text{s}} = 10.0\,\text{m/s}$$

A car travelling 100 kilometres in 2 hours has an average speed which is $100\,\text{km}/2\,\text{h} = 50\,\text{km/h}$.

In science, we divide quantities into two classes: **scalars** and **vectors**.

A scalar is a quantity which has size (magnitude) but not direction. In motion, speed is a **scalar** – we are concerned only how big the speed is, not its direction. So you may have walked home from a friend with an average speed of 4 m/s, no matter in which direction you walked.

'Distance' is a scalar. A distance of 20 metres, for example, could be in any direction and, as we stated before, speed = distance/time. 'Displacement', however, is a **vector**. It refers to a distance in a **particular direction**. So in Fig 1.1(a), OA represents a displacement of

Fig 1.1 Scalars (distance, speed) and vectors (displacement, velocity)

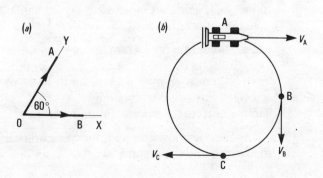

50 m in a direction OY inclined at 60° to OX. OB is a displacement of 50 m in a direction OX. Both OA and OB have equal distances but different displacements.

1.2 VELOCITY

Velocity is a vector, unlike speed. Velocity has both size and direction. By definition,

$$\text{velocity} = \frac{\text{displacement}}{\text{time}}$$

For example, in Fig 1.1(*b*) a racing car is travelling round a circular track at a constant **speed** of 100 km/h. The speed is the same at say A, B, and C. But its **velocity** is different at these points. The velocity directions are along the tangents to the circle at A, B, and C, as shown. So although they have the same magnitude, 100 km/h, the velocities v_A, v_B, and v_C are different from each other.

When a car travels with a constant, or uniform, velocity, it travels in a fixed direction.

1.3 EXAMPLE ON VECTORS

In Fig 1.2, A, B, C, D, E each represent speeds of 5 m/s in certain directions. Which of the five are equal **vectors**?

B and E are equal vectors. They have the same direction and the same speed.

Fig 1.2 Example on vectors

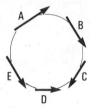

1.4 UNITS OF MASS, LENGTH, TIME

At this stage it would be useful to list some of the main physics units to be used. They are needed in experiments. In calculations, always give the units of the final answer.

Mass   kilogram (kg), gram (g) $1\,\text{g} = \frac{1}{1000}\,\text{kg} = 10^{-3}\,\text{kg}$
Length metre (m), centimetre (cm), millimetre (mm), kilometre (km)
        $1\,\text{cm} = \frac{1}{100}\,\text{m} = 10^{-2}\,\text{m}$, $1\,\text{mm} = \frac{1}{1000}\,\text{m} = 10^{-3}\,\text{m}$
        $1\,\text{km} = 1000\,\text{m} = 10^{3}\,\text{m}$
Time   second (s), minute (min), hour (h)

In scientific measurement, the basic units are the kilogram (kg), the metre (m), and the second (s).

1.5 ACCELERATION

Starting from rest on their blocks, sprinters aim at high acceleration in order to reach their maximum speed in the shortest time. Racing cars have high acceleration for the same reason. Road tests on new cars always include measurement of their acceleration.

Acceleration is defined by

$$\text{acceleration} = \frac{\text{velocity change}}{\text{time taken}}$$

So acceleration is the 'velocity change per second'. The units of acceleration are 'metres per second per second' or 'm/s²' because the second is repeated twice.

Fig 1.3 Acceleration and measurement

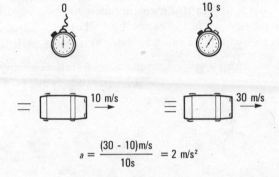

$$a = \frac{(30 - 10)\text{m/s}}{10\text{s}} = 2 \text{ m/s}^2$$

So if the velocity increases from 10 m/s to 30 m/s in 10 s with a uniform (constant) acceleration (Fig 1.3)

$$\text{acceleration} = \frac{(30-10) \text{ m/s}}{10 \text{ s}} = \frac{20}{10}\text{m/s}^2 = 2 \text{ m/s}^2$$

Remember that velocity has a unit 'm/s' but acceleration has a unit 'm/s²'.

If a car slows down its velocity decreases. We say that the car **decelerates**. We calculate deceleration in the same way as acceleration, but in this case the answer is negative. So deceleration is a 'negative' acceleration.

For example, a car may slow steadily from 40 m/s to 20 m/s in 10 s. Then

$$\text{deceleration} = \frac{(40-20) \text{ m/s}}{10 \text{ s}} = 2 \text{ m/s}^2$$

Or we can say, acceleration of car $= -2 \text{ m/s}^2$

1.6 EXAMPLE ON ACCELERATION

A train accelerates steadily from rest at 2 m/s².
(a)   How long does it take to reach 40 m/s?
(b)   If the train then continues at the same acceleration for another 10 s, what is its final velocity?

(*a*)   With a steady acceleration of 2 m/s², the velocity of the train increases by 2 m/s every second. So time to reach 40 m/s

$$= \frac{40}{2} = 20 \text{ s}$$

(*b*)   With the same acceleration of 2 m/s², in 10 s the velocity increases by 10 × 2 m/s = 20 m/s. So

final train velocity = 20 m/s + 40 m/s = 60 m/s

DISTANCE WITH UNIFORM ACCELERATION

Suppose a car, moving with a velocity of 10 m/s, then accelerates uniformly (steadily) at 2 m/s² for 10 s.

To find the distance travelled in this time, we first calculate the final velocity of the car at the end of 10 s. Since 2 m/s² means a rise in velocity of 2 m/s every second, at the end of 10 s,

final velocity = increase + initial velocity
= (10×2 m/s) + 10 m/s = 30 m/s

Fig 1.4 Distance with uniform (constant) acceleration

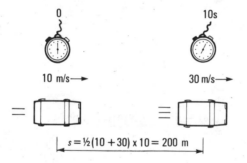

Since the velocity changes steadily under uniform acceleration, we can say that during the 10 s

average velocity = ½(10+30) = 20 m/s

So the distance travelled is given by

average velocity×time = 20×10 = 200 m

1.7 MAXIMUM HEIGHT UNDER GRAVITY

Suppose that a rocket, fired vertically, leaves the ground with an initial velocity of 30 m/s. To find the maximum height it reaches, we need to find the time taken to reach this height and the average speed during this time.

Suppose *g*, the acceleration due to gravity is 10 m/s², so the rocket moving upward decelerates at this rate, or decreases in velocity at 10 m/s every second. Now the decrease in velocity to the maximum height is 30 m/s to zero or 30 m/s. So

$$\text{time taken} = \frac{30}{10} = 3 \text{ s}$$

The average velocity of the rocket during this time = $\frac{1}{2}(30+0)$ = 15 m/s.

So   maximum height = average velocity × time
$$= 15 \times 3 = 45 \text{ m}$$

1.8 MOTION GRAPHS. DISPLACEMENT–TIME GRAPH

Graphs are useful for studying motion. As we see later, velocity and acceleration can be found from graphs.

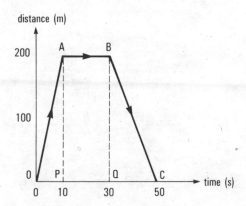

Fig 1.5 Displacement (s)–time (t) graph

Fig 1.5 shows a displacement (s)–time (t) graph OABC for the motion of a car. The vertical axis represents the distance s travelled in a constant direction and the horizontal axis represents the time t starting from O.

The straight line OA shows that for 10 s (OP) from rest at 0, the car moved steadily or uniformly for a distance of 200 m (AP). So

$$\text{uniform velocity} = \frac{\text{displacement (AP)}}{\text{time (OP)}} = \frac{200 \text{ m}}{10 \text{ s}}$$
$$= 20 \text{ m/s}$$

We call the ratio AP/OP the **slope** or **gradient** of the straight line OA. So generally,

velocity = slope or gradient of displacement–time graph

From P to Q, 10 s to 30 s, the graph AB is horizontal. The slope of AB is zero. So the velocity is zero. In fact, the car is stationary for 20 s. From Q to C, in the time 30 s to 50 s, the line BC falls steadily to zero. So the car returns to the place it originally started from. The straight line BC shows that it travels with constant velocity in the opposite direction to that represented by OA, because the slope of BC is a downward or negative slope, whereas OA is an upward or positive slope.

1.9 VELOCITY–TIME GRAPHS

A velocity (v)–time (t) graph shows how the velocity of moving objects varies with time. Fig 1.6 shows the velocity v of a train which starts from rest ($v=0$) and accelerates uniformly (steadily) until it reaches a velocity of 40 m/s, represented by A; the time taken, 10 s, is OD on the time-axis. The train then keeps a uniform (constant) velocity for a time DE of 30 s, so the graph AB is horizontal. The brakes are now put on and the train decelerates steadily from B to C in 20 s, when it comes to rest ($v=0$).

Fig 1.6 Velocity–time graphs of (a) car and (b) lift (elevator)

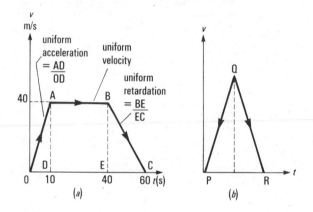

ACCELERATION AND DISTANCE FROM VELOCITY–TIME GRAPHS

In Fig 1.6(a), the straight line OA represents a steady rise in velocity. So it represents an acceleration given by

$$\frac{\text{velocity change}}{\text{time}} = \frac{\text{AD}}{\text{OD}} = \frac{40 \text{ m/s}}{10 \text{ s}} = 4 \text{ m/s}^2$$

Now AD/OD is the **slope** or **gradient** of the line OA. So in a velocity (v)–time (t) graph, remember that

>the **acceleration is numerically equal to the slope or gradient of the graph at the particular time**

Along AB, the slope or gradient is zero and so the acceleration is zero. This is because the velocity is uniform here. Along BC the slope or gradient is downward or negative. So this is a deceleration. Its value numerically is BE/EC = 40/20 = 2 m/s².

We can also find the distance travelled from a velocity–time graph. In Fig 1.6(a), the distance gone in a time OD = average velocity × time = $\frac{1}{2}$AD×OD = area of triangle OAD. The distance gone in the time DE = AD×DE = area of rectangle DABE. The distance gone in the time EC = area of triangle BEC. The total distance travelled from O to C is therefore the total area of OABCA. So remember that

>the **distance travelled is the area between the velocity–time graph and the time-axis**

Fig 1.6(*b*) shows the graph of the velocity of a lift against time. The acceleration of the lift is the slope of the line PQ and the deceleration is the slope of QR. The total distance travelled is the area of triangle PQR, which is in metres if the v-axis is in metres/second and the time-axis in seconds.

1.10 EXAMPLE ON VELOCITY–TIME GRAPH

A train starts from rest at a station, accelerates at 0.2 m/s² for 2 min or 120 s, then keeps a constant velocity for 10 min or 600 s, and finally comes to rest with a uniform deceleration in another 3 min or 180 s. Draw a velocity–time graph of the motion. From the graph, find the deceleration and the total distance travelled by the train.

Fig 1.7 Velocity–time graph

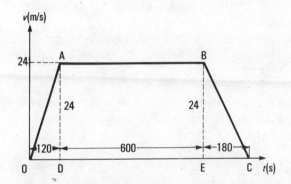

Graph. After 120 s, velocity = 0+0.2×120 = 24 m/s. This helps to plot point A, and by joining O to A we obtain the part OA of the graph showing the uniform acceleration (see Fig 1.7).

Now draw the line AB parallel to the time-axis so that AB or DE represents 10 mins or 600 s. Finally, join B to C, which is 3 min or 180 s further than E on the time-axis.

Calculations

(*a*)   Deceleration along BC = gradient of BC

$$= \frac{BE}{EC} = \frac{24 \text{ m/s}}{180 \text{ s}} = 0.13 \text{ m/s}^2$$

(*b*)   Total distance   = area OABC = area of triangle OAD + rectangle ABED + triangle BCE

$= (\frac{1}{2} \times 120 \times 24) + (600 \times 24) + (\frac{1}{2} \times 180 \times 24)$

= 1440 + 14 400 + 2160

= 18 000 m or 18 km

CHECK LIST ▶   Make sure you can answer the following questions.

1   What is the difference between **speed** and **velocity**?
2   In a **velocity–time** graph, how would you find the acceleration and the distance travelled? What information can be obtained from a **displacement–time** graph?
3   A ball is thrown vertically upwards with a velocity of 30 m/s. How high does it go and how long does it take to reach its maximum height, assuming g = 10 m/s²?

1.11 EQUATIONS OF MOTION

Formulae are very useful. They give the relationship between quantities using letters instead of writing out words. As an example, consider a tennis ball falling vertically with a uniform (constant) acceleration g under gravity of about 9.8 m/s² or 10 m/s² in round figures. Fig 1.8.

Suppose the falling ball has a velocity of 20 m/s at some instant. Then in 3 s, its velocity increases by 3×10 m/s or 30 m/s. The new velocity is now (20+30) or 50 m/s.

To state the relationship in letters, suppose u is the initial velocity, a is the uniform acceleration, and t is the time. Then its final velocity v at the end of the time t is always given by

$$v = u + at \qquad\qquad (1)$$

In the above example, $v = 20 + (10 \times 3) = 20 + 30 = 50$ m/s. If the object is simply released at a height, its initial velocity $u = 0$. Then in 2 s its velocity v is given by

$$v = u + at = 0 + (2 \times 10) = 0 + 20 = 20 \text{ m/s}$$

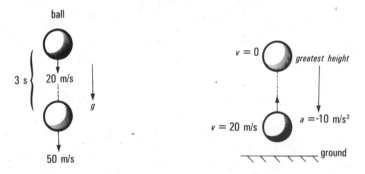

Fig 1.8 Calculation   Fig 1.9 Acceleration under gravity

Suppose a ball is thrown vertically upwards with a velocity of 20 m/s as it leaves the hand, as shown in Fig 1.9. This time the ball *decelerates*, that is, its velocity decreases by 10 m/s per second as the ball rises. So $a = -10$ m/s². In a time of 1 s, then, its velocity v is given by

$$v = u+at = 20+(-10\times1) = 20-10 = 10 \text{ m/s}$$

When the ball reaches its greatest or maximum height, its velocity v becomes zero. The time, t, taken to reach the maximum height is therefore given by putting $v = 0$ in $v = u+at$. So

$$0 = 20+(-10\times t)$$
$$= 20-10t$$

So $\qquad 10t = 20$, or $t = 20/10 = 2$ s

1.12 FORMULA FOR DISTANCE

We can get a useful formula for the distance s travelled with uniform acceleration a. From numerical cases, we see that

$$\text{average velocity} = \tfrac{1}{2}(u+v) = \tfrac{1}{2}[u+(u+at)] = u+\tfrac{1}{2}at$$

So $\qquad \text{distance } s = \text{average velocity} \times \text{time}$
$$= (u+\tfrac{1}{2}at)\times t$$

or $\qquad s = ut+\tfrac{1}{2}at^2 \qquad\qquad (2)$

MEASUREMENT OF g

This formula can be used to help find the acceleration due to gravity, g. A steel ball bearing is allowed to fall a known distance, s. The time taken, t, to fall this distance is measured using apparatus as described in question 12, p.38. The starting speed, u, is zero since the object falls from rest. So using (2)

$$s = 0\times t+\tfrac{1}{2}gt^2$$

where we have used g instead of a as g is the acceleration in this case. This gives

$$g = 2s/t^2$$

from which g may be calculated. The experiment would be repeated for several values of s, and the average value of g found.

EXAMPLE OF HOW TO USE $s = ut+\tfrac{1}{2}at^2$

Suppose $u = \text{initial velocity} = 10$ m/s, $a = 2$ m/s^2, and $t = 10$ s. Then, from (2),

$$s = (10\times10) + (\tfrac{1}{2}\times2\times10^2)$$
$$= 100+100 = 200 \text{ m}$$

If the time t is not given when an object moves with uniform acceleration, we can calculate the distance s from

$$s = \text{average velocity} \times \text{time} = \frac{v+u}{2} \times \frac{v-u}{a}$$

Simplifying, $\qquad s = \dfrac{v^2-u^2}{2a}$

so $\qquad\qquad v^2 = u^2 + 2as$ $\qquad\qquad\qquad\qquad$ (3)

1.13 EQUATIONS OF MOTION

The three equations of motion,

$$v = u+at \qquad\qquad\qquad (1)$$
$$s = ut+\tfrac{1}{2}at^2 \qquad\qquad\qquad (2)$$
$$v^2 = u^2+2as \qquad\qquad\qquad (3)$$

help us to work out problems on uniform acceleration.

In solving problems,

(a)   Write down from the question the values of the quantities given: u, v, t, a or s,

(b)   then write down the formula, (1), (2), or (3), you think will be needed, and

(c)   substitute the values in the formula.

Here are some worked examples to show you how to do typical questions.

1.14 EXAMPLES ON MOTION

1   A train travelling at 20 m/s accelerates uniformly for 5 s and reaches a velocity of 30 m/s. Calculate (a) the acceleration, and (b) the distance travelled in 5 s.

Here initial velocity u = 20 m/s, final velocity v = 30 m/s, time t = 5 s.

(a)   From $\qquad\qquad v = u+at$
         we have $\qquad 30 = 20+5a$
         So $\qquad\qquad 5a = 30-20 = 10$, or $a = 2$ m/s^2

(b)   From $\qquad\qquad s = ut+\tfrac{1}{2}at^2$
         we have $\qquad s = (20\times5) + (\tfrac{1}{2}\times2\times5^2)$
$\qquad\qquad\qquad\qquad\quad = 100+25 = 125$ m

2   A ball is thrown vertically upwards with an initial velocity of 15 m/s. Assuming the acceleration of free fall g is 10 m/s^2, find (a) the time to reach the greatest height, (b) the greatest height, (c) the time to return to the thrower.

When the ball is moving upwards, it has a *deceleration*. So a = -10 m/s^2. The initial velocity u = 15 m/s. The final velocity v = 0, because the ball's velocity decreases to zero at the greatest height.

(a)   From $v = u+at$, we have

$$0 = 15+(-10+t) = 15-10t$$

So $\quad 10t = 15$, or $t = \dfrac{15}{10} = 1.5$ s

(b)   From $v^2 = u^2+2as$, we have

$$0^2 = 15^2 + (2 \times -10 \times s) = 225 - 20s$$

So $\quad 20s = 225$, or $s = 11.25$ m

(c)   The time taken to return to thrower = 2 × time taken to reach
                                                greatest height
                                            = 2 × 1.5 s = 3 s

(a) YOU SHOULD KNOW:

1   A scalar quantity has size but no direction. A vector quantity has both
    size and direction.
2   Distance and speed are **scalars**. Displacement, velocity and acceler-
    ation are **vectors**.
3   Velocities are **different** if they have (a) the same direction but dif-
    ferent size or (b) the same size but different direction.
4   Distance = average speed × time. Displacement = average velocity ×
    time.
5   Acceleration = velocity **change**/time taken.
        In deceleration (retardation) the velocity decreases with time, so it
    is a 'negative' acceleration.
6   In a displacement–time graph, velocity = slope (gradient) of graph.
7   In a velocity–time graph, (a) acceleration = slope (gradient) of graph,
    (b) distance travelled = area between graph and time-axis.
8   With uniform acceleration, the three equations of motion are:

$$v = u+at, \quad s = ut+\tfrac{1}{2}at^2, \quad v^2 = u^2+2as$$

In problems, when an object starts from rest, then $u = 0$; if it comes
finally to rest, then $v = 0$; and if it decelerates, then a is negative.

(b) YOU SHOULD UNDERSTAND:

1   The difference between a scalar and a vector quantity.
2   The difference between distance and displacement, and between
    speed and velocity.
3   The definition of acceleration and of uniform acceleration.
4   In free fall, the acceleration due to gravity g is about $9.8 \, \text{m/s}^2$ or
    $10 \, \text{m/s}^2$ in round figures. A ball thrown vertically upwards decelerates
    at about $10 \, \text{m/s}^2$.
5   How to find the distance travelled when the velocity is uniform or
    when it increases steadily and the acceleration is uniform.
6   How to use (a) distance–time graphs to find speed or velocity and (b)
    velocity–time graphs to find acceleration and distance travelled.
7   How to apply the three equations of motion to problems.

(c) APPLICATIONS

You should be able to do the following calculations.
1   A car does 4 laps of a circular track 1000 m long in 100 s. What is the
    average speed? How long does it take to do 6 more laps at the same
    average speed? Is the velocity the same all round the track.

2   A ball is thrown vertically upwards with an initial velocity of 20 m/s. How high does it go? What height does it reach? What is the velocity in 1.5 s?

3   A train starts from a station X, travels with a uniform acceleration of 2 m/s² for 15 s, then keeps a constant velocity for 20 s, and finally decelerates to a station Y steadily where it comes to rest in 30 s. Draw the velocity–time graph. Use it to find the average velocity over the whole journey.

QUESTIONS 1A MOTION

MULTIPLE-CHOICE QUESTIONS

1   Which of the following is a **scalar**?
      A   velocity   B   acceleration   C   speed   D   displacement

2   A bicycle travels 40 m in five seconds and then 24 m in three seconds. What is the average speed for the whole journey?
      A   5 m/s   B   6 m/s   C   7 m/s   D   8 m/s

3   The graph, Fig 1A, represents the velocity (v)–time (t) graph for the motion of a lift which takes a total time of 8 s between two floors in a tall building. For what period of the time is the lift travelling with zero acceleration?
      A   2 s   B   3 s   C   5 s   D   8 s

Fig 1A

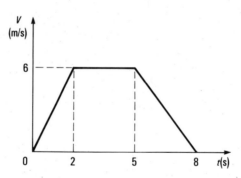

4   From the graph in Fig 1A, the retardation or deceleration of the lift is
      A   4 m/s²   B   3 m/s²   C   2 m/s²   D   1 m/s²

5   From the graph in Fig 1A, the distance travelled by the lift between the two floors is
      A   12 m   B   30 m   C   33 m   D   48 m

6   A car leaks oil at the rate of 4 drops every second. If the car starts from rest with a constant acceleration, which pattern of drops, A, B, C or D, is obtained? (Fig 1B)

Fig 1B

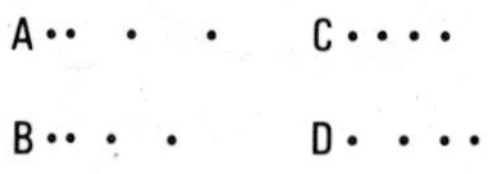

A ·· · ·   C · · · ·

B ·· · ·   D · · · · ·

SHORT ANSWER QUESTIONS

7   A ball is dropped from a height above the ground and takes 2 s to reach the ground. What is (*a*) the velocity of the ball just before it hits the ground, (*b*) the height from which it was dropped?
(Assume $g = 10$ m/s^2)

8   During constant acceleration, a train travels (*a*) 40 m in 4 s and then (*b*) 160 m in the next 4 s. Calculate the average velocity of the train in (*a*) and (*b*).

   Using your results for average velocity, estimate the acceleration of the train.

9   In Fig 1C, OABC represents the velocity (*v*)–time (*t*) graph for the motion of a car.

Fig 1C

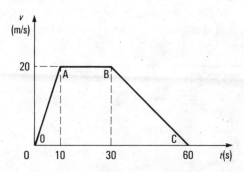

(*a*)   Describe the motion during the time O to P and P to Q.
(*b*)   Find the acceleration and retardation (deceleration) of the car.
(*c*)   What is the total distance travelled by the car?

10   Two cars A and B undergo speed tests round a racing circuit, starting at the same time. A graph of distance (*s*)–time (*t*) travelled by the cars is shown in Fig 1D.

Fig 1D

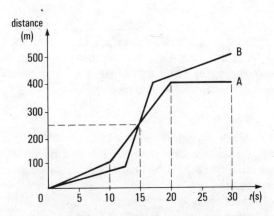

(*a*)   After 30 s, what is the distance between A and B?
(*b*)   What is the average speed of A in the first 10 s?
(*c*)   At what time are the two cars side by side?

(d)   What is the average speed of each car after 15 s?
(e)   What is the difference between the motion of A and B in the interval 20 s to 30 s?

11 A ball is thrown vertically upwards from the ground with an initial velocity of 30 m/s.
(a)   What is the velocity 2 s after it is thrown?
(b)   How long does it take to reach its maximum height?
(c)   Calculate the maximum height.
(d)   From the time it is thrown up, how long does it take for the ball to return to the thrower?
      (Assume $g = 10 \text{ m/s}^2$)

12 In an experiment to measure the acceleration of free fall due to gravity (g), a steel ball B is held between two electrical contacts C by an electromagnet M (Fig 1E). When M is switched off, B falls and then starts an electronic stop-watch A. After B falls a distance 0.75 m, it hits a metal trapdoor T and stops the clock. The time on the clock was 0.39 s.

Fig 1E

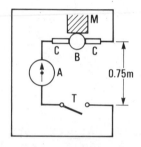

(a)   What is the calculated acceleration of the ball B as it fell?
(b)   What was the velocity of the ball as it hit T?
(c)   Name two possible sources of error in measuring g in this experiment.

FORCES IN MOTION

In this section we deal with objects such as cars, trains and aeroplanes which are kept moving by **forces**. Forces produce acceleration proportional to the size of the force and we shall see how accelerations are found.

1.15 MASS. INERTIA

The **mass** of a car, whether it is big or small, affects its acceleration when a force acts on it. Masses are measured in kilograms (kg) or grams (g).

A box of chocolates, securely wrapped, will have the same amount of eating matter or mass if it is taken from London to the Equator or the North Pole, or even if it is taken to the Moon. You should remember that **the mass of an object is constant**, wherever it may be. So the mass of a man is the same at the North Pole as at the Equator.

A heavy sandbag, suspended from a beam, needs a greater effort to push than a light sandbag. We say that the heavy sandbag has more 'inertia' than the light sandbag. **Mass** is a measure of the inertia of objects. So in a rugby scrum, a forward of mass 80 kg is more difficult to push than one of mass 60 kg.

1.16 FORCES. THE NEWTON

There are many different kinds of forces. Engines produce forces which move the masses of cars or trains, for example. Leg muscles produce forces which move the masses of runners. A common force is **weight**. This is the force on the masses of objects due to the Earth's gravitational field.

As we see shortly, a force produces an **acceleration** proportional to the size of the force. Aeroplanes have the fast acceleration needed for take off because their engines produce a powerful force. Forces are measured in **newtons**, symbol N. By definition,

1 newton is the force which produces an acceleration of 1 m/s² in a mass of 1 kg.

In the Earth's gravitational field, near its surface all masses fall freely with an acceleration of about 10 m/s². The gravitational pull on a girl of mass 50 kg, her weight, is therefore $50 \times 10 = 500$ N. The weight of a car of mass 1000 kg is about 10 000 N. 1 newton is the weight of a mass of about 100 g (0.1 kg), which is about the weight of an average-size apple. Generally, then,

weight in newtons = mass in kg × gravitational field strength in N/kg

On the Earth's surface, the gravitational field strength is about 10 N/kg, the same numerical value as the acceleration due to gravity. On the Moon's surface, the gravitational field strength is only about 1.6 N/kg. So here the weight of a mass of 100 kg is 160 N but on the Earth the same mass has a weight of 100×10 or 1000 N.

Spring balances can be calibrated in newtons by hanging known masses on them, when the spring is pulled out by the weights of the masses.

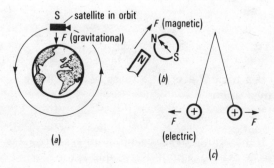

Fig 1.10 Forces acting at a distance (a) gravitational (b) magnetic (c) electric

1.17 FORCES AT A DISTANCE

When a football is kicked or a tennis ball is hit, the forces make direct contact with the ball.

Gravitational forces, however, act at a distance. For example, they pull a man at the end of a parachute downwards when he is not in contact with the Earth. Satellites S in orbit, high above the Earth, have a force F on them due to Earth's gravitational attraction.

Fig 1.10(*a*). **Magnetic forces** also act at a distance. A magnet attracts a magnetic compass without any contact. Fig 1.10(*b*). **Electric forces** act at a distance. Two positive electric charges repel each other without any contact. Fig 1.10(*c*).

1.18 RELATION BETWEEN FORCE, MASS, ACCELERATION

When you make contact with a ball by hitting or kicking it, you usually change its speed or its direction or both its speed and direction. So the velocity is changed. You have therefore given the ball an **acceleration**.

As we see later, the acceleration produced in a given mass is directly proportional to the force. Also, the acceleration produced by a given force is inversely proportional to the mass on which it acts – the greater the mass, the smaller is the acceleration produced by the same force. Both these laws, which can be verified experimentally, are summarized in one equation:

Force = mass × acceleration

or $\qquad F = ma,$

where F is the force in newtons, m is the mass in kg and a is the acceleration in m/s^2. If F is the **weight** (force due to gravity) of a mass m, then, from $F = ma$,

$$\text{Weight} = mg,$$

where g is the gravitational field strength or acceleration due to gravity. Fig 1.11.

Fig 1.11 Weight and mass

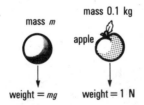

mass m

mass 0.1 kg

apple

weight $= mg$ weight $= 1$ N

If a force F acts on a mass of 5 kg and gives it an acceleration of 2 m/s^2, then

$$F = ma = 5 \times 2 = 10 \, \text{N}$$

If a force of 3000 N acts on a car and produces an acceleration of 3 m/s^2, the mass of the car is given by

$$F = ma, \text{ or } 3000 = m \times 3$$

So $\quad m = \dfrac{3000}{3} = 1000 \text{ kg}$

1.19 MOTION UNDER BALANCED FORCES. TERMINAL VELOCITY

Suppose a car starting from rest is accelerated steadily by a constant force F due to the engine. The total frictional force on the car due to the air and the ground is very small at first. So the net or resultant force on the car keeps it accelerating.

As the velocity increases, the total frictional opposing force R increases. Fig 1.12. So at one particular velocity, the opposing force R just balances the force F due to the engine. Since the net or resultant force is then zero, **the car no longer accelerates**. It then continues to move with the same velocity. This is called the **terminal** (end) **velocity** of the car. In Fig 1.12 (*a*), $F = R$ and v is the terminal velocity. Fig 1.12 (*b*) shows roughly how the velocity of the car varies with time from the start.

Fig 1.12 Terminal velocity

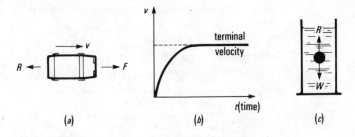

(*a*)   (*b*)   (*c*)

An object released from an aeroplane at a height reaches a maximum or terminal velocity as it falls, for a similar reason. When first released from the aeroplane, its weight makes it accelerate downwards. As the velocity increases, the air friction increases. So at one particular velocity, the frictional force balances the weight. The object no longer accelerates and has then reached its terminal (maximum) velocity.

Fig 1.12 (*c*) shows a simple laboratory experiment on terminal velocity. A steel ball-bearing X is released in a tall jar having a thick liquid such as glycerine inside it. At first, the weight W makes X accelerate. In a short time, however, the frictional force R due to the liquid balances the weight and the ball X now falls with a constant or terminal velocity. This can be shown by timing the fall over a known distance measured on the jar.

CHECK LIST ▶
Make sure you can answer the following questions:

1 What is the difference between **mass** and **weight**? What weight has a girl of mass 50 kg if $g = 10$ m/s^2?
2 A car has a mass of 1000 kg and the force due to the engine is 800 N. What is the car's acceleration, neglecting frictional forces?
   If the acceleration is actually 0.5 m/s^2, what is the frictional force on the car?
3 Why does a parachutist fall with a constant velocity after a short time? What name is given to this velocity?

1.20 HOW TO USE $F = ma$ WITH SEVERAL FORCES

In practice, more than one force acts on an object when it is moving. For example, a travelling car has a force due to the engine pushing it forward and wind resistance and tyre friction, both of which are forces acting the opposite way to the engine force. In '**force = mass × acceleration**', or $F = ma$, the force F is the **net** force or **resultant** force on the object. So we often have to add or subtract all the forces on an object to find the value of F in $F = ma$.

The following examples show how this is done.

1 A sledge of mass 40 kg is pulled along the ground by a horizontal force of 50 N. Due to friction, the opposing force is 30 N. Calculate the acceleration of the sledge.

   We first find the resultant force F on the sledge. Here $F = 50$ N $- 30$ N $= 20$ N. Now we use $F = ma$ to find a. We have, since $F = 20$ N and $m = 40$ kg,

   $$20 = 40 \times a$$

   So $a = \dfrac{20}{40} = 0.5$ m/s^2

2 A box B of mass 10 kg is raised by a chain from the ground (see Fig 1.13). If the tension (force) in the chain is 120 N, find the acceleration of the box as it rises.

   What tension in the chain would produce an acceleration of 3 m/s^2? What tension produces a steady velocity?

Fig 1.13 Calculation on $F = ma$

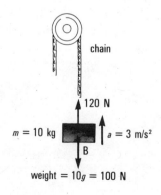

chain

120 N

$m = 10$ kg $a = 3$ m/s^2

B

weight $= 10g = 100$ N

(a)   There are two forces on the box as it rises. One is the force of 120 N pulling it upwards. The other is its weight, mg, which acts **downwards**. The weight $= mg = 10 \times 10 = 100$ N. So the resultant upward force $F = 120 - 100 = 20$ N. From $F = ma$,

$$20 = 10 \times a, \text{ so } a = \frac{20}{10} = 2 \text{ m/s}^2$$

(b)   Suppose T is the tension (force) in newtons in the chain when the acceleration is 3 m/s^2.
Then

resultant force $F =$ tension$-$weight $= T-100$, in newtons
From $F = ma$
               $T-100 = 10 \times 3 = 30$
So $T = 30+100 = 130$ N

(c)   When the box rises with a steady velocity, its acceleration is zero. So the resultant force F on it is zero. The upward tension in the chain is therefore exactly balanced by the downward weight of the box, 100 N. So the tension $= 100$ N.

SUMMARY

(a) YOU SHOULD KNOW

1   Mass is constant all over the world but weight varies.
2   Weight $= mg$ and g may be given as about 9.8 N/kg on the Earth.
3   Gravitational, magnetic and electric forces can act at a distance from objects.
4   In $F = ma$, F is the *resultant* force in newtons, m is the mass of the object in kilograms and a is its acceleration in metre per second^2.
5   When the object falls in air, the frictional force on it increases with its velocity. At one velocity the frictional force becomes equal to the weight of the object, so the resultant force is zero. The acceleration is then zero. So the object now falls with a constant velocity called its 'terminal velocity'.

(b) YOU SHOULD UNDERSTAND

1   The difference between 'mass' and 'weight' and how to find weight from mass.
2   How contact forces differ from those in gravitational, magnetic and electric fields.
3   The units in $F = ma$ for F, m and a and how to apply $F = ma$ in problems.
3   Why there is a terminal (maximum) velocity when a parachutist falls.

(c) APPLICATIONS

You should be able to do the following calculations.

1   A climber reaches the top of a high mountain. What do you know about his **mass** and his **weight** compared with their values when he was at the foot of the mountain.

2   A car has a force of 1000 N on it due to the engine and the frictional force is then 200 N. If the acceleration of the car is 1 m/s^2, what is the mass of the car?

3   A parachutist falls with a terminal velocity. The mass of the parachute is 10 kg and the frictional force due to the air is 700 N. Calculate the mass of the parachutist if $g = 10$ N/kg.

QUESTIONS 1B FORCE AND ACCELERATION

MULTIPLE CHOICE QUESTIONS

1   When a climber reaches the top of a mountain,
   A   his mass is now greater
   B   his weight is now greater
   C   his mass is now slightly smaller
   D   his weight is now slightly smaller

2   Which statement in A to D is NOT true?
   When a force acts on an object, it may produce a change in
   A   velocity   B   shape   C   mass   D   length

3   A steady force of 6 N accelerates a mass of 2 kg from rest. The acceleration is
   A   6 m/s^2 B   3 m/s^2 C   2 m/s^2 D   1 m/s^2

4   A force of 400 N due to the engine acts on a car moving with a uniform velocity of 20 m/s. The total frictional force on the car is then
   A   8000 N   B   800 N   C   600 N   D   400 N

5   An astronaut X has a mass of 60 kg. If the gravitational field strength is about 10 N/kg on the Earth and about 1.6 N/kg on the Moon, then
   A   X has a weight of 50 N on the Earth
   B   X has a mass of 60 kg on the Moon
   C   X has a weight of 61.6 N on the Moon
   D   X has a mass of 600 kg on the Earth

6   A parachutist soon reaches a steady (terminal) velocity after leaving the aeroplane. This is because
   A   his weight is counterbalanced by the frictional force of the air
   B   his weight is supported by strings
   C   his mass is constant
   D   the parachute exerts a downward force

SHORT ANSWER QUESTIONS

7   In Fig 1F, two trolleys A and B are pushed together tightly to compress the spring S. When the trolleys are released together, the initial

acceleration of A, mass 3 kg, is 2 m/s² and that of B, mass m, is 1.5 m/s².

Fig 1F

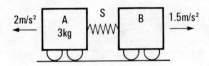

(*a*)   Calculate the mass m of B.

(*b*)   Why do the velocities of A and B decrease as they move further along the plane XY?

8   While practising for a high-jump competition, a girl athlete produces a force of 600 N jumping vertically upwards from the ground. If her mass is 50 kg, calculate (*a*) her weight, (*b*) her initial acceleration leaving the ground.

9   Fig 1G shows the forces acting on a car while travelling with uniform (constant) velocity. The weight of the car is W, the vertically upward forces of the ground on the wheels are 7000 N and 4000 N respectively, 500 N is the frictional force and P is the forward force on the car.

Fig 1G

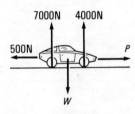

(*a*)   Assuming $g = 10$ m/s², what is the mass of the car?

(*b*)   What is the value of the force P?

(*c*)   If P increases to 600 N, calculate the acceleration of the car, assuming no change in the other forces.

10   A crate C of mass 20 kg is lowered by a rope AB into the hold of a ship with a uniform acceleration of 0.5 m/s². Fig 1H.

Fig 1H

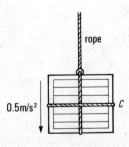

(*a*)   Copy the diagram and show on it the force F in the rope and the weight of the crate C.

(*b*)   Calculate the value of F.

(c)   If the crate C moves down with a uniform **velocity** of 0.5 m/s, what is the new force in the rope? (Assume $g = 10$ m/s^2)

Work, energy and power are important topics in physics. Although we are discussing mechanical work, mechanical energy and mechanical power here, the same ideas occur in all branches of physics; for example, later on we shall deal with electrical work, electrical energy and electrical power.

1.21 WORK

Work is done when a force moves. The amount of work done is calculated from (see Fig 1.14)

work = force × distance moved in direction of force

So, if a model engine exerts a force of 20 N and steadily pulls a train 4 m along a track, then the work done = $20 \times 4 = 80$ units. The unit of work is the **joule**, symbol J; it is the work done when a force of 1 N moves through a distance of 1 m in the direction of the force. So the work done by the engine is 80 J. Remember that

1 newton × 1 metre = 1 joule

Fig 1.14 Work done

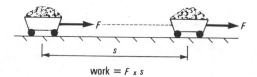

work = $F \times s$

So if F is the force in newtons and s is the displacement (distance moved) in the same direction as the force in metres, the work done W in joules is calculated from

$$W = F \times s$$

1.22 ENERGY

When work is done, **energy is transferred**. For example, in Fig 1.14 the work done in moving the model engine along smooth rails is transferred to it and the engine now has motion energy or kinetic energy, discussed shortly. If the work done is 80 J, then the energy transferred is 80 J.

The reverse is also true. **Energy can be transferred to work.** For example, if a moving train hits an obstacle in its path and pushes the obstacle along the track before coming to rest, the kinetic energy of the train is transferred largely to work.

So work and energy have the same unit, which is the joule, J. Note that work and energy are **scalars** – they have size or magnitude but no direction.

EXAMPLE

A skater on ice is pushed by a horizontal force of 30 N for 2 m. How much work is done? How much energy has the skater gained, neglecting friction?

$$\text{Work done} = F \times s = 30 \times 2 = 60\,\text{J}$$
$$\text{Energy gained} = \text{work done} = 60\,\text{J}$$

1.23 KINETIC ENERGY

There are two kinds of mechanical energy – **kinetic energy** and **potential energy**.

Kinetic energy is the energy of an object due to its motion. A moving train and a moving ball have kinetic energy. We have already shown that a moving train has kinetic energy because it can move objects in its path. If a cricket ball crashes into stumps, its kinetic energy is largely transferred to work as it moves the stumps.

We can show that the kinetic energy of a mass when it has a particular speed is calculated from

$$\text{kinetic energy} = \tfrac{1}{2} \times \text{mass} \times \text{speed}^2$$
or $\quad$ Kinetic energy $= \tfrac{1}{2} mv^2$,

where m is the mass and v is the speed or velocity value. The energy is in joules, J, when the mass m is in kg and the speed or velocity v is in m/s. So a tennis-ball of mass 0.2 kg, hit with a speed of 30 m/s (108 km/h) by a Wimbledon player on serving, will have a kinetic energy

$$= \tfrac{1}{2} mv^2 = \tfrac{1}{2} \times 0.2 \times 30^2 = 90\,\text{J}$$

1.24 PROOF OF KINETIC ENERGY FORMULA

Suppose an object at rest is pushed a distance s by a steady force F. Then, from the transfer of energy,

$$\text{work done} = \text{kinetic energy of object} = F \times s$$

If m is the mass of the object and the force F produces an acceleration a, then $F = ma$ (p.40). Starting from rest, $a = v/t$, where v is the gain in velocity in the time t. So $F = ma = mv/t$.

The distance s = average velocity × time = $\tfrac{1}{2} v \times t$

So $\quad$ work done $= F \times s = \dfrac{mv}{t} \times \tfrac{1}{2} v \times t = \tfrac{1}{2} mv^2$

1.25 POTENTIAL ENERGY. GRAVITATIONAL AND ELASTIC (MOLECULAR)

When an object is raised steadily, the force used to move it is equal to the **weight** of the object. So when the object is moved to a height above the ground, work is done on the object and so **energy** is transferred to it.

The energy of the object due to position, in this case its height above the ground, is called **potential energy**. Here we are dealing with gravitational potential energy because work is done against the gravitational pull of the Earth. Since work done = force × distance moved in direction of force,

gravitational potential energy = weight of object × height

This is the gain in potential energy from the ground position. If m is the mass, g is the gravitational field strength or acceleration due to gravity and h is the height, then, since the weight = mg (p.40),

$$\text{gravitational potential energy} = mg \times h = mgh$$

So a ball of mass 0.2 kg at a height of 30 m above the ground has a potential energy = mgh = 0.2 × 10 × 30 = 60 J, assuming the value of g to be 10 N/kg or 10 m/s^2.

Fig 1.15 Potential and kinetic energy changes

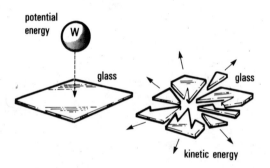

A heavy weight held stationary above a glass sheet has potential energy. When the weight is released and crashes into the glass, pieces are thrown in different directions, shown in Fig 1.15. The weight in a grandfather clock has gravitational potential energy. As the weight falls slowly, wheels and levers are moved.

Another kind of potential energy is obtained when an elastic band is stretched. The molecules in the band are then strained and work is done in moving the molecules farther apart against their force of attraction. The potential energy of the stretched band is called **elastic** or **molecular** potential energy. After winding a watch, the coiled spring inside has gained elastic or molecular potential energy equal to the work done in moving the molecules against their forces of attraction.

1.26 TRANSFER OF POTENTIAL AND KINETIC ENERGY

A ball, thrown vertically upwards from the ground, initially has kinetic energy. As it rises, the ball gains gravitational potential energy and this comes from the transfer of some of the kinetic energy. So the kinetic energy becomes less or decreases. At the top of its height, the ball comes to rest at this instant. So all the kinetic energy is now transferred to potential energy. We can illustrate the transfers by a numerical example.

Fig 1.16 Conservation of energy under gravitational forces

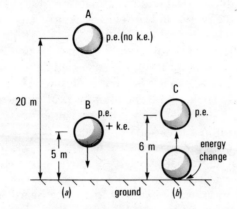

Suppose a ball of mass 0.1 kg is thrown vertically upwards and reaches a maximum height of 20 m at A (Fig 1.16a). At this height the ball has only potential energy as its velocity is then zero. So if $g = 10 \text{ m/s}^2$,

$$\text{energy of ball} = \text{p.e.} = mgh = 0.1 \times 10 \times 20 = 20 \text{ J}$$

When the ball falls and reaches a point 5 m above the ground, it then has both potential energy, p.e., and kinetic energy, k.e. If we assume that no energy is used up in falling (not strictly true because there is friction between the falling ball and the air), then

$$\text{energy of ball} = \text{k.e.} + \text{p.e.} = 20 \text{ J}$$

But at 5 m above ground,

$$\text{p.e.} = mgh = 0.1 \times 10 \times 5 = 5 \text{ J}$$
So $\quad \text{k.e.} = 20 - 5 = 15 \text{ J}$

Just before it hits the ground, the ball has only kinetic energy, k.e. So since the energy is constant,

$$\text{k.e.} = \text{initial p.e.} = 20 \text{ J}$$

When the ball hits the ground, suppose it bounces to a height of 6 m at C (Fig 1.16b). At this height the energy of the ball = p.e. = mgh = $0.1 \times 10 \times 6 = 6 \text{ J}$. So on contact with the ground the ball lost energy of $20 \text{ J} - 6 \text{ J} = 14 \text{ J}$. This amount of energy is transferred to heat and sound energy on collision with the ground. A lump of putty falling to the ground would transfer all its energy to heat and sound and would not bounce up.

1.27 ENERGY TRANSFORMATION. THE PRINCIPLE OF CONSERVATION OF ENERGY

Energy has many different forms, for example, mechanical, electrical, light, sound, chemical and nuclear energy. Energy can be transferred from one form to another. For example, an electrical motor transfers electrical energy to mechanical energy; a battery transfers chemical energy to electrical energy; a microphone transfers sound energy to electrical energy; and an electric lamp transfers electrical energy to heat and light energy.

A nuclear reactor transfers nuclear energy to heat (thermal) energy, which in turn is transferred to electrical energy. Electromagnetic radiation is a form of energy which can be obtained (a) from lamps as visible (light) radiation or heat (infra-red) radiation or ultra-violet radiation, (b) from X-ray machines as X-radiation and (c) from unstable atoms as gamma-radiation.

Hydroelectric power stations produce electrical energy from the potential energy of water high above them. The human body transfers chemical energy from the food we eat to mechanical energy needed by muscles in use and by the heart pump. Fig 1.17 shows some energy transfers and the device or apparatus needed.

Fig 1.17 Some energy transfers by devices

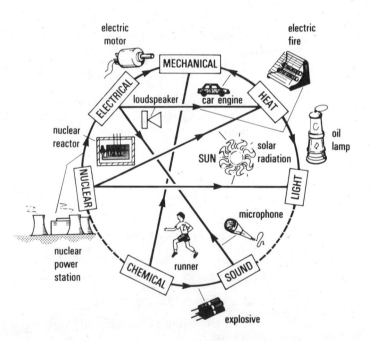

In an electric motor, the electrical energy supplied is transferred mostly into mechanical energy for driving machines, for example. The rest of the energy is transferred to heat energy due to frictional forces inside the motor and to sound energy due to air movement inside. We can never obtain more energy than the amount supplied. This important principle is expressed by the Principle of Conservation of Energy: **In a closed system, energy can be transferred from one form to another but the total amount of energy remains constant.**

1.28 POWER

Engines produce energy which moves a car along. The **power** of an engine is the **rate of producing energy or doing work**. The power of any machine is

$$\text{power} = \frac{\text{work done (or energy produced)}}{\text{time}}$$

If two cars X and Y have the same mass, but X has a greater engine power than Y, then starting from the same place O, X can reach the top of an inclined road quicker than Y (Fig 1.18).

Fig 1.18 Power

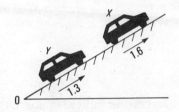

An electric lamp of 100 W uses 100 joules per second from the mains supply.

The **kilowatt**, symbol kW, is a larger unit of power used in industry. An electric heater may have a power of 1 kW; a car engine may have a power of 2 kW at a particular speed.

When the force due to an engine on a car is 60 N and the velocity is then 20 m/s,

power = work done per second
= 60 N × 20 m/s = 1200 joules per second
= 1200 W = 1.2 kW

Generally, to find the power produced,

power = force × velocity

1.29 EFFICIENCY OF MACHINES

Some energy or work is needed to overcome frictional forces in an engine when its piston and other parts are rotating. This energy is transferred to heat energy. From the engine point of view, the energy is 'wasted'. Lubrication with oil can reduce the amount of energy wasted but the **input power** to a machine is always greater than the **output power** owing to frictional forces. The **efficiency** of any machine is defined as

$$\text{efficiency} = \frac{\text{power output}}{\text{power input}} \text{ or } \frac{\text{work (energy) output}}{\text{work (energy) input}} \times 100\%$$

If the power output is 600 W and the power input is 1000 W, the efficiency = (600/1000) × 100% = 60%. If the work or energy output is 800 J and the work or energy input is 1000 J, the efficiency = (800/1000) × 100% = 80%.

CHECK LIST ▶

Make sure you can answer the following questions:

1 How is **work** calculated? What is the **power** of an engine?
2 A girl of mass 50 kg walked up a flight of stairs of total height 6 m. What is the change in her gravitational potential energy if g = 10 m/s²? What transfer of energy took place in this case?
3 Define **kinetic energy**. Is it a scalar or vector quantity?
   A car of mass 1000 kg has a velocity of 20 m/s. What is its kinetic energy? If the car uses 300 000 J in braking, what kinetic energy is left and what is then the velocity of the car?

1.30 MACHINES. FORCE MULTIPLIERS

Machines such as levers and pulleys enable large loads or forces to be overcome by using only a small force or effort. An effort or force of 20 N, for example, may then overcome a force of 200 N, which is ten times as big. So these machines are **force multipliers**.

Fig 1.19 Levers (force multipliers)

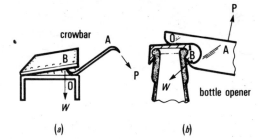

(a)   (b)

Figure 1.19(a) shows a crowbar used to open the lid of a case. The effort or force P is applied at the end of a long arm OA and O is the pivot. If P moves a distance 10 cm when the crowbar is used, work input = force × distance = P × 10 units. Suppose the lid is then raised 2 cm to B. Then work output = resistance W of nails × 2 units.
    Assuming 100% efficiency, work in = work out. So

$$P \times 10 = W \times 2$$
$$P = \frac{W}{5}$$

So if the resistance W = 50 N, then the effort P = 50/5 = 10 N. The crowbar as a lever therefore multiplies the force P by 5 when used.

Levers are force multipliers, as this example shows. The multiplying number is the ratio OA/OB or *long arm/short arm*. So a good lever has a long arm for force and a short arm for the resistance to be overcome. Fig 1.19(*b*) shows a bottle-opener working as a lever.

Fig 1.20 Wheel and axle machine

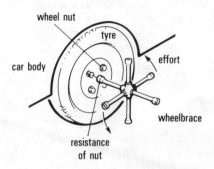

Fig 1.20 shows a wheelbrace, used for unscrewing the wheelnuts of a car. This is an example of a type of machine called a **wheel and axle**. Here the applied force or effort P turns through a circle ('wheel') of large radius R and then overcomes the large resistance W of the nut, which turns through a circle of small radius r, the axle radius of the wheelbrace. If $P = 5\,\text{N}$ and the circumference of the circle of radius R is 90 cm or 0.9 m, then work input = force × distance = 5 × 0.9 = 4.5 J.

If the circle of radius r has a circumference of 3 cm or 0.03 m, then work output = W × 0.03 J, assuming the machine is 100% efficient. Since work output = work input in this case,

$$W \times 0.03 = 4.5, \qquad \text{so } W = 4.5/0.03 = 150\,\text{N}$$

So a small force of 5 N is multiplied 30 times by using the brace.

1.31 GEARS

Gears are used to make a car start, accelerate and climb a hill and to make it move with a suitable high speed.

Fig 1.21 shows a simple gear arrangement. Two parallel shafts A and B each have a gear wheel A' and B' fixed on them, with 12 and 30 teeth respectively which intermesh. So when A turns round once, the 12 teeth on A' have turned 12 teeth on B' and so B has turned through only $\frac{12}{30}$th of a revolution. So, generally,

$$\frac{\text{speed of shaft B}}{\text{speed of shaft A}} = \frac{\text{number of teeth in A}}{\text{number of teeth in B}}$$

So Fig 1.21 illustrates a 'step-down' gear ratio of 12/30 or 1/2.5.

When a car reaches a hill or up-gradient, the road speed decreases because of the downward force due to the weight of the car. If the force due to the engine remains the same, the car would soon stop or stall. To climb the hill, the driver changes down to a lower gear. If shaft B is connected to the car wheels, shaft A connected to the

Fig 1.21 Gears

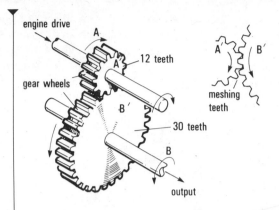

engine now increases in speed. So the engine speed now increases and the output power from the engine therefore increases. This extra power keeps the car moving at a good speed up the hill. A low gear helps the car to start or to accelerate.

1.32 EXAMPLE ON WORK AND EFFICIENCY OF A MACHINE

A load of 100 N is raised 1 m by a machine when the force or effort F applied to the machine moves 5 m in its own direction. The efficiency of the machine is 80%.

Find (a) the work or energy output, (b) the work or energy wasted in the machine, (c) the value of F.

(a)   Work or energy output = load × distance = $100 \times 1 = 100$ J

(b)

$$\text{Since } \frac{\text{work out}}{\text{work in}} = 80\% = \frac{80}{100}$$

$$\text{So work in } = \frac{100}{80} \times \text{work out} = \frac{100}{80} \times 100 \text{ J}$$

$$= 125 \text{ J}$$

Work wasted = $125 - 100 = 25$ J

(c)   Work in   = $F \times 5 = 125$

So $F = 125/5 = 25$ N

1.33 ACTION AND REACTION – NEWTON'S LAW

If you lean on the table with your elbow, your elbow exerts a downward force on the table. Newton called this force the 'action' of the elbow. The table exerts an upward force on your elbow. Newton called this force the 'reaction' of the table and stated that:

Action and reaction are always equal and opposite.

Any contact between two objects produces equal and opposite forces. If you kick a football, as in Fig 1.22, on impact the force on the ball is equal and opposite to the force of your foot. The ball moves

Fig 1.22 Action and reaction

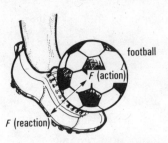

forward due to this 'action' force. Since the ball is light, the reaction force on your foot is hardly noticeable. But if you were to kick a heavy stone, you *would* feel the reaction force!

Reaction forces are widely used. In the case of a firing rocket, for example, the downward force on the gas pushed out at the rear is equal to the upward force on the rocket. The same principle applies to the jet engine: the aeroplane moves forward on account of the force of reaction. Lawn sprinklers throw jets of water forward and rotate backwards on account of the reaction force.

The lift on a hovercraft on the ground is provided by a force of reaction. The rotating blades are tilted so as to hit the air molecules in a downward direction and the and opposite reaction force lifts the hovercraft for take-off.

Forces of action and reaction can occur at a distance. For example, a falling ball is attracted downwards by the Earth's gravitational field. An equal and opposite force acts upwards on the Earth. If a magnet A attracts another magnet B near it, then B will attract A with an equal and opposite force.

1.34 FORCE AND MOMENTUM

The **momentum** of an object is defined as:

momentum = mass × velocity

So a boy of mass 50 kg running with a velocity of 2 m/s has a momentum of 50×2 or 100 units. We can write the momentum as '100 kg m/s' because we multiply mass (kg) by velocity (m/s).

Newton recognized that a force changes the momentum of an object. His second law of motion said that:

$$\text{force} = \frac{\text{momentum change}}{\text{time}}$$

or **force is the rate of change of momentum**.

Momentum is a **vector** quantity, that is, it has both direction and magnitude. A ball of mass 0.2 kg moving towards a wall with a velocity of 10 m/s has a momentum of 0.2 × 10 or 2 kg m/s. If it rebounds straight back with a velocity of 10 m/s after hitting the wall, its momentum is −2 kg m/s, the minus showing that the direction of the momentum has reversed. So due to the impact with the wall,

change in momentum $= 2-(-2) = 2+2$
$$= 4 \, \text{kg m/s}$$

Note that momentum is a **vector** quantity.

1.35 EXAMPLES ON MOMENTUM

1 In a collision test, a car of mass 1000 kg travelling at 10 m/s is brought to rest in 2 s. Calculate the average force on the car.

$$\text{Force } F = \frac{\text{momentum change}}{\text{time}}$$

$$= \frac{(1000 \times 10) - 0 \, \text{kg m/s}}{2 \, \text{s}}$$

$$= \frac{10\,000}{2} = 5000 \, \text{N}$$

The 0 in the momentum change arithmetic represents the zero momentum of the car when it comes to rest. If the car had slowed down to 2 m/s, for example, in 2 s, then the momentum change would have been ($10\,000 - 2000$) or 8000 kg m/s. The average force is then 8000/2 or 4000 N, which is less than before.

2 A force of 20 N acts for 4 s on an object. What momentum change is produced?

$$\text{Since force } F = \frac{\text{momentum change}}{t}$$

where t is the time, then

$$F \times t = \text{momentum change}$$
So $\quad 20 \times 4 = 80 \, \text{kg m/s} = \text{momentum change}$

1.36 CONSERVATION OF MOMENTUM

As we have seen, momentum (mass×velocity) is a vector quantity; it has the same direction as the velocity. So a mass of 2 kg moving with a velocity of 3 m/s from left to right has a momentum of, say, $+2 \times 3$ or +6 units, and a mass of 4 kg moving with a velocity of 2 m/s from *right to left* will then have a momentum of -4×2 or -8 units. Their total momentum is given by

$$+6 - 8 = -2 \, \text{units}$$

The momentum of colliding objects can be investigated by using the impact between a moving and a stationary small trolley in a laboratory experiment, with which we assume the reader is familiar. In Fig 1.23, a moving trolley X of mass 250 g has a velocity of 20 cm/s. After colliding with the stationary trolley Y of mass 200 g, X and Y stick together and move off with a velocity of 11 cm/s. Then, using units of gram for mass and cm/s for velocity,

momentum of X and Y before collision $= 250 \times 20 = 5000$ units momentum of X and Y after collision =

$$(250+200)\times11 = 4950 \text{ units}$$

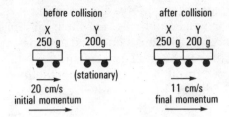

Fig 1.23 Conservation of
momentum

So, allowing for experimental errors, *when two objects collide their total momentum remains constant*. This is always the case when no forces act on the objects other than those due to the collision. We call this the 'principle of conservation of momentum'.

The reason for this result is that, from Newton's law of action and reaction, the colliding objects exert equal and opposite forces F on each other for the same time t. Now $F\times t$ = momentum change (see Example 2, p.56). The momentum change in one object is therefore cancelled out by the momentum change in the other object. So the total momentum of both objects is the same after collision as before.

A trolley of mass 5 kg and velocity 4 m/s collides with a trolley of mass 3 kg and velocity 2 m/s moving in the opposite direction (Fig 1.24). If both trolleys stick together, calculate their common velocity after collision.

Total momentum before collision = $(5\times4) - (3\times2) = 14$
Total momentum after collision = $(5+3)\,v = 8v$

$8\,v = 14$ from the conservation of momentum

So $\qquad v = \dfrac{14}{8} = 1.75$ m/s

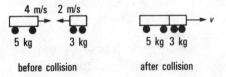

Fig 1.24 Calculation on
momentum

SUMMARY

(a) YOU SHOULD KNOW

1 Work = force $\times$ distance in direction of force. Unit: joule, J.
2 Work done = energy transferred.
3 Kinetic energy = energy due to motion = $\frac{1}{2}mv^2$.
4 Gravitational potential energy change = mgh, where h is the change in height or level.

5   Elastic (molecular) potential energy change is due to change in position of molecules.
6   Power = work done per second = work/time taken. Unit: watt, W.
7   Power of car engine = force due to engine × velocity.
8   Levers, or wheel and axle, are force multipliers. The force applied moves through a large distance and overcomes a big resistance or force which moves through a small distance.
9   Gears work through interlocking toothed wheels. The speed of the shaft driving the wheels is inversely proportional to the number of teeth.

(b) YOU SHOULD UNDERSTAND

1   The definition of **work** and the connection between work and energy transfer.
2   The meaning of kinetic energy.
3   The meaning of potential energy change in the gravitational field and how to calculate them.
4   The meaning of potential energy change in molecular fields, which is elastic energy.
5   Devices which transfer energy of one kind to another.
6   The meaning of the principle of conservation of energy.
7   The definition of **power** and **efficiency** of a machine.
8   How levers act as force multipliers and how gears work.

(c) APPLICATIONS

You should be able to
1   define **gravitational potential energy change**. A ball of mass 0.5 kg is released at a height of 10 m. At a height of 4 m above the ground, find the potential energy relative to the ground and the kinetic energy of the ball.
2   define the **power** of a machine. A crate of weight 500 N is hauled from the ground to a height of 12 m in 20 s by a crane. What is the output power of the crane? What is the efficiency of the crane if it is driven by a motor of $\frac{1}{2}$ kW power?
3   do this calculation: A car is moving with a velocity of 25 m/s and the force due to the engine is then 100 N. What is the power of the engine?

QUESTIONS 1C WORK. ENERGY. POWER

(Assume g = 10 m/s^2 or 10 N/kg where necessary)

MULTIPLE CHOICE QUESTIONS

1   A metal block of mass 4 kg is moved 5 m in the direction of a pulling force of 2 N. The work done in moving the block is
     A 22 J   B 12 J   C 11 J   D 10 J

2   The unit of power is

    A   joule   B   newton   C   watt   D   kilogram

3   A lifting truck takes 10 s to raise a crate of mass 8 kg steadily through a vertical height of 5 m. The output power of the truck is

    A   8000 W   B   400 W   C   40 W   D   23 W

4   When an arrow is fired from a bow, the energy transfer is

    A   elastic potential energy to kinetic energy
    B   chemical energy to elastic potential energy
    C   kinetic energy to elastic potential energy
    D   heat energy to kinetic energy

5   When the small mass at the end of a simple pendulum is pulled to one side and then released, after several oscillations the mass does not rise as high as at the start. This is because

    A   some of the gravitational potential energy is transferred to kinetic energy
    B   some of the potential energy is transferred to heat energy by air resistance
    C   the kinetic energy is transferred to potential energy
    D   the string of the pendulum reduces the potential energy

SHORT ANSWER QUESTIONS

6   A girl diver of mass 50 kg stands on a diving board which is 3 m above the surface of the water.

    (a)   What is her potential energy?
    (b)   As the girl dives into the water, does her potential energy increase, decrease or stay the same?
    (c)   Calculate the speed of the diver as she is about to enter the water, using energy transfer.

7   A boy of mass 40 kg takes 8 s to climb steadily three flights of stairs from the ground floor. Each flight is 4 m high.

    (a)   What was the average power of the boy?
    (b)   What energy transfer took place in the climb?
    (c)   If the boy slid down the banisters to the ground floor, write down the energy transfer which occurs.

8   A lifting crane uses an electric motor and raises a pile of bricks of total weight 1500 N steadily through a vertical height of 25 m.

    (a)   What work is done by the crane?
    (b)   If the efficiency of the motor is 50%, what amount of work was done in turning the motor?
    (c)   The crane takes 10 s to lift the bricks. Calculate the power of the motor.

9   A ball of mass 0.5 kg is dropped from a height of 10 m.

    (a)   What is the initial potential energy of the ball?
    (b)   What are the potential and kinetic energies of the ball when it is 2 m from the ground?
    (c)   What is the speed of the ball when it is 2 m from the ground?
    After the ball hits the ground it bounces up vertically to a height of 6 m.

(d)   What mechanical energy is lost on hitting the ground and what energy transfer then takes place?

10   A girl turns the button winder of her wrist-watch six times to wind up her watch. Each time she exerts a force of 2 N and the button turns 1 cm or 0.01 m.

(a)   Calculate the total work she does in winding the watch.

(b)   Describe the energy transfers which take place when the watch is wound.

11   A small model car, mass 0.2 kg, is held at A, the top of a runway or slope. Fig 1I. On releasing the car, it moves down the runway to the bottom B and then 'loops the loop' and **just** reaches the top C of the loop P. The diameter of P is 0.6 m.

Calculate (a) the potential energy at A relative to B, (b) the kinetic energy at B if 0.4 J is used against frictional forces from A to B, (c) the change in potential energy from B to C.

Fig 1I

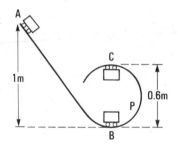

Fig 1J

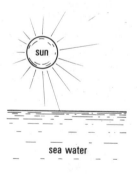

12   The Sun evaporates seawater, Fig 1J, and forms clouds. These clouds produce rainwater which fills a reservoir and the water here is used in a hydroelectric plant to produce electricity.

(a)   Draw a sketch of all the changes just described, starting with the Sun.

(b)   Label the **energy transfer** which takes place each time, starting with the Sun and finishing with the production of electricity.

FORCES, PRESSURE AND MATERIALS

CONTENTS

MOMENTS OF FORCES. CENTRE OF GRAVITY. PARALLEL FORCES

In this section we deal with the turning-effect or **moment** of a force about a point or axis. The turning-effect of forces keep machines such as lathes and printing presses working in industry. It also plays an important part in keeping structures such as bridges in balance.

We start with the meaning of 'moment' and then show how it is used when forces are in balance and when objects are stable or unstable.

2.1 MEANING AND CALCULATION OF MOMENT

When you push open a door, the force you exert has a turning-effect or moment about the hinges. By definition:

moment about a point = force × perpendicular distance from that point to the line of action of force

So $$\text{moment} = F \times p$$

where F is the force and p is the **perpendicular** distance from the point to the line along which the force acts. When F is in newtons (N) and the distance p is in metres (m), then the moment is in newton metre (N m).

Fig 2.1(a) shows a spanner round a nut and about to screw it up. The perpendicular distance from the centre of the nut to the line of action of the force may be 0.6 m and the force F may be 5 N. In this case

$$\text{moment} = F \times p = 5 \times 0.6 = 3.0\,\text{N m}$$

Fig 2.1(b) shows a wheel W with centre O and radius 0.5 m. A rope is tied to W at A and is pulled with a force of 10 N in a direction AT

Fig 2.1 Moments of forces

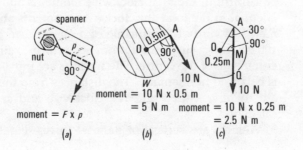

tangential to the wheel, that is, AT is perpendicular to the radius OA. Suppose the wheel can turn about an axle through O. Then

$$\text{moment about O} = \text{force} \times \text{perpendicular distance from O}$$
$$\text{to 10 N force}$$
$$= 10 \times 0.5 = 5 \,\text{N m}$$

Suppose, however, the rope at A is now moved so that the 10 N force pulls in the direction AQ at 30° to the radius OA as in Fig 2.1(c). The moment is now $F \times$ OM, where OM is the perpendicular distance from O to the line AQ of the force. Now

$$\frac{\text{OM}}{\text{OA}} = \sin 30°, \text{ or } \text{OM} = \text{OA} \sin 30° = 0.5 \times 0.5 = 0.25 \,\text{m}$$

So   moment about O = 10 N $\times$ 0.25 m = 2.5 N m

2.2 PIVOTED OBJECTS IN EQUILIBRIUM. PRINCIPLE OF MOMENTS

Fig 2.2 Principle of moments

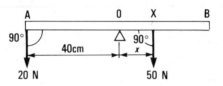

Fig 2.2 shows a uniform horizontal beam AB pivoted at its centre O where its weight has no turning-effect or moment. A vertical force of 20 N at A, 40 cm from O, and a vertical force of 50 N at X, x cm from O, keep AB in equilibrium.

Moments can turn clockwise or anticlockwise. Here the clockwise moment of the 50 N force about O = the anticlockwise moment about O of the 20 N force, since the beam is in equilibrium or balanced. The perpendicular distances from O to the two forces are respectively x cm and 40 cm. So

$$50 \times x = 20 \times 40$$

So $$x = \frac{20 \times 40}{50} = 16 \,\text{cm}$$

For the pivoted beam, we have used the so-called **principle of moments**. This principle (law) states that **when a pivoted object is in equilibrium, the total clockwise moments about the pivot (fulcrum) is equal to the total anticlockwise moments about the pivot.** Experiments to verify the principle of moments can be carried out using a 100 cm ruler suspended from its centre, with known weights on either side of the centre. The weights are moved along until the ruler is balanced horizontally. The distances from the weights to the centre are then measured and the clockwise and anticlockwise moments calculated.

Weights are vertical or **parallel forces**. Fig 2.3 illustrates how the

Fig 2.3 Three parallel forces in equilibrium

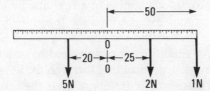

principle of moments can be verified when three parallel forces keep a pivoted uniform ruler balanced horizontally. In this case

total clockwise moments about O = $(2 \times 25) + (1 \times 50) = 100$

and   total anticlockwise moments about O = $5 \times 20 = 100$

So the total clockwise and anticlockwise moments about O are equal.

CHECK LIST ▶

Make sure you can answer the following questions.

1 When a 'moment' is calculated, what 'distance' is used?
2 When a pivoted object is in balance, what is the relation between the forces?
3 What measurements are made in verifying the 'principle of moments'?

CENTRE OF GRAVITY. STABILITY OF OBJECTS

2.3 CENTRE OF GRAVITY

Any object such as a ball, a bicycle or a person has its mass and weight spread all over it. The point where we can consider the whole of the weight to act, or appear to act, is called the **centre of gravity** of the object.

Fig 2.4 Centre of gravity

uniform rod   disc   ring   rectangle   triangle

Fig 2.4 shows the positions of the centre of gravity, G, of some uniform objects. Except for the ring, all the objects can be balanced on a point at G, where the whole of their weight appears to act.

Fig 2.5 Finding the centre of gravity

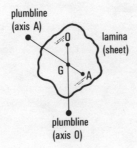

To find the c.g. of a lamina of any shape by experiment, suspend it from a horizontal axis O passing through a hole near one edge, making sure the lamina swings freely (Fig 2.5). Use a plumbline (a thread with a small heavy weight tied to one end) suspended from the axis to mark a vertical line through O. Repeat with another axis, such as A. The centre of gravity, c.g., is then the point of intersection of the two lines because the lamina always comes to rest with its c.g. vertically below the axis. To check this, try balancing the lamina with its c.g. resting on the horizontal edge of a glass prism.

2.4 STABILITY OF OBJECTS. STABLE EQUILIBRIUM

As we shall see, the stability of an object such as a racing car, for example, depends on the height of its centre of gravity (c.g.) and on the width or size of its base. If an object is slightly displaced and then released, it is in **stable equilibrium** if it returns to its original position. Examples are shown in Fig 2.6. In (*a*), a cone slightly tilted about an edge at O will return to its original position when released. The weight *W* acting through the centre of gravity G has a moment about O which restores the coner to its original position, as shown. In Fig 2.6(*b*), a chair tilted backwards slightly about two legs, A, will return to its original position if released because the weight *W* has a moment about the legs which brings it back. Both the cone and the chair in Fig 2.6(*b*) have a **wide base**, which helps to make stable equilibrium.

Fig 2.6 Stable equilibrium – wide base

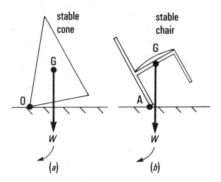

Generally, a *low* c.g. will help stable equilibrium. Fig 2.7 shows a toy with a heavily weighted base. When it is pushed down, as

Fig 2.7 Stable equilibrium – low c.g.

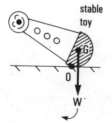

shown, it springs up again when released and returns to its original position. The weight W always has a restoring moment about O. Racing cars have a low c.g. and a wide base to help stable equilibrium when going round bends at high speed, otherwise the car would topple over.

2.5 UNSTABLE EQUILIBRIUM

If an object is slightly displaced and then released, it is said to be in **unstable equilibrium** if it moves farther away from its original position.

In Fig 2.8(a), a chair was rocked back too far and is in unstable equilibrium. Its weight W now has a moment about the legs which makes it move farther away. So it topples over. A cone resting on its apex O is in unstable equilibrium, as in Fig 2.8(b).

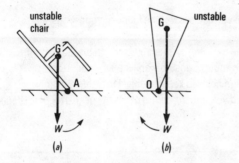

Fig 2.8 Unstable equilibrium

Unstable equilibrium occurs when the c.g. is high above the base and the base is narrow. When the object is displaced, the weight acting downwards then has a moment about the base which topples the object.

2.6 EXAMPLES ON STABLE AND UNSTABLE EQUILIBRIUM

1 What type of equilibrium has a marble in the middle of a bowl or a tightrope walker without a pole? Explain your answers.

The marble has **stable equilibrium**. Reason: When the marble is displaced from the middle and released, it always rolls back to the centre of the bowl.

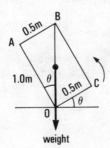

Fig 2.9 Calculation on unstable equilibrium

The tightrope walker has **unstable equilibrium**. Reason: When the walker is displaced sideways away from the rope, his weight will make him move farther away and he will fall off.

2 A heavy solid rectangular box rests on a horizontal surface. The height of the box is 1.0 m and its base is 0.5 m wide (see Fig 2.9). The box is tilted about one edge on the surface until it just topples over under its own weight. Through what angle has the box been turned?

Fig 2.9 shows the box when it is just about to topple over under its weight about the edge of O. The angle θ through which the box has turned equals angle AOB. Now

$$\tan \theta = \frac{AB}{OA} = \frac{0.5}{1} = 0.5$$

So, from Tables, $\theta = 27°$ (approx).

CHECK LIST ▶ Make sure you can answer the following questions.

1 What is the meaning of 'unstable' and 'stable' equilibrium?
2 Give an example of unstable and stable equilibrium.
3 What design helps to keep an object in stable equilibrium?
4 How would you find the centre of gravity of an irregular-shaped metal sheet?

PARALLEL FORCES IN BALANCE

Bridges and beams resting on supports are examples of structures where parallel forces are in balance. The weight of a bridge and the weight of cars and lorries on it are all parallel forces acting vertically downwards. So there must be upward parallel forces at the bridge supports which balance all the weights and so keep the bridge in equilibrium.

2.7 EQUILIBRIUM WITH PARALLEL FORCES

As a typical example, consider a horizontal beam AB resting on supports at O and B, Fig 2.10(a). The beam is in equilibrium under three parallel forces. These are (a) the weight, say 12 N, of the beam acting vertically downwards at G (see p.65), (b) the upward forces, P

Fig 2.10 Parallel forces in equilibrium

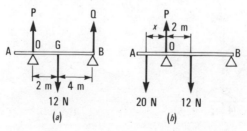

and Q at O and B. These are the reactions of the supports on the beam. Two conditions for equilibrium are:

1 The total upward forces equal to the total downward forces.
2 The total clockwise moments of the forces about any any point or axis equal the total anticlockwise moments of the forces about the same point or axis.

So, from 1,

$$P + Q = 12\,\text{N}$$

Using 2, take the moments *about B* to avoid having Q in the equation. Then

$$P \times 6 \text{ (clockwise moment)} = 12 \times 4 \text{ (anticlockwise moment)}$$

So
$$P = \frac{12 \times 4}{6} = 8\,\text{N}$$

Thus
$$Q = 12 - P = 4\,\text{N}$$

Suppose we want to know the distance x from O where a load of 20 N just makes the beam in Fig 2.10(*b*) leave the support at B. The reaction Q then disappears; and taking moments about O to avoid having P in the equation, we have

$$20 \times x = 12 \times 2 = 24$$

So
$$x = \frac{24}{20} = 1.2\,\text{m}$$

EFFECTS OF FORCES. FORCES IN BALANCE

2.8 TYPES OF FORCE

As we saw previously, a force can produce a change in motion. A force can also be a **push**, for example, when a door is pushed open, or a **pull**, for example, when a tug pulls a ship. Forces can also cause a **change of shape**, for example, when a rubber cord or a spring is twisted.

2.9 ADDING FORCES. VECTOR ADDITION

Force is a vector quantity, that is, a force has both direction and size (magnitude). Often we need to add two or more forces so as to find their total or **resultant** force. Since forces are vectors, we need **vector addition**.

Fig 2.11 Vector addition – parallelogram of forces

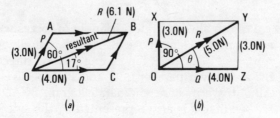

(*a*)   (*b*)

Fig 2.11(*a*) shows two forces *P*, 3.0 N, and *Q*, 4.0 N, at 60° to each other, pulling an object at O. We draw a line OC to represent 4.0 N, *Q*, to scale, then a line OA to represent 3.0 N, *P*, on the same scale. Now we complete the **parallelogram** OABC by drawing parallel lines from A and C to OC and OA respectively. Then OC is the vector sum, or resultant, of the two forces *P* and *Q*. Measurements from an accurate drawing show that the diagonal OC represents 6.1 N and its direction is about 17° to the larger force *Q*.

OABC is called a '**parallelogram of forces**' and this is the parallelogram way of adding vectors. We can also add *P* and *Q* vectorially by drawing OC to represent *Q* to scale and then CB, drawing CB to scale to represent *P*. Then the third side of the triangle OBC is the sum or resultant. This is the '**triangle**' way of adding vectors.

The angle between the two forces *P* and *Q* affects their resultant R. In Fig 2.11(ii), the angle is 90°. So the parallelogram of forces is now a **rectangle** OXYZ. From Pythagoras' theorem for triangle OYZ, $R^2 = P^2 + Q^2$. So

$$R = \sqrt{3.0^2 + 4.0^2} = 5.0 \, \text{N}$$

Also, from triangle YOZ, the angle θ which *R* makes with *Q* is given by

$$\tan \theta = \frac{YZ}{OZ} = \frac{3.0}{4.0} = 0.75, \text{ so } \theta = 37°$$

2.10 EQUILIBRIUM OF THREE FORCES. TRIANGLE OF FORCES

Suppose a 20.0 N weight *W* is suspended by two strings inclined at 30° and 45° to the horizontal respectively, as in Fig 2.12. If *P* and *Q* are the tensions (forces) in the strings, the resultant of *P* and *Q* must be exactly equal and opposite to *W* for equilibrium.

Fig 2.12 Triangle of forces

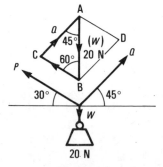

We can always draw a **triangle of forces** when three forces are in equilibrium. Here the side AB of triangle ABC is first drawn to represent *W* or 20.0 N in magnitude and direction, and then AC and BC are drawn parallel to *Q* and *P* respectively to form the triangle ABC. If we imagine the parallelogram BCAD completed as shown, we see that *Q* is also represented by the side BD. The resultant of *P*

and Q is BA, so AB, which balances the resultant, is 20 N. Hence ABC is the triangle of forces.

We now measure the lengths of the sides BC and CA, and change them to newtons from the scale used for 20 N, represented by AB. From a scale drawing,

$$P = 14.6 \text{ N and } Q = 17.9 \text{ N}$$

CHECK LIST ▶ Make sure you can answer the following questions.

1 How would you find the *resultant* of two forces?
2 If two known forces are in balance with a third force X, how would you find X?

Fig 2.13 Forces in balance on ladder

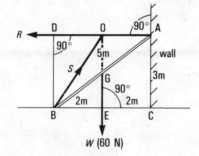

W (60 N)

2.11 LARGE OBJECTS IN EQUIILIBRIUM

In problems on equilibrium, always keep in mind that:

1 A **smooth** surface has a reaction (force), when objects rest on it, which is always **perpendicular to the surface**.
2 Three forces which keep an object in equilibrium must all pass through one point – otherwise the resultant of two of the forces cannot balance the third force.

As an example, consider the ladder AB in Fig 2.13, which is 5 m long. It rests against a smooth wall at A, so the reaction R is perpendicular to the wall AC. The weight W of 60 N acts vertically downwards at its midpoint G if the ladder is uniform. The reaction S at the ground at B must pass through the point of intersection O of R and W. So BO is the line of action of S as shown.

A simple way of finding R is to take moments about B for all the forces. We choose B because S passes through B and therefore has no moment about B – so we eliminate S from our moment equation. R has an anticlockwise moment about B of $R \times$ BD or $R \times 3$, since BD = CA = 3 m. W has a clockwise moment about B of $W \times$ EC or 60×2, where BC is 4 m. So, for equilibrium,

$$R \times 3 = 60 \times 2, \text{ from which } R = 40 \text{ N.}$$

S is equal to the resultant of W (60 N) and R (40 N). W and R are at 90° to each other. So, from Pythagoras, $S = \sqrt{60^2 + 40^2} = 72$ N.

2.12 EXAMPLES ON FORCES IN BALANCE

1 Two horizontal forces of 5 N and 7 N respectively pull together on a block O.

(a)   What is the greatest and the least possible values of their resultant?

(b)   If the two forces pull at an angle to each other, is the resultant force direction nearer the 5 N or the 7 N force?

(a)   Maximum resultant = 5+7 = 12 N (both forces pull in same direction).

Minimum resultant = 7−5 = 2 N (the forces pull in opposite directions).

(b)   The resultant force is nearer the 7 N force, from the parallelogram of forces drawing.

2

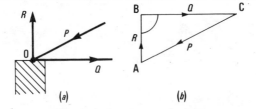

Fig 2.14 Forces in balance

                        (a)   (b)

In Fig 2.14(a), P, Q and R are three forces in balance at a joint O of a structure. Triangle ABC in Fig 2.14(b) is a triangle of forces for P, Q and R, that is, the sides AB, BC and CA represent the forces in magnitude and direction.

(a)   Copy the triangle ABC and put on it arrows pointing in the direction of the forces P, Q and R.

(b)   If $R = 30$ N and $Q = 40$ N, what is the size of P?

(a)   AB is the direction of R, BC is the direction of Q, CA is the direction of P.

(b)   Triangle ABC has 90° at B. So, from Pythagoras' theorem, $AC^2 = CB^2 + AB^2$.

So $P^2 = 40^2 + 30^2$

So $P = \sqrt{40^2 + 30^2} = 50$ N

3 A trap-door AO, with a hinge at O, is kept open by a horizontal rope AL tied to A. Fig 2.15. The weight 80 N of the door acts at the middle, G.

(a)   With the dimensions shown, calculate the force F in the rope.

(b)   Calculate the new value of the force in the rope if the door is now kept open by the rope pulling in the direction AC at 90° to AO.

(a)   To keep the door in equilibrium, the moment of the weight W

Fig 2.15 Calculations on moments

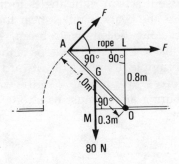

about O must be exactly counterbalanced by the moment about O of the force F in the rope, which turns in the opposite direction to W.

Moment of W about $O = 80\,\mathrm{N} \times OM = 80 \times 0.3\,\mathrm{m} = 24\,\mathrm{N\,m}$
Moment of F about $O = F \times OL = F \times 0.8\,\mathrm{N\,m}$

So $\qquad\qquad F \times 0.8 = 24$, or $F = 24/0.8 = 30\,\mathrm{N}$

(*b*) If the trap-door was held by a rope pulling in the direction AC at A, the moment of F about O would be $F \times$ perpendicular distance from O to line of $F = F \times OA$. So, for equilibrium,

$$F \times 1.0\,\mathrm{m} = 80 \times 0.3 = 24, \text{ or } F = 24\,\mathrm{N}$$

F would be less than before, when the rope at A pulled in the direction AL, because the perpendicular distance OA is greater than the perpendicular distance OL.

2.13 SHEAR FORCES

With beams fixed in a wall at one end, or on supports as in bridges, engineers need to consider forces in the beam called **shear forces**.

Fig 2.16 Shear forces

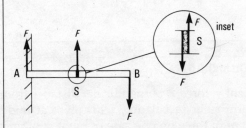

As an example of shear forces, consider a beam AB with one end A built into a wall and a load F at the free end B. Fig 2.16. Any part such as SB of the beam is in balance. So for equilibrium of SB, there must be a force acting upwards at S equal to F. This force at S is called a shear force because it acts at right angles to the beam and tends to shear or cut across the beam. Unlike shear forces, tensile and compressive forces act along the length of a beam, as we saw previously.

Shear forces equal to F act at all sections of the beam. In the part AS of the beam, for example, there is a downward force F at S (see inset) and an upward force F at A provided by the wall. The internal forces between neighbouring atoms must be strong enough to counteract the shearing forces.

2.14 BENDING OF BEAMS

Beams which are supported tend to **bend** under loads. In Fig 2.17(a), a horizontal wooden ruler AB fixed at A will bend as shown when a load W is placed at the other end B. In Fig 2.17(b), a horizontal ruler XY, placed symmetrically on supports at C and D, will bend or sag as shown when a load W is placed in the middle at O.

Fig 2.17 Bending moments

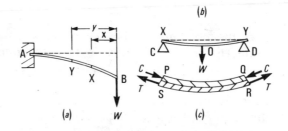

The bending is due to the turning-effect or **moment** of the load W about the different sections of the beam. For example, W has a moment $W \times x$ about the section X and a greater moment $W \times y$ about the more distant section Y.

Fig 2.17(c) shows the internal forces in a bent beam PQRS. The middle section MN is unchanged in length so there are no forces in MN. But the sections of the beam between MN and SR are longer than normal. So they are under **tension** forces T as shown. As can be seen, the sections between MN and PQ are shorter in length than MN. So these sections are under **compressive** forces C, as shown.

SUMMARY

(a) YOU SHOULD KNOW

1   Moment = force × perpendicular distance from axis (pivot) to force.
2   Uniform ruler in balance, with pivot at middle (centre of gravity), moment of force on one side of pivot = moment of other force about pivot.
3   Centre of gravity is the point where the total weight of an object appears to act.
4   In stable equilibrium, an object will return to its original position if

slightly displaced and then released. A low centre of gravity and a wide base help stable equilibrium. High centre of gravity and a narrow base will produce unstable equilibrium.

5 With several parallel forces keeping an object in balance, (a) total force in one direction = total force in opposite direction, (b) total clockwise moments about a point = total anticlockwise moments about the same point.

6 The resultant of two forces can be found by adding them vectorially. Using the parallelogram of forces, the diagonal represents the resultant and its direction.

7 If three forces keep an object in balance, (a) a triangle can be drawn to represent the forces, (b) the total clockwise moment about a point = the total anticlockwise moment about the same point.

(b) YOU SHOULD UNDERSTAND

1 The definition of moment and how to apply the principle of moments to the forces keeping a pivoted object in balance.

2 The meaning of centre of gravity and its position for rectangles, circular discs and circular rings, and uniform rods.

3 How a chair can be in stable or unstable equilibrium and the way in which the height of the centre of gravity and the width of the base may produce stable or unstable equilibrium.

4 How to find the resultant of two (or more) forces by adding them using vectors or the parallelogram of forces.

5 How to find an unknown force if three forces keep an object in balance and (a) the forces are parallel, or (b) non-parallel.

6 The meaning of compression, tension and shear forces.

(c) APPLICATIONS

You should be able to solve the following problems.

1 A light beam of length 2 m is pivoted in the middle O at its centre of gravity. A weight of 8 N is placed 0.5 metre from O and a weight W is placed 0.4 m on the other side of O. Calculate W and the force at the pivot.

2 A racing car is usually low and has a wide base. Explain the reason for this design.

3 Two men pull a cart along by two ropes inclined at 60° to each other. The forces in each rope is 200 N. Find by drawing the resultant pull. What single force, and in which direction, will stop the cart moving?

QUESTIONS 2A – MOMENTS. CENTRE OF GRAVITY. PARALLEL FORCES

MULTIPLE CHOICE QUESTIONS

1   In Fig 2A, a girl presses a bicycle pedal P with a vertically downward force of 10 N when P is horizontal. The moment about the axle C is calculated in newton metres by
    A 10×0.15
    B 10×0.09
    C 10×0.12
    D $10 \times 0.09 \times 0.12$

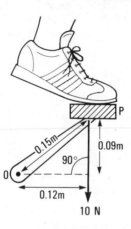

Fig 2A

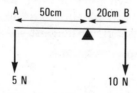

Fig 2B

2   Fig 2B shows a uniform beam AB 100 cm long pivoted at its centre O. To balance the beam horizontally
    A   the 10 N force should be moved 5 cm towards O
    B   the 5 N force should be increased to 10 N
    C   the 5 N force should be decreased to 3 N
    D   the 10 N force should be moved 5 cm towards B

3   When crossing a high horizontal wire in a circus act, the performer will sometimes carry a horizontal pole. This is because the pole helps to
    A   get a firmer grip on the wire with his feet
    B   counteract any unbalance
    C   move forward along the wire
    D   increase the force on the hands

4   Passengers are not allowed to stand on the top deck of a bus because they may
    A   lower the centre of gravity of the bus
    B   move forward if the bus suddenly stops

C   cause instability when the bus turns corners

D   weigh the bus down too much

5   Fig 2C shows a beam of weight 8 N with weights of 10 N and 20 N at its ends. The beam is balanced at O. The force at O on the beam is

A   38 N upwards

B   22 N downwards

C   28 N upwards

D   30 N downwards

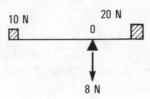

Fig 2C

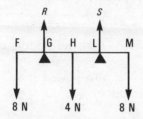

Fig 2D

6   Fig 2D shows a uniform beam FM of weight 4 N on supports at G and L. Weights of 8 N are placed at the ends. R and S are the reaction forces at G and L. To calculate S, the best point to take moments for all the forces is

A   G

B   F

C   H

D   L

SHORT ANSWER QUESTIONS

7   A wheelbarrow has a load of 130 N. Fig 2E. O is the wheel and H is the end of the handles.

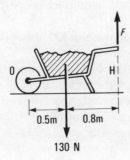

Fig 2E

Calculate
(a)   the force F to just raise the wheelbarrow load,
(b)   the reaction force between the ground and the wheel when the force F is applied.

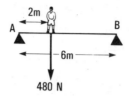

8   A light beam 6 m long rests on supports at its ends A and B. Fig 2F. A boy of weight 480 N stands on the beam 2 m from A.
Calculate the reaction forces at A and at B.

9   A horizontal trapdoor ABCD has a weight of 40 N and is hinged at AB. Fig 2G. The trapdoor has its centre of gravity at G and is a square of side 1 m.
(a)   Where is G?
(b)   What vertical force F at the middle of DC will just lift the trapdoor?
(c)   A weight of 20 N is now placed at G. What new vertical force will now just raise the trapdoor?

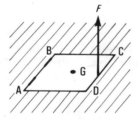

Fig 2G

Fig 2H

P   Q

10   In Fig 2H, OQ represents a billiard cue.
(a)   Copy the diagram and show by a letter X roughly the position of the centre of gravity of the cue.
(b)   Describe how you would check experimentally that your answer for X is right.

11   A horizontal beam AB of weight 500 N is pivoted at O. Fig 2I. The centre of gravity of the beam is at G.
Just to raise AB from the horizontal, one man exerts a downward force of 200 N at A and another man exerts an upward force of 50 N at B.
Calculate the distance x of G from O.

Fig 2I

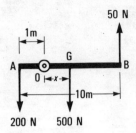

Fig 2J

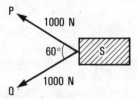

12 Two tugs exert equal forces P and Q of 1000 N at 60° to each other in pulling a ship S from a sand bank. Fig 2J.

By drawing, find the resultant force on the ship.

13 A uniform ladder AB of weight 40 N rests at A on a rough ground and at B on a smooth wall. Fig 2K. The height BC is 8 m and the distance AC is 6 m. R is the reaction force of the wall at B and acts at 90° to the wall.

(*a*) Copy the diagram and show in it the other two forces on the ladder, which are its weight and the force at A of the rough ground.

(*b*) By taking moments about A, calculate R.

Fig 2K

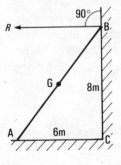

Fig 2L

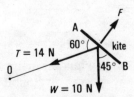

14 Fig 2L shows a kite of weight $W = 10$ N, held in the air by a string OG which has a pulling force or tension $T = 14$ N. W makes an angle of 45° with the kite and T makes an angle of 60°.

If the kite is in balance, find (a) the force F on it due to the air pressure, and (b) the angle F makes with the kite.

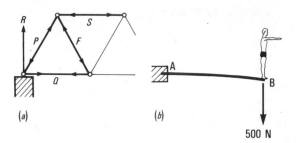

(a)   (b)

Fig 2M   500 N

15   (a)   A bridge rests with one end on a support O. Fig 2M(a). Forces P, Q, R, S, F act in the metal framework and at O.

Write down the forces of (i) tension, (ii) compression, (iii) reaction.
(b)   In Fig 2M(b), a diver stands at one end of a diving board AB. His weight is 500 N. (i) What is the force at A? (ii) Why does AB bend? (iii) Copy the diagram and show the **shearing force** at the board half-way between A and B. (iv) Are there forces of compression and tension in the board? Explain your answer.

PRESSURE OF FLUIDS

In this section we discuss the **pressure** of fluids (liquids and gases). We shall see that the pressure at a place in a liquid depends on both the depth and the density of the liquid. The pressure applied to a liquid can be transmitted to other places in the liquid and this is used in the hydraulic brakes of cars and other vehicles.

In dealing with the pressure of gases, we shall begin with atmospheric pressure and the barometer. We explain the pressure of gases by the gas molecules bombarding the walls of the container. Finally we shall consider Boyle's law, which shows how the pressure and volume of a gas are related when the temperature is constant.

2.15 PRESSURE AND ITS MEASUREMENT

Pressure is defined as the **average force per unit area** at the place concerned, where the force is normal (at right angles) to the area. So

$$\text{average pressure, } p = \frac{\text{force, } F}{\text{area, } A}$$

and   force, F = pressure, p × area, A

The unit of pressure is 'newton per metre$^{2'}$, N/m^2. 1 N/m^2 is called 1 Pa, where Pa represents **pascal**, in honour of the French scientist who made early discoveries about pressure. A unit used in the measurement of atmospheric pressure is the 'bar'. 1 bar = 10^5 N/m^2 or 10^5 Pa. Note that 10^6 N/m^2 = 1 N/mm^2, a unit sometimes used to measure tyre pressures.

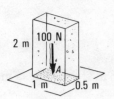

Fig 2.18 Pressure on surface

Suppose a solid block weighs 100 N and has dimensions 2 m × 1 m × 0.5 m. When it is resting on a flat surface, the maximum pressure on the surface occurs when the weight is pressing on the *smallest* area. So (see Fig 2.18)

$$\text{maximum pressure} = \frac{\text{weight } F}{\text{area } A} = \frac{100 \text{ N}}{1 \times 0.5} = 200 \text{ N/m}^2 = 200 \text{ Pa}$$

Also, $$\text{minimum pressure} = \frac{100 \text{ N}}{2 \times 1} = 50 \text{ N/m}^2 = 50 \text{ Pa}$$

The area 2 m × 1 m is the largest surface area the box can press on.

2.16 EXAMPLES OF PRESSURE

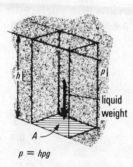

Fig 2.19 Formula for pressure

With narrow heels as in stiletto heels, the weight of a woman is spread over a small area of floor. So the pressure is high and this may mark the floor. Walking shoes have wide heels and the pressure on the ground is moderate. Padded seats yield well to pressure and so feel comfortable.

Egg-slicers and knives have narrow blades. So the forces they exert are over a very small area and the pressure is then high. For a similar reason, if a heavy parcel is carried by thin string, the pressure on the flesh of the hand is high and painful. A thick string or handle produces less pressure.

Ice skates have narrow blades, so that the area in contact with the ice is very small. The pressure due to the skater's weight is then very large and this helps to lower the freezing point of ice. So the ice melts under the blade and the blade moves through a thin film of water. Heat produced by friction between the blade and the ice also helps to melt the ice.

Fig 2.20 Pressure and height

2.17 PRESSURE IN LIQUIDS

At a depth h in a liquid, the pressure is the weight per unit area at that point. So if we consider a horizontal area A at a depth h, then (see Fig 2.19)

$$\text{pressure} = \frac{\text{weight of liquid of volume } (A \times h)}{\text{area } A}$$

Now   mass of liquid, m = volume × density = $Ah\rho$,
and   weight of liquid = mg = $Ah\rho g$

So $\qquad$ pressure $p = \dfrac{\text{weight}}{A} = \dfrac{Ah\rho g}{A}$

or $\qquad\qquad\qquad p = h\rho g$

When h is in metres, ρ in kg/m^3, and $g = 9.8$ m/s^2 or 10 m/s^2 in round figures, then ρ is in N/m^2 or Pa.

The formula $p = h\rho g$ shows that the pressure at a point in a given liquid depends only on the depth h. When a liquid is poured into a U-tube with a narrow and a wide vertical column on each side, as in Fig 2.20, the height of the liquid is the same on both sides. The reason is that the pressure at the bottom of either column depends only on the height of the liquid and does not depend on the area of cross-section of the side.

EXAMPLE

Calculate the pressure (a) at the bottom of a column of mercury 760 mm high, density 13 600 kg/m^3, (b) 100 m below the surface of water, density 1000 kg/m^3, (c) at the bottom of a column of air 2 km high, density 1.2 kg/m^3. (Assume $g = 9.8$ m/s^2.)

(a) $\qquad p = h\rho g = 0.76 \times 13\,600 \times 9.8 = 101\,300$
$\qquad\qquad\qquad = 1.013 \times 10^5$ Pa
$\qquad\qquad\qquad = 1.013$ bar $= 1013$ mb (millibars)

(b) $\qquad p = h\rho g = 100 \times 1000 \times 9.8$
$\qquad\qquad\qquad = 980\,000$ Pa^2 $(9.8 \times 10^5$ Pa$^2)$

(c) $\qquad p = h\rho g = 2000 \times 1.2 \times 9.8$
$\qquad\qquad\qquad = 24\,000$ Pa^2 (approx)

2.18 EXAMPLES OF PRESSURE IN LIQUIDS

Water comes out of taps n the ground floor of a house faster than from taps on the upper floors. This is because the water-tank on the roof has a greater height above taps on the ground floor and so the water pressure here is greater than at upper floors.

Swimming below water, the pressure of the water on ear drums may become painful as the depth increases. At great depths, divers must wear head-gear and special clothing to withstand the water pressure and carry oxygen cylinders for breathing. If a deep-sea diver comes up too quickly to the surface, the pressure of the blood may produce bleeding through the nose and painful 'bends' in the body.

2.19 TRANSMISSION OF PRESSURE. HYDRAULIC BRAKES

A pressure at one place of a liquid is transmitted by the movement of the liquid molecules to other places. So pressure on water at one place of a drum with small holes in its sides will make the water come out of all the holes.

The transmission of pressure in liquids is used in the **hydraulic brake** for cars and other vehicles. Oil is used as the liquid and this connects the small 'master' piston, operated by the brake pedal, to the 'slave' piston connected to the brake drums on the wheels of the car. Fig 2.21. As the following example illustrates, the large area of the 'slave' piston produces a large force on the brake drums or pads by transmission of pressure.

Fig 2.21 Hydraulic brake

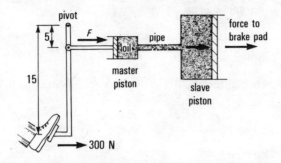

EXAMPLE

In Fig 2.21, a force of 300 N is applied to the brake pedal of a car and the pressure is transferred by oil from the 'master' piston to a brake pad operated by a 'slave' piston. The area of the master piston is 100 cm² and the area of the slave piston is 500 cm².

Calculate (a) the pressure on the master piston and (b) the force applied to the brake pad assuming 100% efficiency.

(a) Suppose F is the force exerted by the rod on the master piston. Then, by moments about the pivot

$$F \times 5 = 300 \times 15, \text{ or } F = 900 \text{ N}$$

Thus pressure on master piston, $p = \dfrac{F}{A}$

$$= \frac{900 \text{ N}}{100 \text{ cm}^2} = 9 \text{ N/cm}^2$$

(b) Force on slave piston = pressure × area
$$= 9 \times 500$$
$$= 4500 \text{ N}$$

2.20 HYDRAULIC PRESS

The hydraulic press uses the transmission of pressure to compress steel and other materials at large engineering works.

Fig 2.22 shows the basic principle of the hydraulic press. One side, B, has a small cross-sectional area A_1 and the other side, C, a much wider cross-sectional area A_2. The lever L applies a force F to the piston of area A_1, so a pressure $p = F/A_1$ is produced. This pressure is transmitted by the liquid to the larger piston of area A_2. If we omit

Fig 2.22 Hydraulic press

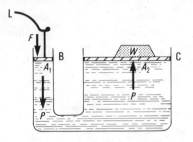

frictional forces, the upward force W produced = pressure × area = p × A_2 = $(F/A_1) × A_2$. So

$$W = \frac{F \times A_2}{A_1}, \text{ or } \frac{W}{F} = \frac{A_2}{A_1}$$

Suppose A_2 = 4000 cm^2 and A_1 = 200 cm^2. Then A_2/A_1 = 200. If F is 100 N, then the load W just raised is 200 × F = 200 × 100 N = 20 000 N. This large force is used, for example, to compress metals placed on the piston.

In practice, with friction and other factors omitted from the calculation, the compression force of the hydraulic press is much less than the value of 20 000 N.

CHECK LIST ▶   Make sure you can answer the following questions.

1   What is *pressure*? How would you calculate the force on an area if you know the pressure? What is the formula for pressure in a liquid?
2   How do a hydraulic brake and a hydraulic press work? Give diagrams.

2.21 ATMOSPHERIC PRESSURE

We now consider the pressure due to gases. We begin with atmospheric or air pressure.

Air cannot be seen but the pressure due to air molecules is shown

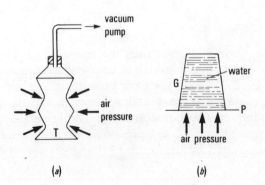

Fig 2.23 Demonstrations of air pressure   (*a*)   (*b*)

by sailing boats, by the movement of leaves on trees, by rotating windmills and by aeroplanes kept in flight by air pressure.

Fig 2.23 shows two simple demonstrations of air pressure. In Fig 2.23(*a*), a thin-walled tin can T collapses when the air inside it is pumped out. The pressure outside is now unbalanced and pushes the walls of the can together. In Fig 2.23(*b*), a drinking glass G is filled to the brim and then covered with paper P to keep all air out of G. When the glass is turned upside down keeping P in place, the air pressure stops the water from falling out.

2.22 SIMPLE BAROMETER

Torricelli was the first person to suggest how the atmospheric pressure could be measured. In the laboratory, a simple barometer can be made as follows:

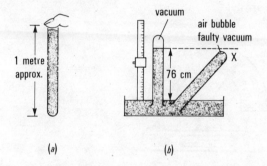

Fig 2.24 Simple barometer   (*a*)   (*b*)

Take a barometer (thick-walled) tube about one metre long and fill it nearly to the top with clean mercury, as in Fig 2.24(*a*). Place a finger over the top and turn the tube upside-down several times so that the air bubble runs along the tube each time and collects any small, air-trapped bubbles present in the mercury. Finally, completely fill the tube to the brim, so that air is completely excluded.

With one finger on the top as before, turn the tube upside-down and place it below the surface of some mercury in small trough. Remove the finger. The mercury level inside the tube falls – it is now about 760 mm (76 cm) above the surface of the mercury in the trough (see Fig 2.24(*b*)).

The empty space at the top of the tube must be a vacuum because it contains no air. The mercury column inside the tube is therefore kept up by the atmospheric pressure. Or, **the atmospheric pressure is equal to the pressure at the bottom of the column of mercury**. When the atmospheric pressure increases, the height of the column increases and when the pressure decreases the height decreases. We can therefore read off the value of the atmospheric pressure by fixing the tube vertically in a clamp and placing a metre rule beside the tube – the rule must be placed a short distance from the tube to avoid the curved mercury meniscus at the glass.

If the barometer has air at the top it will be **faulty**. We can test if this is the case by tilting the barometer until the top, X, of the tube is below the 760 mm vertical height. If the mercury does not completely fill the space at the top, then some air is present, as shown in Fig 2.24(*b*).

2.23 ATMOSPHERIC PRESSURE AND WEATHER. ANEROID BAROMETER

Standard atmospheric pressure is taken as that due to a column of mercury 760 mm or 0.76 m high. As shown on page 82, the pressure at the bottom of this column is given by

$$p = h\rho g = 0.76 \times 13\,600 \times 9.8 = 1.013 \times 10^5 \, \text{Pa}$$
$$= 1013 \text{ millibars (mb)}$$

With very fine weather, atmospheric pressure may be high at about 1050 mb. As the weather worsens the barometer falls. A pressure as low as 920 mb has been recorded in the Caribbean in a tropical storm.

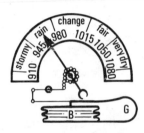

Fig 2.25 Aneroid (no liquid) barometer

Fig 2.25 shows an **aneroid barometer**, used widely in the home. It has no liquid. A strong thin metal box B is partially evacuated and a strong spring G stops the sides collapsing. When the atmospheric pressure varies the sides move in and out slightly. The small movement is magnified by levers and a pointer is made to move over a circular scale previously calibrated to read pressure. Both the mercury and aneroid barometers record changes in atmospheric pressure. The mercury barometer is an accurate type used in scientific laboratories whereas the aneroid barometer is a domestic type only.

The atmospheric pressure is due to air whose height stretches for many kilometres above the Earth's surface. So the pressure decreases with height above the ground. At a height of about 5 km, the pressure falls to about 550 mb. Here the air is also 'thinner' or less dense than at the ground. Altimeters on aeroplanes and on cars in hilly countries are aneroid barometers which now read the height in place of pressure. Aeroplanes have pressurised cabins to counteract the fall of pressure with height so that passengers can breathe comfortably.

2.24 U-TUBE MANOMETER. BOURDON GAUGE

The domestic gas pressure is slightly greater than atmospheric pressure. It is measured by a **U-tube manometer** (pressure gauge) containing water, Fig 2.26(a). One side X of the U-tube is connected to the gas supply and the other side Y is open to the air. The gas pressure forces down the water connected to it so that there is now a difference in levels h between the two water columns, as shown. The gas pressure is therefore greater than the atmospheric pressure A by a height h of water.

Suppose h is about 20 cm. Then, since the density ρ of water is 1000 kg/m^3, the gas pressure is greater than the atmospheric pressure by

$$p = h\rho g = 0.2 \times 1000 \times 9.8 = 1960 \text{ Pa} = 19.6 \text{ mb}$$

Fig 2.26 Gas pressure measurement

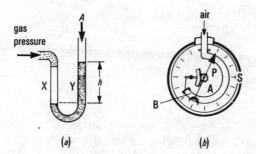

(a)   (b)

The U-tube manometer measures pressure changes slightly greater than atmospheric pressure. The **Bourdon gauge** can measure pressures much greater than atmospheric pressure such as 10 bar, where 1 bar is about the standard atmospheric pressure. This has a coiled thin metal tube A which tends to straighten as the pressure inside it increases and the end B is closed. Fig 2.26(b). A coiled paper toy works on a similar principle – it unwinds when air is blown into it at one end. The movement at B is magnified by a gear arrangement and a pointer P then moves round a circular scale S previously graduated in bars. The gauge is used on gas boilers and on foot-pumps for pumping air into tyres.

CHECK LIST ▶ Make sure you can answer the following questions.

1   Why is mercury and not water used for barometers? How do you calculate the pressure in Pa from a given height of mercury in a barometer?

2   What is the difference between the U-tube manometer, an aneroid barometer and a Bourdon gauge, and what kind of pressure is measured by each?

2.25 GAS PRESSURE.
BOYLE'S LAW

We now consider gas pressure in general and its applications.

In 1660 Robert Boyle, a famous Irish scientist, found that: **For a given amount of gas at constant temperature, pV = a constant** where p is the pressure and V is the volume of the gas; or, as sometimes stated, $V \propto 1/p$, that is, the volume is **inversely proportional** to the pressure. This is known as **Boyle's law**.

Boyle's law can be verified with the apparatus shown in Fig 2.27. Air is trapped above a column of oil and its volume, V, is proportional to the length AB. The pressure is applied by a foot-pump and transmitted to the air through the oil. The pressure readings, p, are read directly on a Bourdon gauge. In this way various values of p and V are measured.

Fig 2.27 Boyle's law
experiment

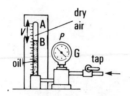

To verify Boyle's law you can either (a) calculate the product pV and see if the results are roughly constant, or (b) plot a graph of V against $1/p$ (or p against $1/V$) and see if a straight line passing through the origin is obtained, as shown in Fig 2.28(a).

Fig 2.28(b) shows how p varies with V, when pV = constant.

Fig 2.28 Graphs
illustrating Boyle's law

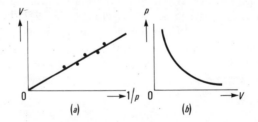

2.26 EXAMPLES ON
BOYLE'S LAW

1 A bubble of air at the bottom X of a pool of water of depth h rises to the surface Y. Fig 2.29(a). The bubble is now twice the volume at X.

Calculate the depth h if the atmospheric pressure A is equivalent to a barometric height of 10 m of water.

At X, pressure of air $p_1 = (A+h) = (10+h)$ in metres of water
and volume $V_1 = 1$ unit
At Y, pressure of air $p_2 = A = 10$ m and volume $V_2 = 2$ units
From Boyle's law, $p_1V_1 = p_2V_2$

So $\qquad (10+h) \times 1 = 10 \times 2 = 20$
and $\qquad\qquad\qquad h = 10$ m

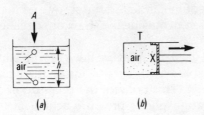

Fig 2.29 Examples on Boyle's law

2 In Fig 2.29(*b*), air trapped in a metal closed tube T is under pressure due to a piston X. If X is now moved slowly outwards so that the volume of air is doubled, what happens to (*a*) the pressure of the air, (*b*) the density of the air, (*c*) the spacing between the molecules of air?

(*a*) From Boyle's law pV = constant, the pressure p is **halved**

(*b*) Density = mass/volume. Since the mass of air is unchanged and the volume is doubled, the density is **halved**

(*c*) Since the air has a greater volume than before, the spacing between the molecules **increases**

3 A cylinder of oxygen has a volume of 30 litres and the gas pressure is 10 atmospheres. Fig 2.30(*a*). Some oxygen is released and the pressure drops to 8 atmospheres. Fig 2.30(*b*).

Calculate the volume of the gas at 10 atmospheres which escaped from the cylinder. What is the volume of the escaped gas at 1 atmosphere pressure?

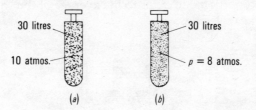

Fig 2.30 Boyle's law calculation

The gas *left* in the cylinder has a volume V_2 of 30 litres at a pressure p_2 of 8 atmospheres. The *same* amount of gas originally had a pressure p_1 of 10 atmospheres and volume V_1. From Boyle's law, $p_1 V_1 = p_2 V_2$. So

$$10 \times V_1 = 8 \times 30$$

So $\qquad V_1 = \dfrac{8 \times 30}{10} = 24$ litres

The volume of gas which *escaped* from the cylinder is therefore $30-24$ or 6 litres at 10 atmospheres. If we wish to find the volume V of this gas at 1 atmosphere, then, from Boyle's law,

$$1 \times V = 10 \times 6$$

So $\qquad V = 60$ litres

2.27 DRINKING STRAW AND SYRINGE

The atmospheric pressure is used when drinking milk with a straw. Each time one sucks upwards, some air is withdrawn. This reduces the pressure of the air left in the straw and the atmospheric pressure acting on the milk outside the straw now pushes some milk higher up the straw.

A **syringe** used for spraying flowers with suitable liquid works on a similar principle. With one end inside the liquid, the piston P in the barrel is raised. This reduces the pressure of air between P and the liquid. The atmospheric pressure acting on the liquid now pushes some liquid into the syringe.

2.28 MOLECULAR EXPLANATION OF PRESSURE

Inside a gas, molecules are moving in different directions. Gas pressure is due to the continual bombardment of the walls of the container by the molecules.

To simplify matters, suppose a molecule of mass m strikes a wall W of a containing cube at right angles with a velocity c (Fig 2.31(a)). It then rebounds with a velocity $-c$. So the collision with the wall has produced a velocity change or **force**. Each time a molecule hits W, a force is exerted on the wall and so the millions of molecules moving to and fro between the walls of the cube produce a **pressure** on the walls which is the average force per unit area.

We can see that the higher the speed, the greater will be the force on the wall at **each** collision. Also, there will then be **more collisions per second**. Each of these factors is proportional to c. So the pressure is proportional to c^2, or to the average of the squares of the speeds of all the molecules.

Fig 2.31 Molecular theory of pressure

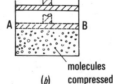

(a)

(b)   molecules compressed

2.29 EXPLANATION OF BOYLE'S LAW

Suppose a gas is inside a rectangular box as in Fig 2.31(b). If the volume is halved by pushing the piston down to AB, and the temperature is kept constant, a molecule will have the same velocity change on collision with the wall but will hit the piston twice as often. So the velocity change per second is **doubled**. Thus the pressure p is doubled when the volume V is halved, or $pV = $ a constant. This is Boyle's law.

QUESTIONS 2B – PRESSURE OF LIQUIDS AND GASES

MULTIPLE CHOICE QUESTIONS

1 A water dam is made thicker at the base because
   A   the concrete is more porous here
   B   the air pressure varies daily
   C   the dam can be filled to different depths
   D   the pressure of water increases with depth

2 Mercury is preferred to water in a barometer because
   A   mercury has a high density
   B   mercury is a better conductor
   C   water has a poor expansion with temperature rise
   D   mercury expands regularly with temperature rise

3 When the hydraulic brake system in a car is used
   A   the pressure on the brake pedal = the force on the wheel brake drum
   B   the force on the brake pedal = the force on the wheel brake drum
   C   oil transmits the pedal pressure to a piston of larger area
   D   oil transmits the pedal pressure to a piston of smaller area

4 The feet of an elephant are very wide because
   A   it can trample better on obstacles in its path
   B   the pressure on the ground is then reduced
   C   it can then turn more easily
   D   the force on the ground is less than its weight

5 In an aeroplane, the altimeter recording height is a form of
   A   electric motor   B   mercury barometer
   C   thermometer   D   aneroid barometer

6 The closed vessel in Fig 2N has water inside it. The pressure
   A   at P is less than at R
   B   the pressure at Q is less than at R
   C   the pressure at Q is greater than at R
   D   the pressures at P,Q,R are equal

Fig 2N

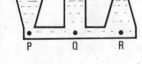

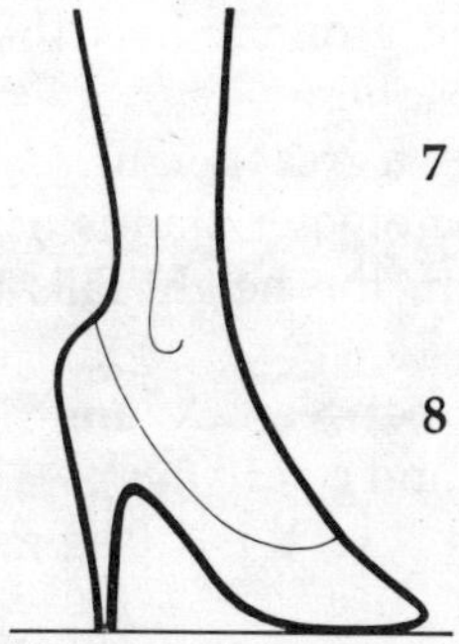

SHORT ANSWER QUESTIONS

7 A girl with stiletto heels of total area $2 \, cm^2$ exerts a pressure of $200 \, N/cm^2$ on the floor. Fig 2P. She then changes her shoes to one whose heels have a total area $40 \, cm^2$.
   What is the new pressure on the floor?

8 A rectangular block of metal M, dimensions $2 \, m \times 0.5 \, m \times 0.8 \, m$, rests on a horizontal surface. Fig 2Q. The weight of M is 40 N.
   (a)   Calculate the pressure on the surface.
   (b)   What is the maximum pressure which the block can exert on the surface when it stands upright?

Fig 2P

Fig 2Q

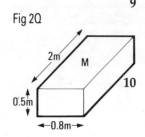

9   A window pane has dimensions 1.2 m × 0.5 m. Assuming atmospheric pressure is 10^5(100 000) Pa, what force is exerted on the outside of the window by the air pressure? Why does the glass not break?
    Explain why the glass of a television tube is much thicker than a window pane.

10 A water manometer M is used to measure the domestic gas pressure. Fig 2R. The heights of the water levels are 20 cm and 45 cm and the height of the manometer is 70 cm.
    (a)   Explain why water and not mercury is used as the manometer liquid.
    (b)   If the atmospheric pressure is 100 000 Pa, calculate the domestic gas pressure using $p = h\rho g$ and assuming the density of water is 1000 kg/m³ and $g = 10$ m/s².

Fig 2R

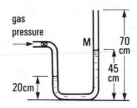

Fig 2S

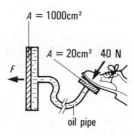

11 In a hydraulic brake system, a force of 40 N is exerted by a motorist on a pedal of area A of 20 cm². Fig 2S. The 'slave' piston has an area of A of 1000 cm².
    Calculate the force F transmitted to the brake drums. What happens if the oil leaks out from the pipe system?

12 A small balloon is filled with hydrogen at the ground. It is then released and begins to float upwards in the atmosphere.
    Explain why the balloon bursts when it reaches a great height.

13 At the bottom X of a mountain, a mercury barometer stands at a height of 0.76 m. At the top Y of the mountain, the height falls to 0.66 m.
    (a)   Calculate the difference in pressure between X and Y, assuming the density of mercury is 13 600 kg/m³ and $g = 10$ m/s².
    (b)   Assuming the average air density from X to Y is 1.0 kg/m³, calculate the height of the mountain.

14 A gas is contained in a cylinder of uniform cross-section by a piston 30 cm from the end. Fig 2T. The piston is now pulled back slowly

until it is 40 cm from the end, so that the gas temperature stays constant. If the pressure of the gas in Fig 2T is 200 kPa,

(a)   calculate the new pressure,

(b)   state the law you used to find the new pressure.

Fig 2T

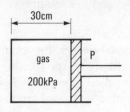

Fig 2U

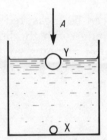

15   A bubble of air X at the bottom of a lake expands to three times its volume at Y where it reaches the top of the lake. Fig 2U.

Assuming the atmospheric pressure is equivalent to a barometric height of 10 m of water, calculate the depth h of the lake.

STRUCTURE OF MATTER

In this section we deal with **matter**, which consists of solids, liquids and gases, and with its structure.

We first show how densities, the mass per unit volume, are measured. We shall then consider the arrangement of molecules in the three states and the way their forces and their separation differ. Experiments showing the existence of molecules (Brownian motion) and their motion (diffusion) then follow. Finally, the molecular theory will be used to explain some common properties of solids, liquids and gases, including their temperature changes and latent heats.

2.30 DENSITY AND MEASUREMENT

Density is defined as **mass per unit volume**, or

$$\text{density} (\rho) = \frac{\text{mass} (m)}{\text{volume} (V)} \qquad (1)$$

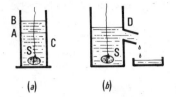

Fig 2.32 Volume by (a) measuring cylinder and (b) Eureka can

The mass of a **solid** can be found by placing it on a balance. If the solid has a rectangular cross-section, its volume = length × breadth × height. If it is an irregularly shaped solid, S, the volume can be found by immersing it completely inside water in a measuring cylinder C. Fig 2.32(a). The volume is read from the original level A of water to the new level B. With a bigger solid, the volume of water displaced can be found by using a displacement or Eureka can D, as shown in Fig 2.32(b).

The density of a **liquid** can be measured by first partly filling a burette or a measuring cylinder with the liquid. A beaker is then weighed empty and again after a known volume of liquid is poured into it. The difference in masses is the mass of the liquid. The density is calculated from mass/volume.

2.31 DENSITY CALCULATIONS

The density of water is 1000 kg/m³ or 1 g/cm³. So a volume of water of volume 50 cm³ has a mass of 50 g. The density of mercury is about 13 600 kg/m³ or 13.6 g/cm³, so its density is 13.6 times that of water.

Fig 2.33 Mass, volume, density

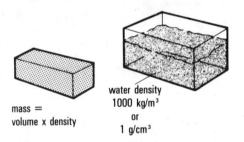

mass =
volume x density

water density
1000 kg/m³
or
1 g/cm³

From the definition of density, you can see (Fig 2.33):

$$\text{mass } (m) = \text{volume} \times \text{density} \tag{2}$$

If the volume is needed from the mass and density, you can use

$$\text{volume } (V) = \frac{\text{mass}}{\text{density}} \tag{3}$$

So if the mass of a metal rod is 100 g and its density is 8 g/cm³, then

$$\text{volume, } V = \frac{100}{8} = 12.5 \text{ cm}^3$$

If the volume of a metal of the same density is 50 cm³, then

$$\text{mass of metal} = \text{volume} \times \text{density} = 50 \times 8 = 400 \text{ g}$$

2.32 MOLECULES AND MATTER

Solids, liquids, and gases – the three 'states' of matter – are made up of very tiny particles called **molecules**. The molecule is so small, that we are unable to imagine it. For example, millions of molecules are on the tip of a pin; it would take about 100 years for the whole population of the world to count the number of molecules in 2 grams of hydrogen gas at the rate of five per second; if a cricket ball was magnified to one thousand metres in diameter, a molecule in the ball would then be magnified to about one two-thousandth of a centimetre!

The existence of molecules can be shown indirectly by experiments on 'Brownian motion', named after a botanist, Brown, who first noticed this motion in 1827.

2.33 BROWNIAN MOTION IN A GAS

To show Brownian motion, some fine particles of burnt cord or tobacco smoke are collected in a small plastic container A (see Fig 2.34(*a*)). The container is illuminated by a lamp B and a lens D. On looking down through a suitable microscope, C, smoke particles can be seen which appear to move rapidly to and fro in different directions. This irregular or random motion is called 'Brownian motion' and is shown diagrammatically in Fig 2.34(*b*).

Fig 2.34 Brownian motion experiment

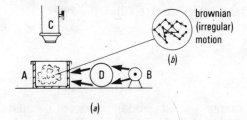

The smoke particle is *very small*. In this case, the number of gas molecules which strike it on one side differs appreciably from those striking it on the opposite side. The particle therefore moves to another place in the direction of the resultant force. Here the same thing happens again. So the particle keeps moving irregularly from side to side. As the particle seems to have 'perpetual motion', we deduce that the molecules of a gas are always moving about in random directions.

For a *large particle*, the number of molecules striking it on opposite sides is not appreciably different. So no Brownian motion is seen in this case. A table-tennis ball suspended from the ceiling in a closed room does not move, although it is bombarded on all sides by molecules of air.

Brownian motion can also be demonstrated for *liquids* – well-diluted aquadag or photopake contain fine carbon particles which show this type of motion due to bombardment by the surrounding molecules of liquid.

2.34 MOVEMENT OF MOLECULES – DIFFUSION

To show that liquid molecules move about, one-third of a small jar can be filled with a colourless concentrated sugar solution, S, the next third can be filled with a blue layer of concentrated copper sulphate solution, C, by means of a pipette, and the last third with a layer of colourless distilled water, W, as in Fig 2.35(*a*). At first the boundaries between the blue and colourless liquids are distinct. After some days, the boundaries become blurred and the sugar solution and water have some blue colour (Fig 2.35(*b*)). We say that 'diffusion' has occurred. So molecules of copper sulphate solution move in different directions.

Fig 2.35 Diffusion experiment

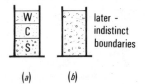

(*a*)   (*b*)

To show the gas molecules are in motion, a gas jar with a cover slip can be filled with brown nitrogen peroxide gas, which is heavier than air. When an empty jar of air is placed over it and the cover slip taken away, a brown colour is seen in the top jar after a few minutes. So the molecules of nitrogen peroxide gas, although heavier than the molecules of air, have moved upwards due to their motion. We say that the gas has 'diffused' into the air.

2.35 MOLECULES IN SOLIDS, LIQUIDS AND GASES

1 SOLIDS

Solids have a fixed geometrical form because, on average, the positions of the molecules are fixed. The molecules are not still, however. They **vibrate** about some average position, as shown in Fig 2.36(*a*), under strong attractive and repulsive forces.

Fig 2.36 Molecules in solids and liquids

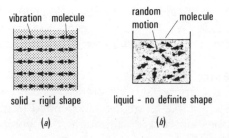

solid - rigid shape   liquid - no definite shape

(*a*)   (*b*)

The maximum displacement from the average position is called the **amplitude** of vibration. The amplitude depends on the temperature of the solid, or its 'thermal energy'. When the temperature rises there is an increase in the energy of vibration of the molecules equal to the heat energy given to the solid.

2 LIQUIDS

Liquids, unlike solids, have no geometrical form; they can be poured into a vessel of any shape. In contrast to solids, the molecules in a liquid have no fixed positions on average but move about in the liquid in different directions (see Fig 2.36(*b*)). So they are continually changing neighbours. When the liquid temperature rises, the average speed of the molecules increases.

3 GASES

Gases, like liquids, have no geometrical form. They fill the space of any vessel into which they are put. Unlike solids and liquids, the molecules in a gas have very little attraction for each other because they are so far apart under normal conditions. So the molecules lead an independent existence and move about freely through the whole volume of their container. As we have seen, the 'pressure' of a gas is due to the collisions with the walls of all the molecules.

2.36 PROPERTIES OF SOLIDS, LIQUIDS, GASES

We now see that because the molecules of solids and liquids are close together but the molecules of gases are very wide apart and free to move, solids and liquids are much less **compressible** than a gas. Further, the molecules of a solid are fixed in position on average, and so solids cannot **flow**, unlike liquids and gases.

As the temperature rises, the molecules have greater speed and energy. The pressure of a **gas** then increases (p.90). For a **solid**, when the temperature reaches its melting point, the increased energy of the molecules is then just sufficient for them to break away from their 'anchored' positions. The molecules then move freely in different directions and the solid has now changed to the liquid state. The energy needed to change from solid to liquid state at the same temperature is called **latent heat of fusion** (p.132).

With **liquids**, some of the more energetic molecules are able to break through the 'skin' of the liquid and exist outside the liquid as vapour or gas. This evaporation occurs at ordinary temperatures. As the liquid temperature rises more molecules gain energy to escape from the liquid and at the boiling point the liquid changes to the gaseous state. The volume increase is then considerable. For example, $1 \, \text{cm}^3$ of water changes to about $1600 \, \text{cm}^3$ of steam (water vapour) when boiling at 100°C.

As the temperature **decreases**, the energy of the molecules decrease. A liquid changes to a solid state at its freezing point. A gas changes to a liquid state at its liquefying point. At the absolute or kelvin zero of temperature, 0 K, the molecular energy is theoretically zero. For a gas, this means that its pressure is theoretically zero at 0 K (see p.116).

2.37 ELASTIC FORCES. STRETCHING OF WIRES

If you twist or squeeze a piece of rubber it returns to its original shape when you release it. The same thing happens when you stretch a rubber band or a coiled metal spring by a small amount. They return to their original length when they are released. In this case we call the the rubber or metal materials *elastic*.

When the metal spring or rubber is pulled out a little, or extended, their molecules are further apart than before. Since the metal returns to its original length, we deduce that the forces between the molecules are *attractive*. If you squeeze a piece of rubber it springs back again after it is released. So when the molecules are closer together than normal, the forces between them become *repulsive*. For this reason, solids (and liquids) are difficult to compress.

HOOKE'S LAW

Over 300 years ago, Robert Hooke carried out an experiment on the stretching or extension of a spring. Figure 2.37(a) shows the basic principle. Increasing weights or loads are added to a scale-pan attached to the spring S and the extension is measured by a pointer P on a vertical half-metre rule M. The weight of the scale-pan is added to find the total load W.

Fig 2.37 Elasticity – Hooke's law

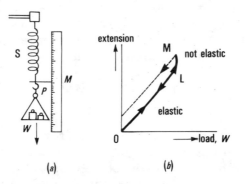

(a)   (b)

The results are shown in Fig 2.37(b). For small loads W, the extension e *from the original length* of the spring varies along a straight-line graph OL. So the extension is directly proportional to the load. Also, the spring returns to its original length when the load is removed anywhere along OL, so the spring is elastic along OL.

But beyond OL, the graph curves along LM, so the extension is no longer proportional to the load. Also, when the load is removed, the spring does not go back to its original length – it is permanently strained. So the load corresponding to L is the 'elastic limit'. As the load is increased further, the metal stretches considerably, or 'yields', and may break.

These results are expressed in **Hooke's law**: *The extension of a spring is directly proportional to the load (or tension in the spring), provided the elastic limit is not exceeded.*

Spring balances use Hooke's law for measuring weight. Manufacturers provide a mechanical 'stop' to prevent loads stretching the spring past its elastic limit.

EXAMPLE

An unloaded spring has a length of 15.0 cm. With a load of 4.0 N, the length increases to 15.8 cm. What would the length be with a load of 1.5 N? (Assume the elastic limit is not exceeded.)

A load of 4.0 N produces an extension of (15.8−15.0) cm or 0.8 cm. So 1.5 N produces an extension of

$$\frac{1.5}{4.0} \times 0.8 \text{ cm} = 0.3 \text{ cm}$$

Thus

$$\text{length of spring} = 15.0 + 0.3$$
$$= 15.3 \text{ cm}$$

SUMMARY

(a) YOU SHOULD KNOW

1 Pressure = force per unit area. Unit: Pa (N/m^2).
2 In liquids, $p = h\rho g$, where h is depth in metres, ρ is density in kg/m^3 and $g = 10$ m/s^2.
3 Pressure is transmitted in liquids. Hydraulic brakes and hydraulic presses have large area pistons since force = pressure × area.
4 Mercury is used in laboratory barometers because the density of mercury is high. Atmospheric pressure is normally about 10^5 Pa or 1000 millibars.
5 A manometer is a pressure gauge. A U-tube with water is used to measure domestic gas pressure (not much above atmospheric) and a Bourdon gauge is used to measure pressure, much greater than atmospheric.
6 Boyle's law: pV = constant at constant temperature. So $p_1 V_1 = p_2 V_2$.
7 Density is mass/volume. Units: kg/m^3 or g/cm^3.
8 Brownian motion shows the random motion of molecules. Diffusion shows that the molecules can move from one place to another.
9 Solids: molecules vibrate about a fixed position. Liquids: molecules move freely and exchange neighbours. Gases: molecules have little attraction for each other and move in all directions freely.
10 Solids are difficult to compress; their molecular bonds are broken as the temperature rises and the solid melts. Liquids are difficult to

compress; their molecular bonds are broken at high temperature and vapour is formed. Gases: easily compressed.

11 Hooke's law: The extension is proportional to the tension (force) provided the elastic limit is not exceeded.

(b) YOU SHOULD UNDERSTAND

1 How to calculate pressure under heavy boxes or inside liquids.
2 How to calculate the big force obtained in a hydraulic brake or press.
3 Which manometer is used to measure domestic gas pressure and which is used to measure large pressures.
4 How to write down Boyle's law and use it in problems on pressure change.
5 The definition of density and calculations using density.
6 The Brownian and diffusion experiments and what they show.
7 The differences between the molecules in solids, liquids and gases and how the molecular theory explains expansion and change of state.

(c) APPLICATIONS

You should be able to answer the following questions.

1 Calculate the pressure at a depth of 8 m in water, given the density is 1000 kg/m^3 and $g = 10$ m/s^2. Why is mercury and not water used in a barometer?

2 The brake pedal in a car has an area of 15 cm^2 and is pressed with a force of 20 N. Calculate the brake force obtained if the master piston has an area of 300 cm^2.

3 Describe an experiment which shows that molecules have motion. Explain how a continuous temperature rise affects the molecules inside solids and liquids.

QUESTIONS 2C – MATTER AND STRUCTURE – MOLECULAR THEORY

MULTIPLE CHOICE QUESTIONS

1 The dimensions of a rectangular steel block are 2 m × 0.5 m × 0.5 m. If the density of steel is 1200 kg/m^3, then
   A the mass of the block is 12 000 kg
   B the weight of the block is 6000 N
   C the mass of the block is 6000 kg
   D the weight of the block is 12 500 N

2 When a large amount of dough X is compressed into a small ball Y, then
   A X has a smaller mass than Y
   B X has a greater density than Y
   C X has a greater mass than Y
   D X has a smaller density than Y

3   Molecules of water are always moving. This can be shown by an experiment on

     A   diffusion   B   density   C   flow   D   weighing

4   In Brownian motion, a large smoke particle X is seen to 'jiggle' around in air. This is because

     A   air molecules are smaller than X
     B   X is more active than air molecules
     C   air molecules hit X in different directions
     D   air molecules are more massive than X

5   When ice melts and forms water, the molecules

     A   lose energy
     B   are now more bonded together
     C   become lighter
     D   move more freely

6   When a metal solid is heated and expands, the molecules

     A   are moving about in the same direction
     B   have a greater separation
     C   have less energy
     D   have a greater attraction for each other

SHORT ANSWER QUESTIONS

7

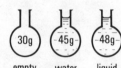

empty   water   liquid

Fig 2V

An empty glass bottle has a mass of 35 g. Fig 2V. Filled with water, the total mass is 45 g. Filled with a liquid, the total mass is 48 g.

(a)   Calculate the liquid density.

(b)   If another liquid of density 0.8 g/cm³ fills the empty bottle, what is the new total mass?

8   Describe the different arrangement of molecules in a solid and in a liquid, drawing diagrams to illustrate your answer.

     What happens to the molecules of a solid and a liquid when they are heated?

9   (a)   Solids have a fixed shape but liquid flow.

    (b)   Liquids have a fixed volume but gases can fill any volume.

     Explain the reasons for (a) and (b).

10   When water vapour is cooled, water liquid is formed. When the water is cooled more, it freezes to ice.

     Using the ideas of energy and molecules, explain the changes which take place from vapour to solid. Draw diagrams to help your answer.

HEAT

CONTENTS

Contents

Temperature and heat play an important part in our daily lives and in our environment. To be in good health, our bodies need to have a temperature of about 37°C. Food storage requires very low temperatures in cold rooms at warehouses and refrigerators provide low temperatures in the home. In winter, when the temperature falls to very low values, we need warm clothing such as woollen or 'thermal' materials. Elderly people then need special care to keep warm. Houses and buildings need good insulation in winter, so that the heat produced inside by heating systems does not escape through windows, for example, into the air outside.

In this Heat section, we begin with thermometers and then consider the effect of heat on expansion of solids, liquids and gases. This is followed by heat transfer in conduction, convection and radiation. We finish with the heat capacity of solids and liquids and their latent heats, and with evaporation and boiling.

3.1 TEMPERATURE SCALES AND FIXED POINTS

If a small glass, X, of hot water is poured into a large tank, Y, of warm water, then the water from X will lose some heat and that in Y will gain the heat. The 'temperature' of an object decides whether it will lose or gain heat when it is placed in contact with another object.

Note that 'temperature' is completely different from 'heat'. Heat transfer, such as the example just considered, is **energy** transfer.

Thermometers measure temperature. The numerical value of a temperature depends on the type of thermometer scale used. On the Celsius scale, the melting point of ice is called '0°C' and the temperature of steam at 760 mmHg pressure is called '100°C'. Between these two lower and upper **fixed points**, as they are known, there are 100 degrees (see Fig 3.1).

Fig 3.1 Celsius and Kelvin scales

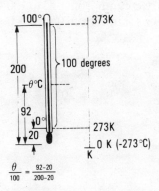

$$\frac{\theta}{100} = \frac{92-20}{200-20}$$

An important temperature scale is the **absolute** or **thermodynamic scale**, suggested by Lord Kelvin. The zero of the scale is '0 K', where K is the kelvin degree – it is called the **absolute zero** of temperature and no lower temperature can be reached. The other fixed point is called '273.16 K'; it is the temperature known as the **triple point** of water, where ice, water and water vapour are all in equilibrium with each other. So, approximately,

$$273 \text{ K} = 0°C \text{ and } 373 \text{ K} = 100°C$$

3.2 MERCURY-IN-GLASS THERMOMETER

When a mercury-in-glass thermometer is made, the bulb is filled with mercury and the top of the narrow-bore or capillary tube is sealed. The level of mercury is marked on the glass when it is placed in melting ice (0°C) and in steam at 760 mmHg pressure (100°C).

Advantages of this thermometer are:

1 mercury expands fairly regularly with temperature rise;
2 it does not 'wet' glass;
3 it has a fairly wide temperature range – about 350°C to −40°C;
4 it has a high thermal conductivity compared to other liquids;
5 mercury is visible and reflects light.

Its disadvantages are:

1 mercury is expensive;
2 it cannot be used in extremely cold temperatures as in the Arctic or Scandinavian countries because it has a freezing point about −40°C, which is not low enough.

3.3 EXAMPLE ON THERMOMETER

At 0°C, the mercury column in a thermometer is 20 mm above the bottom of the bulb and at 100°C the column is 200 mm above the bottom of the bulb (see Fig 3.1).

What is the temperature, θ, of warm water if the mercury column is 92 mm above the bottom of the bulb when the thermometer is placed inside it?

Length of mercury column from 0°C to 100°C = 200−20 = 180 mm
Length of mercury column from 0°C to θ°C = 92−20 = 72 mm

So, by ratio, $\dfrac{\theta}{100} = \dfrac{72}{180} = \dfrac{2}{5}$

Thus $\theta = \dfrac{2}{5} \times 100° = 40°C$

3.4 ALCOHOL-IN-GLASS THERMOMETERS

These can be used in polar regions – alcohol has a freezing point about −112°C. The expansion of alcohol with temperature rise is relatively greater than that of mercury. Its disadvantages are that alcohol has a low boiling point – about 78°C – and the liquid must be coloured to make it visible.

Water is unsuitable as a thermometric liquid because (a) it has an irregular volume change with temperature change – it *contracts* when warmed from 0°C to 4°C; (b) it has a low temperature range – 0°C to 100°C; (c) it is colourless and difficult to see.

3.5 CLINICAL THERMOMETER

This has a small temperature range, for example, 35°C to 45°C, with a marking on it of 36.9°C, normal blood temperature. The capillary tube has a 'kink' or narrow part near the bulb (see Fig 3.2). This allows the mercury to flow past it when the thermometer is used to measure a patient's temperature but the thread remains in the top part of the capillary tube when the thermometer is taken away from the heat because the mercury meniscus stops the mercury flowing past the kink. By jerking the thermometer sharply, the mercury can be forced past the narrow part in the capillary to join up again with the mercury in the bulb.

Fig 3.2 Clinical thermometer

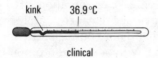

clinical

The glass of the bulb is very thin, so that the mercury quickly reaches the temperature of the patient.

3.6 THERMISTOR. THERMOPILE

Electrical measurements can be made accurately. The **thermistor** is a semiconductor metal whose electrical resistance is sensitive to temperature change. Its resistance can therefore be used to measure temperature or to control the temperature of systems. Fig 3.3(a) shows a thermistor in the form of a small rod, T. A common type of thermistor **decreases** in resistance as its temperature rises – it is said to have a 'negative temperature coefficient'. Other types increase in resistance with temperature rise.

Fig 3.3 (a) Thermistor (b) thermocouple

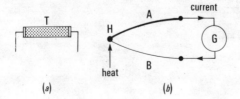

The **thermopile** is another electrical instrument sensitive to temperature change. It is used in heat radiation experiments (see p.125). Basically, it consists of a number of **thermocouples** in series. Fig 3.3(*b*) shows a thermocouple, A and B, with a sensitive current meter or galvanometer G connected to one of their ends. The two different metals are joined at the end H to form a common junction. When the temperature of H rises, an electric current is obtained which flows through G. The size of the current depends on the temperature of H in Fig 3.3(*b*) and so G can be calibrated in temperature values from a previous experiment.

CHECK LIST ▶

Make sure you can answer the following questions.

1   Where is an alcohol thermometer preferred to a mercury thermometer and why?
2   Describe a clinical thermometer, pointing out its special features.
3   What are a 'thermistor' and a 'thermopile'?

THERMAL EXPANSION OF SOLIDS AND LIQUIDS

3.7 EXPANSION OF SOLIDS: MOLECULAR FORCES

Solids usually expand when heated. When the temperature of the solid rises, the amplitude of vibration of the molecules increases (p.156) and so their average distance apart increases.

When a metal expands or contracts, the molecular forces inside it are very large. This is why a cast-iron pin at one end of a metal bar breaks if the metal cannot expand on heating. Telegraph wires are allowed to sag when fixed in summer, so that they do not snap when they contract in winter. In the past, railway lines in open country were laid in sections with a small gap between them to allow for expansion in warm weather. Railway lines may become twisted in very hot summers.

3.8 THE BIMETAL STRIP

When equal lengths of brass and iron are heated through the same temperature rise, the brass expands more than the iron. Fig 3.4(*a*) shows a 'bimetal strip' which has brass on one side and iron on the

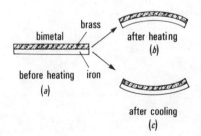

Fig 3.4 Bimetal strip

other. After warming, the strip **curves** with the brass on the outside because brass expands more than the iron (see Fig 3.4(*b*)). After cooling, the strip would curve the other way because the brass contracts more than the iron (Fig 3.4(*c*)).

Invar is an alloy which expands only very slightly with temperature rise. A practical bimetal strip may consist of brass and invar in place of brass and iron, as it will be more sensitive to temperature changes.

3.9 THERMOSTATS

A thermostat is a device which keeps temperatures constant. Fig 3.5 shows the princple of a thermostat which may be used for electric blankets or electric irons. When the temperature is below the desired value, current flows through the bimetal strip and the closed contacts

Fig 3.5 Electric thermostat

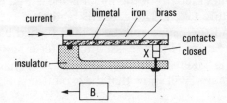

into the wire of the blanket or iron, B, which then becomes hot. When the temperature reaches the value needed, the bimetal strip curves away and the contacts at X are broken. The current is then cut off. When the temperature falls, the bimetal returns to make contact at X again. The current now flows to warm up the blanket or iron. A 'regulator', pushing against the bimetal strip, changes the temperature at which the contacts are broken. For example, if the bimetal has to curve more to break contact at X after the regulator is turned, the temperature of B will have to rise.

Fig 3.6 Gas thermostat

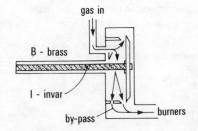

Fig 3.6 shows the principle of a **gas thermostat** for an oven. A brass tube B inside the oven encloses an invar rod I. The rod is attached to one end of B. A valve V is attached to the other end of I. Gas is allowed to flow through to the burners, as shown. When the oven becomes warmer, the brass tube B expands to the left but the invar rod I is practically unaffected. So the valve V moves to the left and

cuts down the flow of gas to the burners. At a particular temperature, which depends on the setting of the thermostat, all the gas is cut off except for a small flow through the bypass.

When the temperature falls the brass tube B contracts and more gas then flows. In this way the temperature is kept constant.

3.10 LINEAR EXPANSIVITY

Physical tables provide the **linear expansivity** of metals. This is defined as the increase in length per unit length (1 m or 1 cm) per °C temperature rise.

Fig 3.7 shows how linear expansivity can be measured in a laboratory. The metal rod AB is fixed at one end A so that it cannot expand there, and the other end B makes contact with a micrometer screw gauge G. The rod is surrounded by a tube with a lagged jacket and steam can be passed round the rod to raise it to steam temperature.

The initial length of the metal is measured by a metre rule and its temperature taken. The gauge is read after contact is made with the end B and the gauge spindle is then turned back to allow the rod to expand. Steam is now passed in. After a sufficient time, the gauge reading is taken when contact with B is made again – a constant gauge reading will show that the expansion of the rod is complete.

Fig 3.7 Measuring linear expansivity

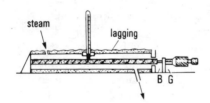

Calculation Suppose the original length of the metal is 102.5 cm, the expansion is 1.50 mm or 0.15 cm, the initial temperature was 15°C and the final temperature was 100°C. Then

$$\text{linear expansivity} = \frac{0.15\,\text{cm}}{102.5\,\text{cm} \times (100-15)\,\text{K}}$$

$$= 0.000\,017 \text{ or } 1.7 \times 10^{-5}/\text{K}$$

This is the value of linear expansivity in the temperature range 15°C to 100°C.

3.11 EXPANSION OF LIQUIDS

Liquids expand relatively more than solids. Fig 3.8 shows how the expansion of three different liquids can be compared. Three large test-tubes of equal volume are filled with the liquids X, Y and Z and their levels are shown by loops of thread round a narrow tube inside the test-tube as shown.

Fig 3.8 Liquids vary in expansion

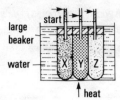

At first, the levels are the same. When the three test-tubes are placed inside a large beaker of hot water, their temperature rises. At first the levels **fall**. This is because the glass becomes warmer than the liquid to start with, but soon the liquids rise above their initial levels. When the temperature is steady, the liquid X has the greatest expansion and Y the least expansion. Alcohol expands more than paraffin oil, which expands more than water.

3.12 VOLUME CHANGE WITH TEMPERATURE

Most liquids increase in volume when their temperature rises. Mercury, for example, has a fairly regular increase in volume with temperature rise (see Fig 3.9). Water, however, is an unusual liquid. From 0°C to about 4°C its volume **contracts** instead of expanding. After 4°C its volume increases in the normal way. So the volume–temperature curve of water has a **minimum** value at about 4°C. Fig 5.14 shows that ice, a solid, expands when its temperature rises from −5°C to 0°C. At 0°C the ice melts and forms water which has a **smaller** volume at 0°C. Also, when the water reaches 100°C, the steam formed has a volume about 1600 times the volume of water.

Fig 3.9 Volume–temperature changes of water and mercury

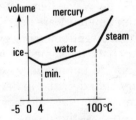

In very cold weather, the water in exposed pipe systems may freeze. The ice formed has a larger volume than the water (Fig 3.9). So the pipe may crack. When the warmer weather returns, the ice melts and contracts, and water now pours out of the crack.

CHECK LIST ▶   Make sure you can answer the following questions.

1   How does a bimetal change when warmed or cooled? Draw diagrams.
2   Draw a diagram showing how a bimetal is used in a thermostat.
3   How does the volume change of water from 0°C differ from that of mercury?

QUESTIONS 3A – THERMOMETRY. EXPANSION OF SOLIDS AND LIQUIDS

MULTI CHOICE QUESTIONS

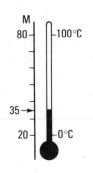

Fig 3A

1   One reason for using mercury in a mercury-in-glass thermometer is
   A   it conducts electricity well
   B   it has a high density
   C   it has an extremely low freezing point
   D   it can easily be seen

2   A rule M is placed beside a mercury thermometer as shown in Fig 3A. 0°C corresponds to a reading on M of 20 divisions and 100°C to 80 divisions. The temperature corresponding to 35 divisions on M is
   A   15°C   B   25°C   C   35°C   D   70°C

3   The capillary tubing of a clinical thermometer is made narrower near the bottom. This is because
   A   the normal body temperature is 37°C
   B   the mercury can then flow more easily
   C   the patient's temperature can be recorded
   D   the thermometer is then more sensitive

4   A bimetal, made of two metals X and Y, can be used in an electric thermostat because
   A   X is a better heat conductor than Y
   B   X and Y have different expansion when heated
   C   X contracts but Y expands on heating
   D   X and Y curve the same way when heated or cooled

5   Equal volumes of water and mercury are heated from 0°C. Then
   A   Water contracts from 0°C but mercury expands
   B   Water and mercury have the same volume at 10°C
   C   Water expands from 0°C but mercury expands more from 0°C
   D   Water and mercury both decrease in density from 0°C

6   In Arctic countries such as Norway, alcohol-in-glass thermometers are preferred to mercury-in-glass thermometers because
   A   alcohol has a greater expansion with temperature than mercury
   B   alcohol has a lower freezing point than mercury
   C   alcohol has a greater boiling point than mercury
   D   alcohol can be seen more clearly than mercury

SHORT ANSWER QUESTIONS

7 In Fig 3A, what reading on the metal scale M beside the thermometer corresponds to a temperature of 40°C?

8 State *one* advantage and *one* disadvantage of using mercury in a thermometer.

9 A bimetal strip curves as shown in Fig 3B when it is cooled. The lengths of the two metals X and Y were initially equal and the bimetal was straight.

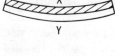

Fig 3B

(a) Which metal, X or Y, has the greater expansion with temperature rise?

(b) Draw a sketch of the bimetal if it was initially heated instead of cooled.

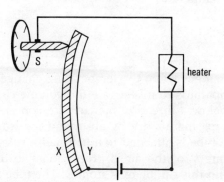

Fig 3C

10 Fig 3C shows a bimetal thermostat, metals X and Y, in an electrical circuit. A screw S can be turned to alter the temperature setting.

(a) Explain how the bimetal can keep the temperature constant.

(b) Describe how S should be turned to get a higher temperature and explain your answer.

11 (a) Fig 3D(a) shows roughly how the volume of a given mass of water varies with temperature from 0°C to 20°C.

Draw a sketch showing roughly how the **density** of water varies from 0°C to 20°C.

Fig 3D (a) and (b)

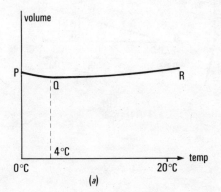

(a)

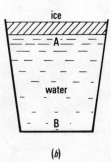

(b)

(*b*)   Fig 3D(*b*) shows a bucket containing water which has frozen at the top in very cold weather. What is the temperature at A and at B? Explain your answers.

EXPANSION OF GASES

Gases are used in heat engines for driving cars and aeroplanes and other machines. The way in which gases behave are therefore carefully studied by mechanical engineers.

Gases expand much more than liquids with temperature rise. Unlike solids and liquids, gases are sensitive to changes in pressure. So we must take into account pressure as well as volume changes when the temperature of a gas varies.

3.13 VOLUME–TEMPERATURE CHANGES AT CONSTANT PRESSURE

First, we keep the pressure of a gas constant, and study the way its volume changes when the temperature changes. Fig 3.10(*a*) shows a simple apparatus to investigate the volume change. Some dry air is trapped below a thread of mercury (or concentrated sulphuric acid, which keeps the air dry by absorbing moisture), inside a capillary tube. The tube is attached to a half-metre rule R by an elastic band. The volume *V* of the air is proportional to the length *l* of the air column and this can be read from R. The tube and rule are placed in water inside a deep beaker and the air temperature is varied and read each time with a thermometer.

The pressure of the gas, whatever its temperature, is always equal to the atmospheric pressure plus the pressure due to the length of mercury thread. So the gas pressure is kept **constant** when the temperature changes.

Fig 3.10 Gas volume–temperature change (pressure constant)

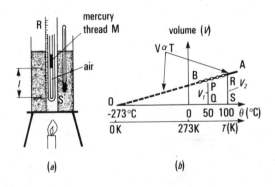

3.14 ABSOLUTE ZERO. ABSOLUTE TEMPERATURE

Fig 3.10(b) shows the results obtained in a typical experiment when the volume V is plotted against the temperature θ in °C. A **straight line** graph BA is obtained. So the volume of a gas at constant pressure varies linearly with temperature rise.

Careful experiments show that when the line BA is produced back to cut the temperature axis, it does so at a temperature of about −273°C. We call −273°C the **absolute zero** because, theoretically, we cannot have a gas at a lower temperature than the one at which its volume would shrink to zero.

The **absolute** or **kelvin temperature scale** has its zero at the absolute zero. So $0\,K = -273°C$, $273\,K = 0°C$ (see Fig 3.10(b)). We use the symbol T for absolute or kelvin temperature and θ for temperature in °C. The relationship is

$$T\,K = 273 + \theta°C,$$

that is, add 273 to the temperature in °C to get the kelvin temperature. So

$$100°C = 273 + 100 = 373\,K$$

and $\qquad 27°C = 273 + 27 = 300\,K$

3.15 RELATION BETWEEN V AND T

From Fig 3.10(b), we can see from the triangles OPQ and ORS that the ratio RS/PQ equals the ratio OS/OQ. This means that if V_2 is the volume of a gas at 100°C (S) and V_1 is the volume at 50°C (Q), then

$$\frac{V_2}{V_1} = \frac{OS}{OQ} = \frac{T_2}{T_1},$$

where T_2 is the kelvin temperature at S and T_1 is the kelvin temperature at Q. So

$$\frac{V_2}{V_1} = \frac{273+100\ (°C)}{273+50\ (°C)} = \frac{373}{323}$$

Generally, **the volume of a gas at constant pressure is directly proportional to its absolute or kelvin temperature**, or

$$V \propto T \text{ (constant pressure)}$$

Always remember that when this relationship is used, the temperature in °C must be changed to K (kelvin).

3.16 EXAMPLE ON VOLUME AND TEMPERATURE

The volume of a gas is 2.0 litres at 27°C. If its pressure is kept constant, find its volume at (a) 87°C and (b) 0°C. (c) At what temperature is its volume 2.5 litres, the pressure being constant?

$$87°C = 273+87 = 360\,K. \qquad 27°C = 273+27 = 300\,K$$

(a)   Since $V \propto T$ at constant pressure,

$$\frac{V}{2.0} = \frac{360}{300} = \frac{6}{5}$$

So $V = \frac{6}{5} \times 2 = 2.4$ litres

(b)   Since $0°C = 273$ K, and $V \propto T$, then

$$\frac{V}{2.0} = \frac{273}{300}, \text{ or } V = \frac{273}{300} \times 2 = 1.8 \text{ litres (approx)}$$

(c)   Suppose the volume is 2.5 litres at a kelvin temperature T. Then

$$\frac{2.5}{2.0} = \frac{T}{300}, \text{ or } T = \frac{2.5 \times 300}{2.0} = 375 \text{ K}$$

so   temperature $= 375 - 273 = 102°C$

3.17 PRESSURE–TEMPERATURE CHANGES AT CONSTANT VOLUME

Now we investigate how the pressure of a gas varies with temperature **when its volume is constant**. Fig 3.11(a) shows how this can be done. The gas, such as dry air, is inside a large bulb B. The whole of B is placed inside water in a large beaker so that its temperature can be varied by warming the water. The pressure p is measured by a mercury gauge or manometer connected to B.

The volume of the gas is kept constant by moving the right-hand side M of the manometer up or down until the mercury level on the other side is level with a fixed mark Y on the rule. The procedure is: (1) warm the gas to a constant temperature read by a thermometer; (2) quickly make the volume constant at Y; and then (3) read the difference, h, in the mercury levels of the manometer. The pressure $p = A + h$, where A is the atmospheric pressure which must be known.

Notice that the **whole** of the bulb B must be under the water in the experiment, so that all the air inside B is at the measured temperature of the thermometer.

Fig 3.11 Gas pressure–temperature change (volume constant)

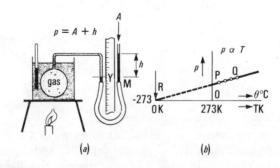

(a)   (b)

3.18 PRESSURE–TEMPERATURE LAW

Fig 3.11(b) shows the results obtained when the pressure p is plotted against the temperature, θ, in °C. The points lie on a straight line PQ which passes through −273°C when PQ is extended to cut the temperature axis at R. So, as in the case of the volume at constant pressure just discussed,

$$p \propto T$$

where T is the absolute or kelvin temperature, when the volume of a gas is constant.

3.19 EXAMPLE ON GAS PRESSURE

The pressure in a bicycle inner tube is 1.40×10^5 Pa at 10°C. (a) What is the pressure at 20°C, assuming the volume of air in the tube is practically constant? (b) If the inner tube breaks when the pressure inside is 2.80×10^5 Pa, at what air temperature would this occur?

(a)   Since the volume is constant, $p \propto T$
Now 20°C = 273+20 = 293 K, 10°C = 273+10 = 283 K.

So $\dfrac{p}{1.4 \times 10^5} = \dfrac{293}{283}$

Thus $p = \dfrac{1.4 \times 10^5 \times 293}{283} = 1.45 \times 10^5$ Pa

(b)   Suppose T is the kelvin temperature when the pressure reaches 2.80×10^5 Pa. Since the volume is constant,

$$\frac{2.80 \times 10^5}{1.40 \times 10^5} = \frac{T}{283}$$

So $T = \dfrac{283 \times 2.80 \times 10^5}{1.40 \times 10^5} = 283 \times 2 = 566$ K

Thus   temperature = 566−273 = 293°C

3.20 KINETIC THEORY OF GASES

In the kinetic theory of gases, we imagine that the molecules are like very tiny spheres moving about freely inside the volume they occupy, and bouncing back with the same speed after hitting the walls of the container.

3.21 PRESSURE–TEMPERATURE CHANGE AT CONSTANT VOLUME

When the gas is heated, the energy supplied makes the molecules move about with greater velocity. If they are inside a cube, the molecules will then have a great momentum change on hitting a wall and bouncing back (see Fig 3.12(a)). They will also make more collisions per second with the wall as they are moving faster. So the molecules now have a greater *rate of change of momentum* as they keep hitting the walls. Now the force is proportional to the rate of change of momentum (p.55). So the force or pressure of the gas on the walls of the vessel increases with increasing temperature.

Fig 3.12 Kinetic theory of pressure

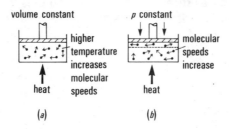

3.22 **VOLUME–TEMPERATURE CHANGE AT CONSTANT PRESSURE**

When the gas is heated at constant pressure, the energy of the molecules increases. Part of this energy is used to push the piston back slowly while the pressure is kept constant (Fig 3.12(b)). The rest of the energy remains in the gas molecules, so that its temperature rises. Although the molecules move faster, they also have to travel farther between successive impacts and the pressure remains constant.

3.23 **GENERAL GAS LAW OR EQUATION OF STATE**

From $p \propto T$ (volume constant) and $V \propto T$ (pressure constant), for a fixed amount of gas it follows that $pV \propto T$ when p, V, and T all vary. So

$$\frac{pV}{T} = \text{constant}$$

This means that if a constant amount of gas has two sets of values of pressure, volume and absolute or kelvin temperature, p_1, V_1, T_1 and p_2, V_2, T_2, then

$$\frac{p_1 V_1}{T_1} = \frac{p_2 V_2}{T_2}$$

The *gas equation* for one mole of an ideal gas is written as $pV = RT$, where R is a constant known as the *molar gas constant*.

3.24 **EXAMPLE ON GAS LAW**

In an experiment, 80.0 cm^3 of oxygen is collected at 17°C and a pressure of 100 kPa (kilopascals).
(a)   What is the volume of the gas at 0°C and 120 kPa?
(b)   At what temperature in °C would the gas have a volume of 90.0 cm^3 and a pressure of 110 kPa?
(a)   Here $p_1 = 100$ kPa, $V_1 = 80.0 \text{ cm}^3$, $T_1 = 273+17 = 290$ K
$p_2 = 120$ kPa, $V_2 = ?$, $T_2 = 273$ K

Since $\dfrac{p_1 V_1}{T_1} = \dfrac{p_2 V_2}{T_2}$

So $\dfrac{100 \times 80.0}{290} = \dfrac{120 \times V_2}{273}$

and $290 \times 120 \times V_2 = 273 \times 100 \times 80.0$

giving $V_2 = \dfrac{273 \times 100 \times 80.0}{290 \times 120} = 62.8 \text{ cm}^3$

(b) Here $p_2 = 110 \text{ kPa}$, $V_2 = 90.0 \text{ cm}^3$, $T_2 = ?$

Since $\dfrac{p_1 V_1}{T_1} = \dfrac{p_2 V_2}{T_2}$

So $\dfrac{100 \times 80.0}{290} = \dfrac{110 \times 90.0}{T_2}$

giving $T_2 = \dfrac{110 \times 90.0 \times 290}{100 \times 80.0} = 359 \text{ K}$

So temperature $= 359 - 273 = 86°C$

QUESTIONS 3B – GASES (PRESSURE, VOLUME, TEMPERATURE). MOLECULAR THEORY

MULTIPLE CHOICE QUESTIONS

1 Oxygen in a gas cylinder has a volume of 1 litre, a pressure of 120 kPa and a temperature of 27°C.

  With the volume constant at 1 litre, the gas is heated to 127°C. The new pressure in kPa is
  A 600   B 247   C 160   D 147

2 Nitrogen in a container has a volume of 2.0 litres and a temperature of 27°C. The gas is heated at constant pressure so that the volume becomes 2.2 litres. The new gas temperature is then
  A 30°C   B 42°C   C 300 K   D 330 K

3 A gas in an engine is compressed to half its volume at constant temperature. The molecules now strike the walls of the cylinder
  A twice as often as before with the same velocity
  B half as often as before with a higher velocity
  C half as often as before with a smaller velocity
  D twice as often as before with a higher velocity

SHORT ANSWER QUESTIONS

4 A gas has a volume of 200 cm^3, a pressure of 100 kPa and a temperature of 27°C. Calculate the new pressure when the volume is 300 cm^3 and the temperature is −73°C.

5 When a car engine is working, at one stage the piston is raised and the gas expands.

Considering the molecules of the gas, explain why (*a*) the pressure is then reduced and (*b*) the temperature of the gas becomes lowered.

6 Before starting a journey, the air in a car tyre has a pressure of 180 kPa and a temperature of 17°C. At the end of the journey, the air temperature rose to 37°C.

(*a*)   Assuming the tube containing the air had a constant volume, find the new air pressure.

(*b*)   What would have been the air temperature if the pressure reached 186 kPa at one stage?

(*c*)   Considering the molecules of air, explain why the pressure has increased.

7 Find the volume at 0°C and 100 kPa pressure of 40 litres of oxygen gas which has a temperature of 17°C and a pressure of 800 kPa.

What is the mass of the gas if 22.4 litres of oxygen at 0°C and 100 kPa pressure has a mass of 32 g?

Fig 3E

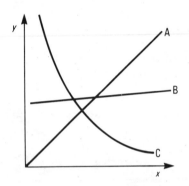

Fig 3E shows three graphs A,B,C which relate to the pressure, volume and temperature changes of a gas. In questions 8, 9, 10, choose **one** graph which fits the way *y* and *x* vary:

8   $y = p$, pressure, and $x = T$, kelvin temperature (volume of gas constant).

9   $y = p$, pressure, and $x = V$, volume (temperature of gas constant).

10   $y = V$, volume, and $x = t°C$ (pressure of gas constant).

TRANSFER OF HEAT: CONDUCTION, CONVECTION, RADIATION

The transfer of heat affects our lives considerably. In cooking, for example, heat is **conducted** from hot gases or heating coils through the bottom of saucepans to the food inside. Bad conductors are needed for heat insulation in the home and in buildings.

Heat is transferred by **convection** in central heating systems and the Sun transfers heat energy to the Earth and its inhabitants by **radiation**.

In this section we shall begin with conduction, follow with convection and finally with radiation.

3.25 THEORY OF CONDUCTION

If one end of a metal teaspoon is heated by dipping it in hot tea, the other end soon feels warm. The hot end gains energy and the free electrons (see p.201) there carry the energy to neighbouring metal atoms. The energy thus passes along the metal to the other end of the spoon by movement of electrons (Fig 3.13(a)).

Fig 3.13 Theory of conduction

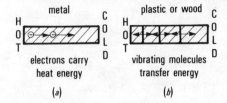

(a) metal — electrons carry heat energy

(b) plastic or wood — vibrating molecules transfer energy

If a non-conductor, such as a plastic teaspoon, is dipped into the hot tea (see Fig 3.13(b)), the molecules at the hot end vibrate with increasing amplitude about their average positions (p.96). So they 'jostle' the neighbouring molecules, and in turn disturb them. This disturbance travels along to the other end of the spoon. So the energy or heat is passed from one layer of molecules to the next, while **the average position of the layers remains the same**.

3.26 GOOD AND BAD CONDUCTORS

1 METALS HAVE DIFFERENT CONDUCTIVITIES

To show that metals have different conductivities, long rods of the same length and diameter but of different materials are pushed into a small tank, as in Fig 3.14.

Fig 3.14 Metals vary in conductivity

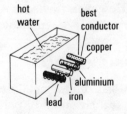

hot water — best conductor — copper — aluminium — iron — lead

The rods are coated with wax and small beads which act as markers are stuck at equal distances along the rods. Hot water is now poured into the tank. The rate at which heat is conducted along the rods is shown by the beads, which fall off as the wax is melted. The heat travels faster along the copper rod than along the others, showing that copper is a very good conductor of heat.

2 WOOD AND METAL CONDUCTORS

The middle of a wooden rod is covered with metal foil, B, which is wound firmly on the wood to make good contact with it as in Fig 3.15(a). Heat-sensitive paper is placed tightly round the metal and partly over the wood. A Bunsen burner flame is then moved to and fro across the whole of the paper.

Fig 3.15 Conduction of metal, wood, water

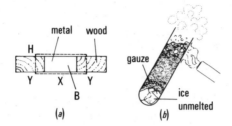

The paper over the metal, X, is seen to be only slightly affected, but the part, Y, over the wood has discoloured. This shows that the metal has conducted the heat from the flame quickly away from the paper, but the wood has conducted the heat away slowly. Wood is therefore a poor conductor. This is why, on a cold day, the wooden handle of a spade feels warmer to the touch than the metal blade, which conducts the heat away from the hand more quickly.

3 WATER IS A POOR CONDUCTOR

This can be shown by placing a piece of ice at the bottom of a test-tube of water and preventing it from rising to the surface by using a metal gauze as in Fig 3.15(b). The water at the top of the tube is now heated until it eventually boils. However, the ice is *not* affected. This shows that heat is conducted very slowly down the water in the test-tube.

4 IGNITION TEMPERATURE OF GAS. MINER'S LAMP

Fig 3.16(a) shows a metal gauze at a small distance above a Bunsen burner. When the gas is turned on and lit *above* the gauze, it burns above the gauze but no flame appears below the gauze. The metal gauze conducts the heat of the flame quickly away, and so the temperature of the gas below the gauze remains below its 'ignition temperature'.

Fig 3.16 Ignition temperature of gas

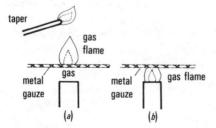

When the gas is turned on and lit **below** the gauze, as in Fig 3.16(*b*), no flame appears above the gauze for a similar reason.

The miner's lamp has a burning wick surrounded by metal gauze. The metal keeps any inflammable gas outside the lamp below its ignition point.

3.27 HEAT INSULATION

Gases such as air are very poor conductors. Woollen blankets are warm because the pockets of air trapped between the strands of wool conduct the heat away from the body very slowly. **Double glazing** traps air between two pieces of glass and reduces appreciably the rate at which heat is lost through the window. In winter birds appear fatter because they fluff out their feathers – this action traps pockets of air and helps keep the bird warm.

In addition to heat losses through windows in the home, reduced considerably by double glazing as just explained, heat can escape through the loft, the floor, the walls and the doors.

The loft should be insulated by fibre glass or felt. Expanded polystyrene, a light material with many pockets of air, is a very good insulator. A thick layer of felt under a carpet will reduce heat loss through the floor. Cavity walls, filled with insulating foam between them, will reduce heat losses through walls. Strips of insulating material can prevent heat losses through gaps in doors.

3.28 CONVECTION. CONVECTION CURRENTS

We now consider transfer of heat by **convection**. Unlike conduction, where the average position of the layers of material remains the same, in convection heat is transferred from one place to another of the substance **by the movement of the substance itself**.

We can illustrate convection by considering the case of water in a kettle when it is heated by the flame on a gas cooker.

The water at the bottom of the kettle becomes warm first (Fig 3.17(*a*)) and expands. This warm water therefore has a **smaller density** than the cold water above it. So the warm water rises, carrying the heat with it, and the colder water falls to the bottom and can be heated in turn.

The water warmed at the bottom of the kettle moves to other parts

Fig 3.17 Convection in liquid and gas

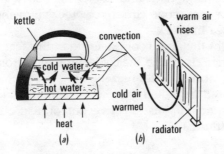

in paths called 'convection currents'. Eventually all the water in the kettle becomes hot and the water boils.

Inside a room, the air in contact with a hot radiator becomes warmed (Fig 3.17(*b*)). Since this air then expands, it has a lower density than the colder air above it. So the warm air rises or circulates in the room and its place next to the radiator is taken by cold air. This becomes warmed and rises. So the air in the room is warmed by convection – not by 'radiation' as the use of the name 'radiator' suggests.

3.29 HOME HOT-WATER SYSTEM

The hot-water system in houses normally warms by convection. Heat passes from the flame through the metal casing at the bottom of the boiler in Fig 3.18 by conduction. The hot water rises from the **top** of the boiler to the top of the storage tank and cold water at the **bottom** of the tank enters the boiler for heating. This is the 'circulating' water system. After some hot water is drawn off, more cold water flows into the tank from the mains. If the water becomes too hot, a steam or expansion pipe discharges the water or steam into the cistern. Thermostats are supplied with boilers to make them run more efficiently at a required hot-water temperature.

Fig 3.18 Hot-water system

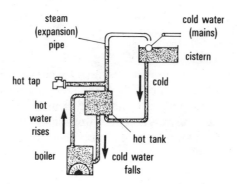

3.30 SEA AND LAND BREEZES

Sea and land breezes are natural convection currents in air.

The land has a smaller specific heat capacity than water. So on a summer's day the land has a higher temperature than the sea. The air above the land rises and cooler air above the sea moves inland, forming a convection current or breeze blowing from the sea. This is called a **sea-breeze**.

At night the land cools faster than the sea. The warmer air above the sea then rises, and the cooler air moves from the land towards the sea. This forms a **land-breeze**.

It should be noted that while conduction of heat can occur in solids, liquids, or gases, convection of heat can only occur in liquids or gases (fluids).

Make sure you can answer the following questions.

1   What is the difference between 'conduction' and 'convection' of heat?
2   Is water a good or a bad conductor? What experiment shows your answer is true?
3   How do double-glazing and a radiator keep a room warm?
4   Why does a sea-breeze occur?

3.31 RADIATION

We now consider the transfer of heat by **radiation**. **Radiation** is the transfer of heat from one place to another without any help from the material between these places. In conduction and convection the material plays an active part, whereas materials (such as glass) can only reduce the amount of radiation passing through them.

The Sun's energy reaches us by radiation through large distances of empty space before it arrives at the Earth. Solar furnaces in hot countries and solar heating for homes both use the Sun's energy.

3.32 EMITTERS AND ABSORBERS OF RADIATION

Some surfaces are good emitters and good absorbers of radiation. Others are poor emitters and poor absorbers. As we now show, for a given temperature the amount of radiation emitted or absorbed depends on the colour of the surface.

Fig 3.19(*a*) shows how to investigate the radiation emitted from different surfaces at the same temperature. The metal cube, L, has black, silver, grey and white surfaces. Hot water is poured into the cube, the radiation is detected by a thermopile with an attached cone C, and the current in the galvanometer, G, is a measure of the radiation. The cone must be **close** to the cube each time, as shown.

The results show that **a dull-black surface is the best radiator and that a highly polished silvery surface is the worst radiator**.

Fig 3.19 Radiation and absorption by different surfaces

(a)   (b)

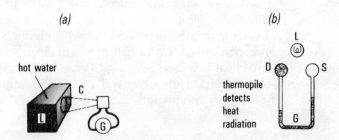

hot water

thermopile
detects
heat
radiation

Fig 3.19(*b*) shows how to demonstrate that a dull-black surface is also a much better **absorber** of radiation than a highly polished, silvery surface. The bulb, D, is painted dull black and the bulb, S, is painted with a silvery coating. The lamp, L, is exactly midway between D and S. The oil gauge G shows that when the lamp is switched on, the level of oil below D is lower than that below S. So the bulb D has absorbed radiation from the lamp much better than the bulb S.

3.33 NATURE AND PROPERTIES OF HEAT RADIATION

The radiation from hot objects consists of electromagnetic waves like light waves but with a **longer** wavelength. These rays, called **infrared rays**, are invisible (see p.159). Infrared rays can be detected by a thermopile and galvanometer, as in Fig 3.19(a).

Infrared rays have the same properties as light rays; for example, they can be reflected and refracted. A hot electric iron, which cannot be seen in the dark, radiates infrared rays. By using a plane glass surface as a reflector, a detector such as a thermopile and galvanometer, and narrow openings to direct the infrared rays at a particular angle of incidence on the surface, the law of reflection can be verified.

3.34 THERMOS FLASK

This flask is mainly used to stop a hot liquid losing heat. It was originally designed to do the opposite, that is, to keep a cold liquid such as liquid oxygen at its low temperature.

Fig 3.20 Design of thermos flask

Fig 3.20 shows the double-walled glass jacket of the thermos flask. It has (a) a **vacuum**, which stops loss of heat by conduction and convection because no matter is present to transfer the heat, and (b) **silvering on the inner sides**, which reduces heat losses by radiation and reflects back any radiation passing through the vacuum. The cork stops heat loss by convection. There are insulating supports between the glass jacket and outer wall of the flask (not shown) to reduce any heat loss by conduction.

3.35 SOLAR ENERGY USES

In very hot countries, large concave mirrors collect energy from the Sun and concentrate the energy on water in a furnace. The steam produced can then be used for generating electricity in power stations.

Fig 3.21 Principle of home solar heating

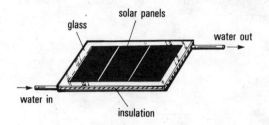

Solar heating for homes need large metal panels painted in black for good absorption of the Sun's radiation. Fig 3.21 shows the basic principle. The inclined panels are placed on the roof and are covered with glass to 'trap' the heat as in greenhouses so that little escapes to the air outside. Insulation below the panels reduces conduction downwards to the roof and house. Water circulates in blackened metal pipes round the panels and the heat absorbed provides hot water for the house.

QUESTIONS 3C – CONDUCTION, CONVECTION, RADIATION

MULTIPLE CHOICE QUESTIONS

1 A radiator warms a room mainly by
   A radiation   B conduction   C convection
   D radiation and conduction

2 Convection can NOT be obtained in a
   A liquid   B gas   C vapour   D solid

3 In a Thermos flask, silvering the jacket walls prevents heat losses by
   A radiation   B convection   C conduction
   D convection and radiation

4 Cavity walls, used in building, have air between the bricks because
   A air becomes warmed by bricks
   B air is an insulator
   C air prevents convection currents
   D radiation can pass through air

5 On hot days in summer the land becomes warmed while the sea is relatively cool. A breeze then occurs because
   A the land radiates heat
   B the sea absorbs heat from the sun
   C conduction takes place from land to sea
   D convection of air takes place

SHORT ANSWER QUESTIONS

6   Fig 3F shows diagrammatically a bungalow which has just been built, where A represents cavity walls with air between bricks.

(*a*)   Explain the purpose of cavity walls.

(*b*)   State **three** other additions by which the house can be kept warm in winter.

Fig 3F

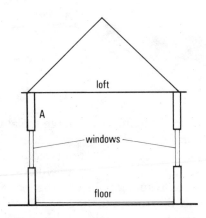

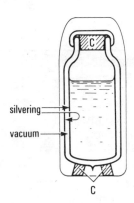

Fig 3G

7   A Thermos flask is shown in Fig 3G. What is the purpose of (*a*) the vacuum, (*b*) the silvering, (*c*) the cork cap and cork supports, C?

8   A thick glass tumbler often cracks when hot water is poured into it. Explain why this happens.

9   (*a*)   The roofs of sheds are often painted with aluminium paint. In summer, what effect would this have on the temperature inside the shed? Explain your answer.

(*b*)   Why are hot-water pipes round kitchen walls sometimes coated with aluminium paint?

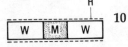

Fig 3H

10   A wooden rod W has a piece of metal foil M round it in the middle. Fig 3H. White heat-sensitive paper H, which turns blue when its temperature rises appreciably, is wound tightly round W and M as shown.

Describe the appearance of the paper after the rod is moved quickly to and fro several times through the flame of a bunsen burner. Explain your answer.

If the paper H were only loosely wound round W and M, what would have been the appearance of the paper in this case after moving it through the flame? Give a reason for your answer.

11 Polystyrene has a lot of fine holes in it and is used as a packing material round a television tube. Explain why the polystyrene feels warm.

12 In winter, the metal part of a spade feels cold and the wooden handle feels warmer. In summer, when the spade is left in the sun, the reverse is the case. Explain why this happens.

HEAT CAPACITY. LATENT HEAT. APPLICATIONS

The temperature rise of water and of metal pipes and tanks in heating systems depends on their **heat capacities**. In this section we first consider heat capacity and its measurement and then show how simple calculations can be made to find the temperature rise on heat transfer.

We then follow with **latent heat**. This is the heat needed to change a substance from a solid to a liquid state (fusion) or from a liquid to a vapour state (vaporization). We conclude with an account of evaporation and how a refrigerator works.

HEAT CAPACITY

The unit of heat is the **joule**, J, the unit of energy. 1 kilojoule, kJ = 1000 J. 1 megajoule, MJ = 1 million (10^6) J.

The **heat capacity** of a substance is the amount of heat needed to raise its temperature by 1°C or 1 K (1°C = 1 K). The unit of heat capacity is J/°C or J/K.

If a block of copper has a heat capacity of 800 J/K, then the amount of heat Q needed to raise its temperature by 5°C is

$$Q = 800 \times 5 = 4000 \text{ J}$$

Generally, Q = **heat capacity** × **temperature rise**

3.37 SPECIFIC HEAT CAPACITY

The specific heat capacity, c, of a substance is the heat needed to raise the temperature of unit mass (1 kg or 1 g) by 1°C (or 1 K). The unit of specific heat capacity is J/kg K (J per kg per K) or J/g K. The specific heat capacity of water = 4200 J/kg K (or 4.2 J/g K) approximately.

Water has a high specific heat capacity. So its temperature rise is relatively small compared with equal masses of other substances given the same amount of heat as water. The sea does not therefore rise appreciably in temperature, even in warm climates, which is an advantage.

You should note that 'specific heat capacity' is always calculated 'per kg' of the substance but 'heat capacity' is not. In fact, if m is the mass in kg of a substance,

$$\text{heat capacity} = \text{mass in kg} \times \text{specific heat capacity}$$
$$= mc$$

Formula The heat Q gained or lost by a substance of mass m when its temperature **changes** by $\theta°C$ is given by

$$Q = mc\theta$$

3.38 EXAMPLES ON HEAT TRANSFER AND TEMPERATURE CHANGE

1 0.5 kg of water is heated from 20°C to 80°C. How much heat is supplied? ($c = 4200$ J/kg K for water.)

Temperature rise $\theta = 80 - 20 = 60°C$

So
$$Q = mc\theta = 0.5 \times 4200 \times 60$$
$$= 126\,000\text{ J}$$

2 A 2 kg mass of copper drops in temperature from 15°C. If the heat lost is 4000 J, calculate the new temperature of the copper ($c = 400$ J/kg K for copper).

From
$$Q = mc\theta,$$

temperature drop, $\theta = \dfrac{Q}{mc}$

$$= \frac{4000}{2 \times 400} = 5°C$$

So   new temperature $= 15 - 5 = 10°C$

3.39 SPECIFIC HEAT CAPACITY MEASUREMENT

Example 3.23 is the basis of an electrical method of measuring the specific heat capacity, c, of a metal in the form of a block. Fig 3.22 shows the apparatus needed. The felt jacket round the aluminium block is an insulator which helps to stop heat leaving the block to the

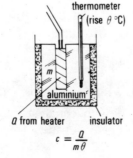

Fig 3.22 Electrical measurement of specific heat capacity

thermometer
(rise θ °C)

m

aluminium

Q from heater   insulator

$c = \dfrac{Q}{m\theta}$

surrounding air. If there were no 'heat losses', all the heat supplied would go to raise the temperature of the block. If some heat is lost, the temperature rise is *less* and so the calculated result from $c = Q/m\theta$ is greater than the true result.

The electrical method can also be used to measure the specific heat capacity of a liquid such as water. Here the water can be placed in a plastic (insulating) container to reduce heat loss to the surroundings.

We can show how the specific heat capacity of the aluminium is calculated in this experiment by the following numerical example:

An aluminium block of mass 0.5 kg is heated electrically by a 100 W supply for 3 min. The temperature of the block rises from 20°C to 60°C. Find the specific heat capacity of aluminium.

Since 100 W = 100 J/s and 3 min = 3×60 s, the heat supplied, Q, is given by

$$Q = \text{power} \times \text{time} = 100 \times (3 \times 60) = 18\,000 \, \text{J},$$

Also,   temperature rise = 60−20 = 40°C

From $$Q = mc\theta,$$

$$c = \frac{Q}{m\theta} = \frac{18\,000}{0.5 \times 40}$$

$$= 900 \, \text{J/kg K}$$

CHECK LIST ▶   Make sure you can answer the following questions.

1   What is meant by 'specific heat capacity'? What are its units?
2   How much heat is transferred from a 24 W heater in 10 min to a block of copper? How would you calculate the specific heat capacity?
3   What would you do to reduce errors in an experiment to measure the specific heat capacity of a metal?

3.40 LATENT HEAT

If a block of ice is heated so that it melts, **its temperature remains at** 0°C, **the melting point**, while the block changes from a solid state to a liquid state. We give the name **latent heat of fusion** to the heat needed to change a substance from solid to liquid **at the melting point**, that is, when a change of state occurs (see Fig 3.23). So if a solid stays as a solid when heated, 'latent heat' is **not** concerned.

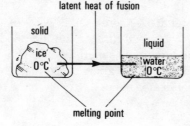

Fig 3.23 Meaning of latent heat of fusion

3.41 MOLECULAR THEORY OF LATENT HEAT OF FUSION

When a solid is heated, its vibrating molecules gain energy. Eventually, the increased energy becomes sufficient for the molecules to break away from their 'anchored' positions (p.96). Now they move freely in different directions, exchanging neighbours, and they are in the liquid state.

3.42 SPECIFIC LATENT HEAT OF FUSION

The specific latent heat of fusion, l, is defined as the heat needed to change unit mass (1 kg or 1 g) of the solid **at the melting point** to liquid at the same temperature. The unit of l is J/kg or J/g.

    The specific latent heat of fusion of ice, l, is about 330 000 (3.3×10^5) J/kg or 330 J/g. So 330 J of heat is needed to change 1 gram of ice at 0°C to water at 0°C.

3.43 MELTING OF ICE TO WATER

Suppose a 10 g mass of ice at 0°C is added to a glass of lemonade to cool it as in Fig 3.24. If all the ice melts and the final temperature of the water and lemonade is 4°C, then

heat transfer from lemonade = heat to melt 10 g ice to water at 0°C + heat to raise 10 g water from 0°C to 4°C

Fig 3.24 Heat exchanges when ice melts to water

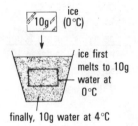

Using 330 J/g as the specific latent heat of ice,

    heat needed to melt ice to water at 0°C (change of state)
    $= 10 \times 330 = 3300$ J

Using 4.2 J/g K as the specific heat capacity of water,

    heat needed to raise 10 g of water from 0°C to 4°C
    $= mc\theta = 10 + 4.2 \times (4-0) = 168$ J

So   total heat transfer from lemonade $= 3300 + 168 = 3468$ J

    If 10 g of **water** at 0°C were used in place of ice, there would be only a slight drop in temperature of the lemonade. Much more heat is taken from the lemonade when ice at 0°C is used, because 330 J of heat is needed to make 1 gram of ice melt to water at 0°C whereas only about 4 J of heat is needed to change the temperature of water by 1°C.

3.44 MEASURING /
FOR ICE

▼ The specific latent heat of fusion of ice can be measured by adding ice to water and observing the temperature drop. Some practical points are:

(a)   the ice must be dried with blotting or filter paper;

(b)   add small pieces of dried ice one at a time and stir the water until it melts before adding another piece;

(c)   warm the water first until it is about 4°C above room temperature and add ice until the temperature is about 4°C below the room temperature – this compensates approximately for any heat exchange with the surrounding air.

The water may be in a polystyrene container and the small heat exchange with this container can be omitted from the calculation to obtain an approximate value. Otherwise, the water may be in a metal vessel called a **calorimeter**, surrounded by insulating material to stop heat losses to the surroundings, and the heat exchange with the calorimeter is taken into account.

Suppose 5.0 g of ice cools 45 g of water, $c = 4.2$ J/g K, from 20°C to 12°C, and the calorimeter has a mass of 200 g, $c = 0.4$ J/g K. Then

heat gained by ice at 0°C changing to water at 12°C
$$= 5l + 5 \times 4.2 \times (12 - 0)$$
$$= 5l + 252 \text{ J}$$
heat transfer by water $= mc\theta = 45 \times 4.2 \times (20 - 12)$
$$= 1512 \text{ J}$$
heat transfer by calorimeter $= mc\theta = 200 \times 0.4 \times (20 - 12)$
$$= 320 \text{ J}$$

Ignoring heat losses to the surroundings,

$$5l + 252 = 1512 + 320 = 1832$$

So $$l = \frac{1832 - 252}{5}$$
$$= 316 \text{ J/g}$$

3.45 MELTING POINT

If the melting point of a pure solid such as naphthalene is needed, a test-tube, A, can be half-filled with it and the solid then melted

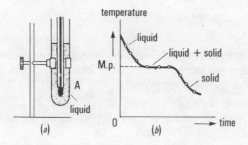

Fig 3.25 How to measure melting-point of a solid

(a)

temperature

liquid
liquid + solid
M.p.
solid
0   (b)   time

completely by placing A in a large beaker of hot water. A thermo-meter can now be placed in the liquid naphthalene as in Fig 3.25(*a*). A is now taken out of the water and allowed to cool in the air while it is stirred. Readings of the temperature are taken at regular intervals of time until all the naphthalene has become a solid again, and a graph of **temperature** against **time** is plotted.

Fig 3.25(*b*) shows a typical result. The flat part of the graph corresponds to the melting point, m.p. The temperature remains constant here because the latent heat of fusion given out by the naphthalene, when changing from liquid to solid, balances the heat lost to the surrounding air.

A very thin wire round a large block of ice, with a heavy weight tied to the wire below the block, gradually sinks into and passes through the ice. **The melting point of ice is lowered by high pressure.** So the ice below the wire melts and the water formed freezes again round the top side of the wire where the pressure is less. Snowballs are made by increase of pressure and then release of pressure. This refreezing is called 'regelation'.

3.46 LATENT HEAT OF VAPORIZATION (EVAPORATION)

If some water in a beaker is heated steadily, its temperature rises until it reaches its boiling point, say 100°C. You can recognize that the water is boiling because bubbles rise to the surface and break open there to form vapour or steam. The temperature of the water now remains constant and the heat supplied goes to change water from the liquid state to the vapour state. This heat is called the **latent heat of vaporization or evaporation** of water.

3.47 MOLECULAR THEORY

Inside a liquid, molecules are moving about in different directions with different energies. When the temperature of the liquid rises, the energy of the molecules increases. At the boiling point, many molecules gain sufficient energy to break the bonds which keep them in the liquid state and they become molecules of vapour.

We shall see later that when a liquid is below its boiling point, some of its molecules have sufficient energy to break through the liquid surface and form a vapour outside. This is known as **evaporation**, not boiling.

3.48 SPECIFIC LATENT HEAT OF VAPORIZATION

The specific latent heat of vaporization, *l*, of a liquid is the heat needed to change unit mass (1 kg or 1 g) from the liquid to the vapour state **at the boiling point**, b.p. (see Fig 3.26). For water, *l* has the large value of about 2 200 000 (2.2×10^6) J/kg or 2200 J/g. So about 2200 J of heat is needed to change 1 g of water at 100°C, its normal boiling point, to vapour at 100°C.

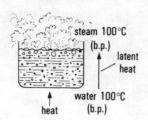

steam 100°C
(b.p.)

latent
heat

water 100°C
(b.p.)

heat

Fig 3.26 Meaning of latent
heat of vaporization

The specific latent heat of fusion of ice, about 330 J/g, is relatively small compared with the specific latent heat of vaporization of water, about 2200 J/g. This shows that much less energy is needed to break the bonds of the solid ice to form water than it is to break the bonds of water to form vapour (steam).

3.49 CONDENSATION: VAPOUR TO LIQUID CHANGE

If, by accident, boiling water spills on the hand, the scald is not as severe as when an equal mass of steam condenses on the hand. We can see this by a calculation.

Suppose 10 g of water at 100°C falls in temperature to 40°C. Then

$$\text{heat given out} = mc\theta = 10 \times 4.2 \times (100 - 40)$$
$$= 2520 \text{ J} \qquad (1)$$

But suppose 10 g of **steam** at 100°C condenses to water at 40°C. Then

latent heat given out in changing to water at 100°C
$= 10 \times 2200 = 22\,000$ J

and   heat given out when water falls from 100°C to 40°C
$= mc\theta = 10 \times 4.2 \times 60 = 2520$ J

So   **total** heat given out by steam $= 22\,000 + 2520 = 24\,520$ J
(2)

If we compare the amount of heat (energy) in (1) and (2), we see why a severe scald is obtained when steam condenses on the skin.

3.50 DIFFERENCE BETWEEN EVAPORATION AND BOILING

Evaporation is the change from liquid to vapour at a temperature below the boiling point at normal atmospheric pressure. Boiling is the change from liquid to vapour at the boiling point. Unlike evaporation, when a liquid boils bubbles can be seen rising from all parts of the liquid to the top, where they burst open. Evaporation, however, takes place only at the liquid surface. The following points must be noted.

1 Evaporation takes place at all temperatures. It increases with surface area, wind (which carries the vapour away), humidity (low air humidity produces more evaporation), and liquid temperature.

2   Boiling takes place only at one temperature, which depends on the atmospheric pressure and not on wind, surface area or humidity.

3.51 COOLING DUE TO EVAPORATION

Evaporation produces cooling. For example, the hand feels cold when a little ether is placed on it and the ether evaporates quickly (the ether is called a 'volatile' liquid because it evaporates quickly at ordinary temperatures).

Fig 3.27(a) shows a demonstration of cooling by evaporation. A beaker with a little ether inside is placed on top of some water on a wooden block. Air is blown through the ether to help it evaporate quickly. After a time, the water is changed to ice and the beaker is stuck to the wood.

Fig 3.27 (i) Liquids cool when they evaporate (ii) Boiling temperature depends on outside pressure

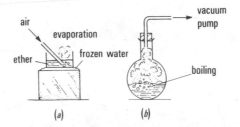

3.52 KINETIC THEORY EXPLANATION

Using the kinetic theory we can explain why cooling takes place. The molecules inside the liquid are moving at different speeds. Some faster molecules near the surface may be moving upwards and have sufficient energy to break through and escape from the liquid. They are then molecules of vapour. The molecules left in the liquid then have *less* kinetic energy on average than before. The average kinetic energy of all its molecules is a measure of the temperature of the liquid. So the liquid is cooled by evaporation. A wind removes molecules in the vapour and other molecules in the liquid can then escape more quickly.

3.53 BOILING-POINT AND PRESSURE

The boiling-point of a liquid depends on the external pressure, that is, the pressure outside the liquid. Fig 3.27(b) shows a simple demonstration. The top of a round-bottom flask is connected to a fast-working pump after a little water has been placed inside the flask. When the pump is switched on, the water begins to boil in a short time, even though no flame is used. The pump removes the air from the flask, so lowering the pressure outside the liquid, and the molecules inside the liquid now have sufficient energy to escape outside from all parts of the liquid.

So water can boil at room temperature if the external pressure is low enough, showing that the **boiling-point of a liquid depends on the external pressure**. At standard pressure, 760 mmHg or 1.013×10^5 Pa, water boils at 100°C. At the top of a mountain, where the pressure is less than at sea-level, water boils at a lower temperature. This is why people living at high altitudes may need a pressure-cooker. This cooker can be set to higher pressures and thus increases the boiling point inside it. It can therefore cook food at higher temperatures and so can speed up the cooking.

3.54 WHY WE PERSPIRE

On occasions, our bodies may reach temperatures well above normal body temperature, for example, in very hot weather or in running races or in hot baths.

We then **perspire**. The moisture evaporates by taking the latent heat of vaporization from the body, so cooling it. Perspiration is therefore the natural way of cooling over-heated bodies.

3.55 THE REFRIGERATOR

The refrigerator also uses the latent heat of vaporization of a liquid when changing to vapour. The cold temperature reached can then preserve food. A volatile liquid, which is a liquid which easily evaporates such as Freeon, is used.

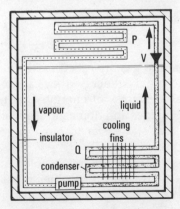

Fig 3.28 Principles of domestic refrigerator

Fig 3.28 shows the principle of the domestic refrigerator. It has a closed pipe system, with low pressure on one side of a valve V and high pressure on the other side.

The liquid expands through V from the high pressure to the low pressure side and then evaporates in coiled pipes P in the freezer compartment. The latent heat of vaporization is taken from P and the compartment, so producing cooling. By means of a pump, the vapour is condensed to liquid in coils Q. This produces heat which is removed by cooling fins. The cycle of changes **vaporization–cooling–condensation** is then repeated as the refrigerant or cooling agent flows round the closed pipe system.

CHECK LIST ▶   Make sure you can answer the following questions.

1   What is the definition of 'specific heat of fusion and of vaporization'?
2   20 g of ice melts to (a) water at 0°C, (b) water at 8°C. How much heat is needed for the ice in both cases. (l = 340 J/g for ice, c = 4200 J/kg K for water.)
3   Describe the experiment to find the melting-point of a pure wax solid.
4   (a)   How does a pressure cooker work?
     (b)   Why do we perspire?
     (c)   Name the chief features of a domestic refrigerator.

3.56 WORLD ENERGY SOURCES

The Sun is the source of most of the world's energy resources. By a process called **photosynthesis**, plants absorb the Sun's ultraviolet rays and make plant material from carbon dioxide and nutrients and water in the soil. Plants are then used for food for humans and animals. Coal stored deep in the Earth comes from plants and trees which have decayed over the past centuries and became buried.

Hydroelectric power is due to the Sun. The Sun makes the seas evaporate and condensation occurs at the top of hills. The rainfall fills the lakes and reservoirs.

3.57 NON-RENEWABLE ENERGY SOURCES

Coal, oil and **natural gas** are called **fossil fuels**. Once they are used up by burning to provide energy, they cannot be used again. So they are non-renewable sources of energy. Oil and natural gas are now widely used for engines and domestic use worldwide. They are easier to extract than coal and easier to move by pipes and are therefore used more than coal.

Nuclear energy is also non-renewable. Atoms which decay and produce nuclear energy may form other atoms which also decay. This process cannot be renewed. Chapter 9 discusses nuclear reactors in detail.

3.58 RENEWABLE ENERGY SOURCES

Some energy sources are renewable, unlike the fossil fuels and nuclear energy.

Wind energy is used for generating energy using windmills or rotating vanes at places where winds are always strong. As explained in Chapter 7, electrical energy is produced by driving turbines.

Wave energy, due to large waves in seas, produces potential and kinetic energy changes as the water rises and falls.

Hydroelectric energy is obtained from the potential energy stored by water at the top of waterfalls or in high lakes or reservoirs. This is used to drive generators which produce electrical energy in places such as Canada, which utilises the Niagara Falls, and in Scotland.

Solar energy is used in hot countries and collected by large concave mirrors. Solar energy is also used for solar heating of homes (p.127), by means of solar panels.

Biomass is the change in energy in complex organic substances when cell growth occurs.

All these energy sources have their origin in the Sun. **Tidal power**, another renewable source, is due to the relative motion of the Moon and the Earth. The gravitational pull between them varies during the monthly cycle of rotation and this makes the tides vary from low to high tide.

Geothermal energy, derived from nuclear energy changes deep in the Earth, is also renewable. In California in the United States, and in the Arctic Circle in the Soviet Union, holes are tunnelled deep into the Earth through hot rocks below. A depth of 12 km or more can be reached. Water or brine is pumped through the holes and steam or hot brine at about 350°C is obtained at the surface. In California, geothermal plants produce about 24 megawatts for use in surrounding areas.

SUMMARY

(a) YOU SHOULD KNOW

1 **Thermometry**
(i)   0°C = 237 K, 100°C = 373 K.
(ii)   the advantages and disadvantages of mercury-in-glass thermometers and the advantage of alcohol-in-glass thermometers.
(iii)   The clinical thermometer has a very thin glass bulb, a narrow restriction and a short temperature scale.
(iv)   How a thermistor is used for measuring temperature.
2 **Expansion** In solids, how a bimetal works in an electric thermostat. In liquids, water has a maximum density of 4°C so seas do not freeze.
   In gases, at constant volume $p_1/T_1 = p_2/T_2$. At constant pressure, $V_1/T_1 = V_2/T_2$. Generally, $p_1V_1/T_1 = p_2V_2/T_2$.
3 **Heat transfer** In conduction and convection, the material itself passes on the heat energy but in conduction the average position remains the same. Radiation passes through a vacuum.
   Insulators are used in double-glazing and in the Thermos flask. Convection helps radiators to warm a room and produces sea and land breezes.

4   **Heat capacity** $Q = mc\theta$, where c is the specific heat capacity and θ is the temperature **change**. Water has a high value for c, so its temperature change is relatively small for a given amount of heat.

5   **Latent heat** $Q = ml$, where l is the specific latent heat and there is only a change from solid to liquid (fusion) or from liquid to vapour (vaporization) but no temperature change. Ice cools water because it takes latent heat from the water to melt. In refrigerators, liquids evaporate and produce cooling.

(b) YOU SHOULD UNDERSTAND

1   How to calculate temperature from a scale alongside an uncalibrated thermometer.
2   The special design of a clinical thermometer and the disadvantage of a mercury-in-glass thermometer.
3   How a bimetal shape changes with temperature change and its use in thermostats.
4   How to apply the gas laws.
5   The difference between conduction, convection and radiation, and the design of a Thermos flask and the use of solar panels.
6   How to use $Q = mc\theta$ where Q may be supplied electrically from a heater and how to use $Q = ml$ in latent heat changes.

(c) APPLICATIONS

You should be able to answer the following questions.

1   Using a metre ruler, the length from the bottom of the bulb of an uncalibrated thermometer to the 0°C mark is 12 mm and to the 100°C mark is 182 mm. What temperature corresponds to a length of 92 mm?
2   Describe how a bimetal is used in an electric thermostat. How is the temperature increased?
3   With the help of a diagram, explain how conduction, convection and radiation losses of heat are prevented in the Thermos flask.
4   0.2 kg of water is heated by a 30 W heater for 7 min. The initial water temperature is 10°C. Find the final water temperature neglecting any heat losses, if the specific heat capacity of water is 4200 J/g K.

QUESTIONS 3D – HEAT CAPACITY. LATENT HEAT. EVAPORATION

(Where necessary, assume specific heat capacity of water is 4200 J/kg K.)

MULTIPLE CHOICE QUESTIONS

1   Equal amounts of heat are transferred to a copper block (specific heat capacity 400 J/kg K) and to an equal mass of water (specific heat capacity about 4000 J/kg K).

The temperature rise of the copper compared with that of the water is about

    A 1/10   B 1/100   C 10/1   D 100/1

2   A block of aluminium in an insulating jacket is heated steadily from room temperature by an electric heater. After a time, the temperature of the block becomes steady. This is because

    A   the insulating jacket is used
    B   the heat per second given to the block reaches a maximum
    C   aluminium does not lose heat because it is a silvery metal
    D   the heat per second given to the block is equal to the heat lost per second

3   The specific latent heat of ice is about 340 000 J/kg. This means that

    A   340 000 J of heat changes 1 kg of ice at 0°C to water at 0°C
    B   1 kg of ice at 0°C needs 340 000 J to change to steam at 100°C
    C   1 kg of water at 0°C changes to ice when given 340 000 J of heat
    D   340 000 J of heat will melt 1 kg of ice at all ice temperatures

4   Which of the following statements is NOT true?

    A   Evaporation produces cooling
    B   Boiling point depends on outside atmospheric pressure
    C   Evaporation and boiling takes place at all temperatures
    D   Evaporation increases with larger surface area

5   On a hot day in summer, the land has a higher temperature than the sea because

    A   the specific heat capacity of the land is less than that of the sea
    B   there is more radiation from the sun to the land
    C   the thermal conductivity of the land is higher than that of the sea
    D   the land is a better absorber of radiation than the sea

SHORT ANSWER QUESTIONS

6   A heater of 25 W is used to heat 0.5 kg of copper from 15°C. The specific heat capacity of copper is 400 J/kg K.

    (a)   How many joules of heat are produced in 4 minutes?
    (b)   Calculate the new temperature of the copper.

   Explain why the measured temperature of the copper in an experiment is less than the calculated value in (b).

7   A candle flame heats 200 g (0.2 kg) of water from 15°C to 55°C and the loss in mass of the candle wax is the 0.5 g.

   Calculate the value these results would give for the **calorific value** of the candle wax, which can be defined as the 'heat per gram' produced when the wax is burned.

8   (a)   The latent heat of steam is 2300 J per gram. What amount of heat is given out when 20 g of steam at 100°C condenses to water at (i) 100°C (ii) 80°C?

    (b)   34 g of steam at 100°C condenses to water at 100°C. This heat is used to melt ice at 0°C to water at 0°C. What mass of ice would be melted? (Assume specific latent heat of ice is 340 J per gram.)

9   Some ice is dropped into 0.34 kg of water at 20°C until the water cools to 0°C.
    (*a*)   What mass of ice was used? (Assume specific latent heat of ice is 340 J/g.)
    (*b*)   Why does the outside of the glass become misty?

10 An electric heater of 40 W is used to warm steadily a 1 kg mass of metal from 15°C. Fig 3I shows the temperature of the metal becomes steady after reaching 35°C.

Fig 3I

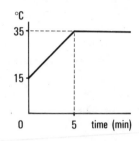

    (*a*)   Using the graph, calculate the specific heat capacity of the metal.
    (*b*)   Explain why the temperature becomes steady.
    (*c*)   Write down two possible errors in this experiment to measure specific heat capacity and describe how you would reduce the two errors.

11 (*a*)   What happens to the boiling point of water when salt is added to it?
    (*b*)   Why is a pressure cooker useful for people living in mountain regions?
    (*c*)   What are **two** differences between boiling and evaporation?

12 In what way is cold produced in a refrigerator?
    The pipes of a domestic refrigerator contain a **volatile liquid** as the fluid or refrigerant and a **high and low pressure side**, and a **pump** and **fins** are used. Explain the purpose of all the items in bold.
    Why is it beneficial to have the freezer compartment at the top of a small domestic refrigerator?

WAVES

CONTENTS

In this chapter we will consider the types and classification of waves. We will look at how waves are produced, how they move and discuss their properties. The main varieties of wave discussed are water, sound and electromagnetic waves.

4.1 PRODUCTION AND MOVEMENT OF WAVES

Waves are produced by **vibrations**. Fig 4.1 shows how a wave may be produced on a very long loose coil – a 'slinky' spring. As the end A of the coil is moved up and down, a wave is set up on the slinky. Note that the motion or vibration of the coils of the slinky is up and down, but the outline or **profile** of the wave travels along to the right.

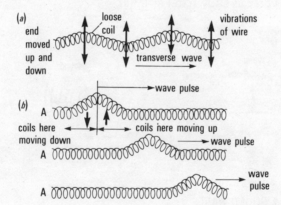

Fig 4.1 Wave on a slinky

If A is moved up and down once only, just a short section of the slinky is disturbed. The wave profile moves along as shown in Fig 4.1(*b*). This short wave is called a **pulse**.

Notice that **energy** from the vibrations of A are transferred along with the wave. All travelling waves carry energy, for example water waves falling on a beach have energy to disturb the pebbles or sand. Sound waves from a loudspeaker have energy to vibrate the sensitive parts of the ear so that we can hear the sound.

4.2 TRANSVERSE AND LONGITUDINAL WAVES

Fig 4.1(*a*) shows a **transverse** wave. In this type of wave the vibrations are at **right angles** to the direction of movement. Fig 4.2 shows another type of wave called a **longitudinal** wave. To produce this type of wave, the end A of the slinky must be moved to and fro in the direction shown by the arrows. Here the vibrations of the coils are in the **same direction** as the wave travels.

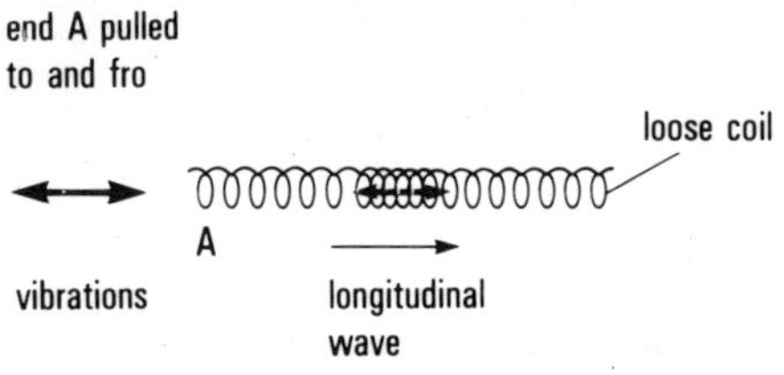

Fig 4.2 Longitudinal wave

end A pulled
to and fro

loose coil

A

vibrations

longitudinal
wave

A longitudinal wave also transfers energy.

4.3 TYPES OF WAVE

1 WATER WAVE

These are set up on the surface of water by some disturbance. Small ripples may be made by dipping something in the water. Waves on the sea are made by the wind in mid-ocean. Water waves are **transverse** as shown in Fig 4.3(*a*).

Fig 4.3 Types of wave

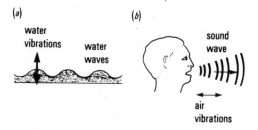

(*a*)

water
vibrations

water
waves

(*b*)

sound
wave

air
vibrations

2 SOUND WAVES

These are due to vibration of molecules in the air or material in which the sound is travelling. They are **longitudinal** waves (Fig 4.3(*b*)). Sound waves are dealt with more fully on p.154.

3 ELECTROMAGNETIC WAVES

There is a wide variety of electromagnetic waves, discussed later, p.157. **Light** waves are one form. **Microwaves** used in telephone communications systems, and in microwave ovens, are another. All electromagnetic waves consist of vibrations of electric and magnetic fields. These fields are directed at right angles to the direction of travel, so the waves are **transverse**. All electromagnetic waves can travel through a vacuum.

| CHECK LIST ▶ | Make sure you can answer the following questions. |

1 What is the difference between a transverse and a longitudinal wave?
2 Give two examples of each of these types of wave.
3 Two examples were given in the text of waves carrying energy. Think of two more different examples.

4.4 WAVE SPEED

The speed of a wave is the distance travelled per second by the wave profile. The waves already mentioned travel at widely different speeds. Water waves are the slowest, followed by sound which travels in air at 340 m/s. Electromagnetic waves all move in a vacuum with the same very high speed of 300 million (3×10^8) metres per second. This is the speed of light, since light is an electromagnetic wave.

4.5 FREQUENCY AND WAVELENGTH

1 FREQUENCY, f

The **frequency** of a wave is the number of complete cycles per second of the vibrating source making the wave. This is equal to the number of complete waves passing a given point per second. The unit of frequency is the hertz, Hz. 1 Hz = 1 vibration per second.

Note that the frequency of a wave is determined by the frequency of the vibrating source. So the frequency of a wave cannot change as it moves along, even if it passes into another material.

Sometimes the **period**, T, of a wave is given. This is the time for one complete vibration of the source, or the time for one complete wave to pass a given point. Frequency and time period are related by $f = 1/T$, or $T = 1/f$.

2 WAVELENGTH, λ

The **wavelength** is the distance between successive crests (tops of waves), or between successive troughs (dips of waves). For all waves their velocity, v, frequency and wavelength are related by the formula:

$$v = f\lambda$$

Proof. In one second f waves are produced each occupying a distance λ. So the total distance moved by the wave profile per second $= v = f\lambda$.

WORKED EXAMPLE

A very low-pitched sound wave has a frequency of about 20 Hz. A very high-pitched sound (too high for some people to hear) has a frequency of 20 000 Hz. Calculate the wavelengths of these sounds. (Speed of sound = 340 m/s.)

Low-pitch
$$v = f\lambda$$
So $\lambda = v/f = 340/20$
$$= 17\,\text{m}$$

High-pitch
$$v = f\lambda$$
So $\lambda = v/f = 340/20\,000$
$$= 0.017\,\text{m}$$
$$= 17\,\text{mm}$$

CHECK LIST ▶

Make sure you can answer the following questions.

1 Explain the meaning of speed, frequency and wavelength as applied to a wave.
2 Calculate the speed of a water wave of wavelength 2 cm having a frequency of 15 Hz.

4.6 WAVE PROPERTIES

Wave properties can be illustrated most easily using water waves or microwaves of 3 cm wavelength.

1 WATER WAVES

Fig 4.4(*a*) shows a ripple tank suitable for producing water waves. A

Fig 4.4 Ripple tank

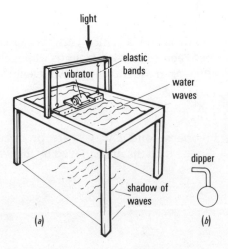

(*a*)

(*b*)

vibrator dipping into water gives **straight** continuous waves. To make **circular** waves the vibrator is lifted clear of the water. A dipper shown in Fig 4.4(*b*) is attached to the vibrator and is adjusted to just touch the surface of the water.

2 MICROWAVE

Fig 4.5 shows a microwave transmitter T, and a probe receiver R. When R receives the microwaves from T, the galvanometer gives a deflection. In most school apparatus the microwaves used have 3 cm wavelength. Remember that microwaves are a form of electromagnetic waves and travel with the speed of light.

Fig 4.5 Microwave transmitter and receiver

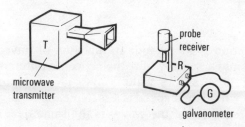

4.7 REFLECTION

Reflection of waves occurs when the waves strike a boundary which they cannot penetrate and which does not absorb their energy.

Fig 4.6(*a*) shows the stages in the reflection of a **straight** water wave at a straight boundary. Note that the wave makes equal angles with the barrier before and after reflection. Fig 4.6(*b*) shows the corresponding experiment with microwaves. You should note that light behaves in a similar way, see p.171.

Fig 4.6 Law of reflection

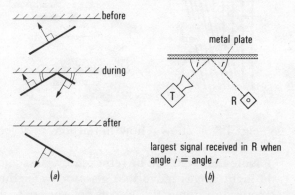

Fig 4.7 shows how a **circular** wave is reflected from straight barrier. Notice that the reflected waves, shown by dotted lines, form parts of circles. The centre of these circles is a point behind the barrier. This point is a distance behind the barrier equal to the distance the wave source is in front of the barrier. Notice again how this

compares with light. For a plane mirror the image is as far behind the mirror as the object is in front, see p.173.

Fig 4.7 Reflection of circular waves

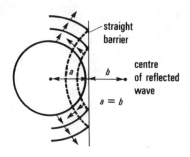

4.8 REFRACTION

Refraction is the change in direction of travel of waves when they move into a region where their speed is different.

Fig 4.8(*a*) shows water waves passing into a region of shallow water where their speed is less. Note that:

1 The frequency of the waves is the same over the deep and shallow water. The reduced speed in the shallow water causes the waves to 'bunch up'. This means the wavelength of the waves **decreases**. You can compare this with traffic on a motorway where cars reach a point where they have to slow down. The cars bunch and the distance between them gets less.

2 The **direction of travel** changes as the waves pass into the shallow region, unless they strike the region 'head on'. This change in direction must occur to enable the wavelength to decrease.

Fig 4.8 Refraction of waves

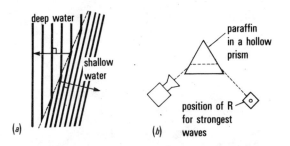

Fig 4.8(*b*) shows how refraction may be demonstrated with microwaves.

Note that light can be refracted by glass and water, see p.178. As the light waves move into glass or water they slow down and so change direction in the way we have just described.

Make sure you can answer the following questions.

1 Describe what happens when a straight water wave reflects from a straight boundary.
2 Draw Fig 4.7 for yourself using ruler and compasses. Make sure you place the compass point at the right place to draw the reflected waves correctly.
3 Draw two diagrams similar to 4.8(a) but make the speed of the waves in the shallow water less in the second diagram than the first. In which case do the waves bend most?

4.9 DIFFRACTION

Diffraction of waves is the change in direction or 'bending' of waves which occurs when they pass through gaps or move round obstacles. Diffraction becomes more noticeable when the wavelength is long compared to the width of the gap or the size of the obstacle.

Fig 4.9 shows the diffraction which occurs when **water waves** of two different wavelengths pass through a gap. The diffraction is greater in the case where the wavelength is longer.

Fig 4.9 Diffraction of water waves

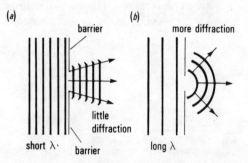

Fig 4.10 shows a similar experiment with **microwaves**. In this case the gap is varied as it is not possible to adjust the wavelength of the waves. There is most diffraction in the second case where the gap is small.

Fig 4.10 Diffraction of microwaves

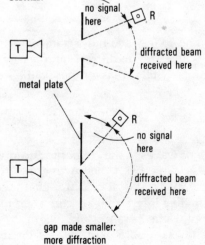

Both of these experiments illustrate the general principle that diffraction is greatest when the wavelength is long compared to the size of the gap or obstacle.

Diffraction can be noticed with **sound waves**. These have wavelength ranging from about 2 cm to 20 m, and can be diffracted round obstacles or through gaps. This is one reason why sound can be heard round corners. (Another reason is reflection of sound from nearby objects.) In open country walking over a hill away from a waterfall there is a gradual change in the sound. The short wavelength or high frequency notes disappear first and the sound gets low and more muffled. This is because these high frequency notes diffract least and do not bend around the brow of the hill.

Light has a much shorter wavelength than sound and so does not diffract significantly around obstacles. This means we cannot see around corners. Diffraction of light can be observed when light passes through very narrow gaps.

TV transmission is by electromagnetic waves of ultra-high frequency (UHF). These have a wavelength of about 25 cm and so will not diffract easily round obstacles. Houses in valleys will therefore find it difficult to receive UHF transmissions, as shown in Fig 4.11(*a*). The problem is solved by using local booster stations as shown in Fig 4.11(*b*).

Fig 4.11 UHF TV reception

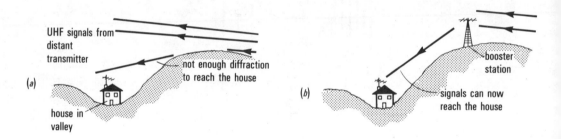

Medium and long wave radio transmissions have a longer wavelength and will therefore diffract more easily. There is less need for booster stations in hilly areas for these radio signals.

4.10 INTERFERENCE

Interference of waves is the effect produced when two waves of the same frequency overlap. **Constructive interference** occurs at points where two wave crests (or two troughs) meet, so reinforcing each other. **Destructive interference** occurs at points where a crest meets a trough. Here the effects cancel and the water is not disturbed.

Fig 4.12 shows the pattern of waves seen in a ripple tank when two dippers A and B vibrate together, each producing circular waves. There are lines, shown bold in the diagram, where there is constructive interference. Large waves are observed on these lines. Between these, on the broken lines, there are lines where the water is undisturbed. These are lines of destructive interference.

P is a point equidistant from A and B. So a crest from A arrives at P at the same time as a crest from B. So there are large waves at P. All other points along this line where $PA - PB = 0$ (i.e. $PA = PB$) will have large waves.

Along the line where $QB - QA = \lambda/2$ there are no waves. Since Q is $\lambda/2$ further from B than from A, crests meet troughs at this point and so there is no resultant disturbance.

R is on the line where $RB - RA = \lambda$. There are large waves along this line because a crest arrives from A at the same time as the crest from B which set out one whole vibration ahead. The difference in distances from the two sources for other lines of 'large waves' and 'no waves' is shown in Fig 4.12.

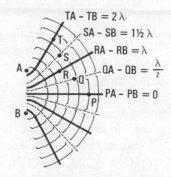

Fig 4.12 Interference of water waves

Interference of microwaves can be shown by the experiment illustrated in Fig 4.13.

Fig 4.13 Interference of microwaves

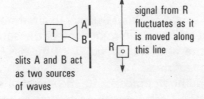

slits A and B act as two sources of waves

signal from R fluctuates as it is moved along this line

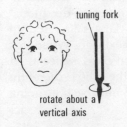

tuning fork

rotate about a vertical axis

Fig 4.14 Interference with sound

Interference occurs with sound and can easily be heard using a tuning fork. The two prongs of the tuning fork act as sources. Hold the sounding tuning fork near the ear and rotate it as shown in Fig 4.14. Alternate loud and quiet sounds will be heard.

Interference of light is more difficult to observe because light has such a short wavelength. Two very narrow slits about 0.5 mm apart can be used to show intereference, when light and dark bands appear on a distant screen. This shows that light is a wave process as interference cannot be explained in any other way. (The true nature of light is, however, more complex.)

1 When does diffraction of waves occur?
2 Diffraction and refraction both involve bending of waves. Explain the difference between them.
3 With two sources of waves, why can there be some regions of no waves, whereas there are waves everywhere with only one source?

SOUND

4.11 PRODUCTION AND PROPAGATION

Sound waves always require a material 'medium' in which to travel. This can be shown by sealing an electric bell into a bell jar, starting the bell ringing, and then pumping out the air. The sound gradually dies down as the air is removed although the bell can still be seen to be operating. Light can travel through the vacuum inside the bell jar, but sound cannot.

Sound is produced by vibrations. A loudspeaker cone vibrates to and fro as shown in Fig 4.15. The cone pushes on the air next to it and makes the air vibrate. A sound wave travels out from the loudspeaker through the air. Sound waves are **longitudinal**, as described on p.145.

To get a loud sound a large volume of air must be set vibrating. Musical instruments and loudspeakers are designed so that loud sound is obtained. For example, in a violin the vibrations from the bowed string are transmitted by the 'bridge' to the body of the violin. The large surface area of the body can then set a considerable amount of air vibrating.

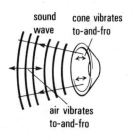

Fig 4.15 Production of a soundwave

4.12 SPEED OF SOUND

The speed of sound is about 340 m/s in air at normal temperatures. It does not depend upon the frequency of the sound wave or upon the pressure of the air. The speed does increase slightly as the temperature of the air rises.

A simple method of measuring the speed of sound is shown in Fig 4.16. The method relies on the fact that sound can be **reflected** to produce echoes. Loud claps are made at regular intervals a distance D in front of a large tall building. The time between claps is altered until the return echo is heard at the same time as the next clap. When this has been done the time, t, for 10 intervals between claps is measured using a stop watch. The time between a clap and the echo is therefore $t/10$. In this time the sound travels to the wall and back again, a distance $2D$. So

$$\text{Speed} = \frac{\text{Distance}}{\text{Time}} = \frac{2D}{t/10} = \frac{20D}{t}$$

Fig 4.16 Speed of sound

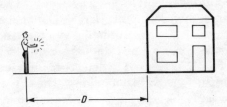

The speed of sound is greater in liquids than in air. It is about 1500 m/s in water. Sound also travels easily through many solids.

In World War II the reflection of sound waves in water was used by the navy for the detection of submarines. This technique is called **sonar**. From the time between the transmitted pulse of sound and the echo, the distance of the submarine could be found, as shown in the following worked example.

WORKED EXAMPLE

In the detection of a submarine the time between the emission of the sonar pulse and its reflection is 1.5 s. The speed of sound in water is 1500 m/s. What is the distance of the submarine?

Distance sound travels = speed×time = 1500×1.5
= 2250 m

The distance of the submarine is half this, since the sound has to travel to and fro. So the distance of the submarine = 1125 m = 1.125 km.

CHECK LIST ▶

Make sure you can answer the following questions.

1 How could you show that sound will not travel through a vacuum?
2 A ship sounds a fog horn near some cliffs. The echo is heard 3 s later. How far away are the cliffs assuming that the speed of sound is 340 m/s?

4.13 CHARACTERISTICS OF NOTES

1 PITCH

This depends on the **frequency** of the sound wave. The higher the frequency the higher the pitch. A very low pitched note has a frequency of about 20 Hz. The highest note that most young people can hear is about 20 000 Hz, although older people will not be able to hear such high pitched sounds. Middle C on the piano has a frequency of 256 Hz. Doubling the frequency raises the pitch by one octave, so a note of 512 Hz is the C one octave above middle C.

A high frequency note will have a short wavelength and vice versa. This means that instruments producing low pitched notes are producing sound waves of a long wavelength. It is easier to do this if the instruments themselves are large. Double-basses, trombones and timpani are all large instruments. Violins and flutes, for example, which make higher pitched sounds are smaller in size.

If a microphone is used to detect a sound, it converts the vibrations of the air into electrical vibrations. These may be displayed on an oscilloscope. Fig 4.17(a) shows the trace obtained when a tuning fork is held in front of the microphone. Fig 4.17(b) shows the effect of using a tuning fork one octave higher.

Fig 4.17 Pitch of a note

tuning fork (a)   tuning fork octave higher (b)

An oscilloscope can be used to measure the frequency of a note as illustrated by the following worked example.

WORKED EXAMPLE

Fig 4.18 Frequency using an oscilloscope

Fig 4.18 shows the trace of a tuning fork obtained with a microphone and oscilloscope. One complete vibration takes up a space of 5 cm on the screen. The time-base on the oscilloscope is set as 0.001 s/cm. What is the frequency of the tuning fork?

The setting of the time base to 0.001 s/cm means that it takes the electron beam in the oscilloscope 0.001 s to cross each cm of the tube face. (See p.263 for oscilloscope details.) The time for one complete vibration of the sound is therefore $5\times0.001 = 0.005 = 5/1000 = 1/200$ s. So the number of vibrations per second = frequency = 200 Hz.

2 LOUDNESS

The loudness of a sound depends on the **amplitude** of the wave. In a vibration the amplitude is the greatest displacement from the centre point of the vibration. A quiet sound has a small amplitude; a loud sound has a large amplitude. Fig 4.19 shows the oscilloscope traces of two sounds of the same frequency. Fig 4.19(a) has a high amplitude and so represents the louder sound.

Fig 4.19 Loudness of a note

loud sound (a)   quiet sound (b)

3 QUALITY OR TIMBRE

The quality of a musical sound depends on the **precise shape of the waveform**. Fig 4.20(*a*) illustrates the waveform of a tuning fork. It is a pure sine curve. A musical instrument producing the same frequency is shown in Fig 4.20(*b*). The difference in shape is responsible for giving the instrument its particular quality.

Fig 4.20 Quality of a note

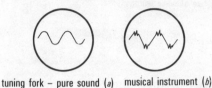

tuning fork – pure sound (*a*)   musical instrument (*b*)

CHECK LIST ▶

Make sure you can answer the following questions.

1 Add arrows to the following diagram to relate words describing musical notes to words describing their waveforms.

LOUDNESS   SHAPE OF WAVEFORM

QUALITY   FREQUENCY

PITCH   AMPLITUDE

ELECTROMAGNETIC WAVES

4.14 NATURE OF ELECTROMAGNETIC WAVES

All electromagnetic waves are due to vibrations of electric and magnetic fields. These fields are at right angles to each other, and at right angles to the direction of travel. Electromagnetic waves are therefore **transverse** (p.145). Unlike sound, electromagnetic waves do not need a material medium in which to travel – they can all travel in a vacuum.

In a vacuum all electromagnetic waves travel at the same speed of about 3×10^8 or 300 000 000 m/s. The difference in properties of the various types of electromagnetic waves is due to their difference in **wavelength**.

4.15 TYPES OF ELECTROMAGNETIC WAVE

The following is a list of the various types of electromagnetic wave: γ-rays, X-rays, ultraviolet rays, visible light, infrared rays, microwaves, radio waves. This list has been arranged in order of increasing wavelength (or decreasing frequency). The whole range of wavelengths is said to form the **electromagnetic spectrum** and is shown diagrammatically in Fig 4.21.

Fig 4.21 Electromagnetic spectrum

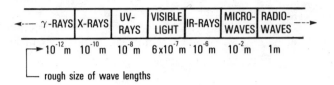

1 γ-RAYS

These have extremely short wavelength, about 10^{-12} m, and are emitted by the radioactive decay of nuclei, discussed on p.295. They are extremely dangerous to health and destroy living cells. They can be detected by a Geiger–Muller tube.

2 X-RAYS

These are produced when electrons with high energies are suddenly brought to rest, for example, by hitting a metal target. X-rays have wavelengths of about 10^{-10} m. They are used in medical diagnosis to detect bone fractures. This is because they are absorbed more by the dense bone structure than by other tissues. More energetic X-rays are used in physics research, for example in the study of crystals. X-rays in large doses can damage cells, and over-exposure must be avoided. They can be detected by a Gieger–Muller tube, or on a photographic film.

3 ULTRAVIOLET (U.V.) RADIATION

This has wavelengths between X-rays and the violet end of the visible spectrum (4×10^{-7} m). U.v. radiation arrives from the sun, and can also be produced by special u.v. lamps. Most of the u.v. radiation from the sun is absorbed by the atmosphere, but that which penetrates causes sun-tan. Over exposure can cause painful sunburn. Too much prolonged exposure to sun can increase the risk of skin cancer. The radiation can be detected as it causes fluorescence of various materials.

4 VISIBLE LIGHT

This ranges in wavelength from about 4×10^{-7} m which is coloured violet, to about 8×10^{-7} m, which is coloured red. So in the case of light the **wavelength** affects the **colour**. The **amplitude** affects the **brightness**. The larger the amplitude of the light, the brighter the light will be. The properties of light are dealt with in the section on Optics.

5 INFRARED (I.R.) RADIATION

This has wavelength of the order of 10^{-6} m. It is emitted by hot bodies and so is called 'heat radiation', discussed on p.125. I.r. radiation gives a sense of warmth when it falls on the skin. I.r. radiation is also used in security systems. Since the rays are invisible it is difficult for a burglar to detect their presence. If the thief walks through a beam an electronic detector can be used to trigger an alarm.

6 MICROWAVES AND RADIO WAVES

These have similar properties but microwaves have shorter wavelengths, about 10^{-2} m ($=1$ cm). Radio waves can have wavelengths up to several kilometres. Both are produced by oscillation electrons in transmitting aerials, and are detected by receiving aerials where they produce an induced voltage. They are used for communication purposes, for example radio, television and telephone signals. Also an intense beam of microwaves produces heat when it is absorbed by moist materials. For this reason microwaves are used for cooking in microwave ovens. They cook quickly because the microwaves can penetrate the food being cooked, and produce heat throughout the whole of the material inside the oven.

CHECK LIST ▶ Make sure you can answer the following questions.

1   Use arrows to join the type of electromagnetic wave in the left hand column, to any effect it can produce in the right hand column.

γ-RAYS	Detected by the eye
	Causes sun tan
X-RAYS	
	Used for communications
U.V. RAYS	Damages living cells
	Used in medicine
VISIBLE LIGHT	
	Produces a sensation of warmth
I.R. RAYS	Used in cooking
	Produces fluorescence
MICROWAVES	
	Used in security systems
RADIO WAVES	Produce a voltage in an aerial

(a) YOU SHOULD KNOW

1   Waves carry energy.
2   Waves are produced by vibrations.
3   The difference between transverse and longitudinal waves.
4   Water waves and electromagnetic waves are transverse, but sound waves are longitudinal.
5   Waves can be reflected.
6   Waves can be refracted.
7   Waves can be diffracted.
8   Two sources of waves of the same frequency can produce interference.
9   Sound requires a material through which to travel.
10 Sound is produced when vibrating sources set the air vibrating.
11 Echoes are produced by reflection of sound.
12 The pitch of a sound is greater if the frequency is greater.
13 How the oscilloscope traces of high and low pitched notes differ.
14 The loudness of a sound is greater if the amplitude is greater.
15 How the oscilloscope traces for quiet and loud notes differ.
16 The quality of a note depends on the shape of its waveform.
17 All electromagnetic waves can travel in a vacuum.
18 All electromagnetic waves travel at the same speed in a vacuum.
19 The properties and uses of the various types of electromagnetic wave.

(b) YOU SHOULD UNDERSTAND

1   The terms speed, frequency and wavelength applied to waves.
2   How refraction is caused by a change of wave speed.
3   How the size of the gap or obstacle alters the amount of bending of waves in diffraction.
4   The reason for the regions of large waves and the regions of no waves in interference.
5   How an oscilloscope can be used to measure frequency.

(c) APPLICATIONS

You should be able to:
1   use the equation speed = frequency × wavelength.
2   describe what happens when straight or circular waves reflect from a straight barrier.
3   describe an experiment to show that sound requires a material to travel.
4   describe an experiment to measure the speed of sound.
5   do simple calculations involving the speed of sound.
6   list the various types of electromagnetic wave in increasing order of wavelength.

MULTIPLE CHOICE QUESTIONS

The following are four types of wave

    A microwaves

    B sound waves

    C water waves

    D waves on a rope

Which one of these

1   is a longitudinal wave?

2   travels at the same speed as light?

The following are four physical phenomena

    A reflection

    B refraction

    C dispersion

    D total internal reflection

Which of the above is most closely associated with

3   echoes?

4   the production of a rainbow?

Fig 4A(a) shows the trace produced when a tuning fork is placed near to a microphone connected to an oscilloscope. Fig 4A(b) shows four alternative traces.

Fig 4A

(a)

    A   B   C   D

(b)

Compared with the tuning fork, which one of these traces shows a note which has

5   double the frequency?

6   a louder sound?

7   Two toy boats X and Y float on the surface of a pond as shown in Fig 4B.

Which of the following correctly describes the motion of X and Y just after the instant shown?

    A X moves to the left and Y to the right.

    B X and Y both move to the left.

Fig 4B

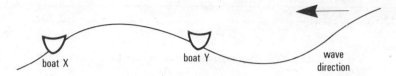

boat X   boat Y   wave
                                                    direction

    C   X moves up and Y moves down,
    D   X moves down and Y moves up.

8   A circular ripple approaches a straight barrier. Which of the diagrams in Fig 4C shows the ripple after it has been partly reflected?

Fig 4C

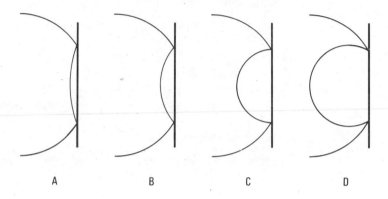

    A   B   C   D

9   A group of water waves move into a region where the water is shallow. Which of the diagrams in Fig 4D best shows what is seen?

    A   B   C   D

Fig 4D

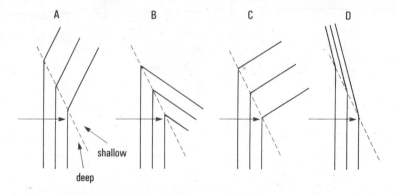

shallow

deep

10   The following are three types of electromagnetic wave.
    1 Radio waves
    2 X-rays
    3 Light waves
  Which one of the following correctly arranges these in increasing order of wavelength?
    A   1 2 3
    B. 2 3 1
    C   3 1 2
    D   2 1 3

Below are four types of electromagnetic wave.

A Light
B Microwaves
C U.V. rays
D I.R. rays

Which of these

11 causes sun tan?

12 is also called heat radiation?

SHORT ANSWER QUESTIONS

13 (*a*) Describe the difference between transverse and longitudinal waves, and give two examples of each.

(*b*) Waves carry energy. Give two practical uses of this property of waves.

(*c*) Calculate the speed of water waves of frequency 5 Hz and wavelength 2 cm.

14 Fig 4E(*a*) shows a straight wave about to hit a straight barrier. Fig 4E(*b*) shows the unreflected part of the wave a little later. Complete Fig 4E(*b*) to include the reflected wave.

Fig 4E

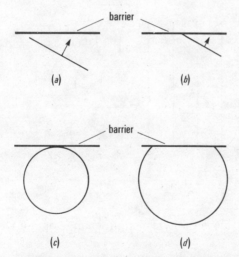

Fig 4E(*c*) shows a circular wave about to hit a straight barrier. Fig 4E(*d*) shows the unreflected wave a little later. Complete Fig 4E(*d*) to include the reflected wave. Mark on the diagram the point where the reflected wave appears to come from.

15 Waves made some distance away in a swimming pool arrive at the edge of the pool where there is a step over which the water is very shallow.

(*a*) Fig 4F shows the waves over the deep water only. Add to the diagram the positions of the three wave crests over the shallow water.

(*b*) Why do the waves change direction over the shallow water?

(*c*) What is the physical name given to this process?

Fig 4F

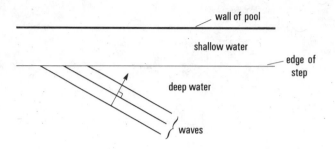

16 Water waves arrive at a narrow gap in a barrier as shown in Fig 4G(*a*).

Fig 4G

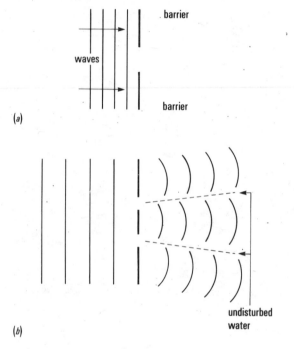

(*a*)

(*b*)

(*a*) Does the wavelength change as the waves pass through the gap?

(*b*) Sketch the appearance of the waves after they have passed through the gap.

(*c*) What is the name given to this process?

(*d*) If there are two gaps in the barrier as in Fig 4G(*b*) the pattern of waves appears as shown. Explain why there are some regions where the water is undisturbed.

17 A ship is using sonar to search the sea bed for a sunken wreck. When an echo is discovered it is found that the shortest time between the sound and the echo is 0.2s. If the search ship moves the time increases.

(*a*) How do you know that the sunken ship is directly underneath the search ship?

(b)   The speed of a sound wave in water is 1400 m/s. What is the depth of the sunken ship?

(c)   The sea bed is very soft and sandy around the wreck. Why would it be much more difficult to detect the wreck if the sea bed had been hard or rocky?

18   Fig 4H shows the electromagnetic spectrum.

Fig 4H

RADIO	MICRO	A	VISIBLE	U.V.	X-RAYS	B

(a)   What is the name of the missing region A?

(b)   What is the name of the missing region B?

(c)   Which radiation has the shortest wavelength?

(d)   Which radiation is used in medical diagnosis?

(e)   Which radiation is used in security systems?

(f)   Why can a microwave oven cook much more quickly than a conventional oven?

OPTICS

CONTENTS

Contents

INTRODUCTION

In this chapter we consider rays of light and how they are used to explain the images obtained in plane mirrors, in curved mirrors and in lenses. Optics has wide practical application. Plane mirrors are used as looking-glasses, curved mirrors are used for make-up and by the dentist as a magnifier, and by astronomers in the design of reflector telescopes. Curved reflectors are also used to collect radio waves from world-wide transmitting stations. Lenses are used in microscopes and telescopes and are needed to correct defects in vision in people.

Glass lenses work because light is **refracted** (changes direction) when it travels from air to glass. We discuss refraction before lenses and show how it is used in the design of prisms for submarine periscopes and in the design of optical fibres which are now used in place of copper cables for telephone systems.

We start with the way light rays travel and how eclipses are explained.

5.1 SHADOWS AND ECLIPSES

Shadows are formed because light usually travels in straight lines. They are produced when the light rays are unable to pass through an object, such as a solid sphere. A **small** light source in front of such an opaque object produces a sharp shadow. None of the light reaches the area on which shadow falls, and this dark region is called the **umbra** or full shadow. A **large** light source produces two regions, an umbra and a **penumbra** (partial shadow), as we can see for the case of the Sun.

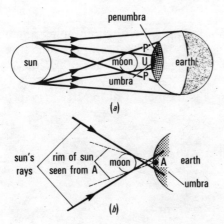

Fig 5.1 Eclipses of Sun

Figure 5.1(*a*) shows the eclipse of the Sun by the Moon, which is an opaque, non-luminous, object (the Moon is seen by light from the Sun which is reflected off the Moon's surface). As the Moon passes between the Sun and the Earth, a 'total eclipse' is seen by people living in the region U of umbra and a 'partial eclipse' is seen by people living in the region P of penumbra. People living outside P and U see no eclipse of the Sun.

When the Moon is in a position slightly further from the Earth, an 'annular' eclipse can be seen from the region A in Fig 5.1(*b*). Only the rim of the Sun is seen since a black shadow covers the centre.

5.2 PINHOLE CAMERA

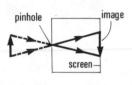

Fig 5.2 Pinhole camera

This first camera had only a pinhole on one side of a closed box and a light-sensitive film or screen on the opposite side, as in Fig 5.2

(*a*)   If the hole is **small**, a sharp inverted image is obtained. Every point on the object produces an image of very small area, and no overlapping of images occurs.

(*b*)   If the hole is **large**, a blurred image is obtained. The blurring is due to the overlapping of images. The same effect is produced by having several small pinholes near each other – each pinhole produces its own image which overlaps with others.

Cameras use a converging lens, whose aperture or opening is relatively large. The image, however, is sharp because the lens is able to bring all the light rays incident on it from one point on the object to a sharp focus or point on the film, so that no overlapping occurs.

Fig 5.3 Calculation on pin-hole camera

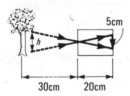

5.3 EXAMPLE ON PIN-HOLE CAMERA

A tree is photographed with a pin-hole camera placed 30 m from the tree (see Fig 5.3). The distance of the hole from the camera screen is 20 cm and an image 5 cm long is produced. What is the height of the tree?

Suppose *h* is the height of the tree. Then, using similar triangles, we have

$$\frac{h}{30\,\text{m}} = \frac{5\,\text{cm}}{20\,\text{cm}} = \frac{1}{4}$$

So
$$h = \frac{1}{4} \times 30\,\text{m}$$
$$= 7.5\,\text{m}$$

Make sure you can answer the following questions.

1 Draw a sketch showing how the Sun can be in total eclipse.
2 In a pin-hole camera use, give two reasons why the image may appear blurred. What decides the size of the image obtained?

REFLECTION AT PLANE MIRRORS

5.4 LAWS OF REFLECTION

By using light rays from a light-ray box, it can be shown that the rays are reflected from a plane mirror according to the following **laws of reflection:**

1 The angle of incidence (i) = the angle of reflection, (r).
2 The incident and reflected rays and the normal all lie in one plane.

The 'normal', or reference line for angles, is the line perpendicular (normal) to the reflecting surface at the point where the incident ray strikes it. The angles of incidence and reflection are always measured from the normal, as shown in Fig 5.4(a).

Fig 5.4 (a) Reflection (b) deviation of light

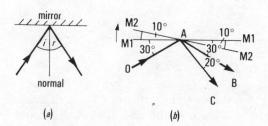

(a)   (b)

5.5 HOW A ROTATING MIRROR DEVIATES (TURNS) LIGHT

Fig 5.4(b) shows a ray OA incident on a plane mirror M1 and reflected along AB. If OA makes an angle of 30° with M1, then AB makes the same angle of 30° with the mirror as shown.

Now suppose the mirror is turned through 10° to a position M2. If the direction of OA is unchanged, it will now be reflected along AC. Because OA makes an angle of (30° + 10°) or 40° with M2, AC makes an angle of 40° with M2. So AC makes an angle of (40° + 10°) or 50° with the mirror M1. Now the reflected ray AB makes an angle of 30° with M1.

So   deviation = angle CAB = 50° − 30° = 20°

The reflected ray is therefore deviated (turned through) **twice** the angle 10° which the mirror turned through. Although we took a special case, this result is always true. So if a mirror is turned through 25° and the direction of the ray on it is unchanged, the reflected ray will be deviated through 2 × 25° or 50°.

5.6 IMAGE IN A PLANE MIRROR

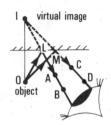

Fig 5.5 Image in plane mirror

Figure 5.5 shows an object O, such as a pin, in front of a plane mirror. The shading shows the silvering behind the mirror. Light rays from O emerge in all directions. For convenience we show only two of the rays, OL and OM, which strike the mirror. The ray is reflected at L along LB so that the angle of reflection equals the angle of incidence. At M, where the angle of incidence is larger than at L, the ray is reflected along MD. Now the eye always sees rays in the direction they travel. Since the rays LB and MD meet at I **behind** the mirror, the object O is seen at I, that is, I is the **image** of O in the plane mirror. Note that OI is at right angles to the mirror.

In practice, the position of I can be located by lining up two pins with I at A and B, and then lining up two more pins with I at C and D. I is then the point of intersection of the two lines DC and BA. Experiment (and theory) shows that IM = OM, that is, **the image is as far behind the mirror as the object is in front**.

5.7 EXAMPLE ON IMAGE POSITION

Fig 5.6 Example on image position

Fig 5.6 shows a plane mirror XY with a small object O in front of it.
(*a*)   Which of the positions A, B, C and D represents the image position?
(*b*)   If the object O is moved to P, where is the new image position?

(*a*)   The image is at D, the same distance behind the mirror.
(*b*)   The image is at A. If YX is extended upwards, A will be the same distance from the mirror as P but behind it.

5.8 LIGHT BEAMS; REAL AND VIRTUAL IMAGES

A beam of light which spreads out from a light source is called a **diverging beam**. In Fig 5.5, the beam between OL and OM is a beam diverging from O. The reflected beam between LB and MD is also a diverging beam and appears to come from a point I behind the mirror. I is called a **virtual image** – a screen placed immediately in front of the mirror will not have an image of O on it on account of the diverging beam.

In Fig 5.5 the light rays are drawn with arrows on them to show their direction. Lines which lead to the image, I, behind the mirror are drawn as broken lines – they are not rays. Virtual images are represented by broken lines, real images by full lines.

A **real image** is formed by a beam converging to a point **in front of** a mirror. An image can then be produced on a screen in front of the mirror. A plane mirror produces a virtual image of an object placed in front of it, as we have seen, but a curved, concave mirror can produce a real image (p.176). Remember the rule, which holds for plane mirrors, curved mirrors, and lenses:

A **real** image is produced by a **converging** light beam.
A **virtual** image is produced by a **diverging** light beam.

5.9 IMAGE OF A LARGE OBJECT

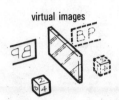
virtual images

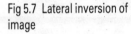

Fig 5.7 Lateral inversion of image

Figure 5.7 shows the images of large objects, represented by the letters P and B, in a plane mirror. The letters have become 'laterally inverted', that is, the right side of the object has become the left side of the image. For this reason the writing on blotting paper can be read when held up to a mirror and a right-handed person holding a tennis racket appears to be left-handed when viewed in a mirror. Summarizing, the image of an object in a plane mirror is

1 as far behind the mirror as the object is in front;
2 laterally inverted;
3 the same size as the object;
4 virtual.

5.10 USES OF PLANE MIRRORS. PARALLAX

Plane mirrors are used as looking-glasses, in simple periscopes, and in other optical instruments. They are also used in some electrical meters. This is because an error will be made when reading the deflection of the pointer along the scale if the observer is not *directly* over the pointer. We say the error is due to '**parallax**' between the pointer and the scale. If a plane mirror is placed below the pointer, however, and the observer takes the reading when the pointer covers its image in the mirror, the observer will then be directly over the pointer and there is no possibility of a mistake.

CHECK LIST ▶
Make sure you can answer the following questions.

1 What is the law of reflection at a plane mirror?
2 Where is the image of an object in a plane mirror? Is the image **exactly** the same as the object? Is the image real or virtual?

CURVED MIRRORS

5.11 CONCAVE AND CONVEX MIRRORS

A shaving mirror and the mirror a dentist uses for examining teeth are **concave** mirrors. They both curve inwards as in Fig 5.8(*a*). A driving mirror is a **convex** mirror; it curves outwards as in Fig 5.8(*b*).

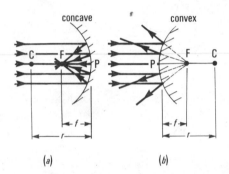

Fig 5.8 Concave and convex mirrors

(*a*)   (*b*)

These mirrors are spherical, so they are part of a sphere of a particular radius. The centre of the sphere, C, is called the **centre of curvature** of the mirror and the radius of the sphere is called the **radius of curvature**, r, of the mirror. The middle of the mirror is its pole, P. Figure 5.8 shows that C is real for a concave mirror but virtual (behind the mirror) for a convex mirror.

The line PC is called the principal (chief) axis of the mirror. As shown in Fig 5.8(*a*), a narrow beam of rays parallel to the principal axis is reflected to a focus F on the principal axis when incident on a **concave** mirror. But when this parallel beam is incident on a **convex** mirror, the reflected beam diverges and appears to come from a focus F **behind** the mirror.

You should remember that the focus F (and centre C) are real for a concave mirror but virtual for a convex mirror. Also, in both concave and convex mirrors F is **midway** between C and P. The distance FP is known as the **focal length**, f, of the mirror. So $r = 2f$ or $f = r/2$

A mirror of 30 cm radius of curvature has a focal length of 30/2 or 15 cm.

5.12 PARABOLIC MIRRORS AND AERIALS

As we stated, a **narrow** beam of light is reflected to a point of focus F when incident on the central part of a concave mirror. A **wide** parallel beam, however, is **not** reflected to a point. The paths of light rays are reversible, so that a light ray will retrace its path exactly if its direction is reversed. Hence light from a small bright lamp at the focus of a large concave spherical mirror will spread outwards from the *edges* of the mirror. The intensity of the light beam will diminish with distance from the mirror.

Fig 5.9 Parabolic mirror and aerial dish

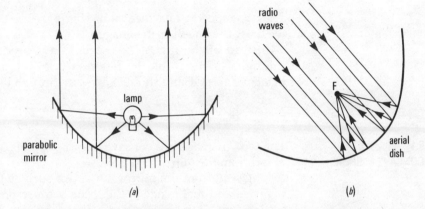

A curved spherical mirror is therefore unsuitable for use as a searchlight or as a motor headlamp reflector. A mirror of **parabolic** shape, shown in Fig 5.9, is used for these purposes. The parabolic mirror reflects all the light from a lamp at F into a parallel beam, which has a constant intensity over long distances.

Radio dish aerials, high above sea level, are positioned at suitable places round the coast to collect messages from transmitters in foreign countries. Fig 5.9(*b*). The large dish aerials are shaped like a parabola to collect radio waves from all parts and to reflect them to a sensitive radio detector at the focus F. Radio waves are electromagnetic waves like light waves but with a much longer wavelength (p.146). Large reflector telescopes all over the world also use a parabolic mirror to collect the light from distant stars or galaxies and reflect them to a focus, where they may be magnified by an eyepiece.

5.13 DRAWING IMAGES IN MIRRORS

Always represent the mirror by a straight line as in Fig 5.10(*a*). Two rays are needed from the top point of the object. One ray AX is drawn parallel to the principal axis – this is reflected from X through F. The second ray, AC, can be drawn to pass through C, the centre of curvature – this is reflected back along its own path, BC, because any ray from the centre of curvature strikes a spherical mirror at right angles or along the normal.

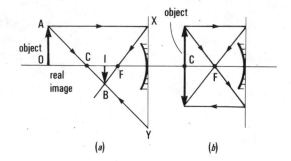

Fig 5.10 Real images in concave mirrors

(a)   (b)

The two reflected rays meet at B. This is the top point of the image. So we draw the line BI as the image.

Instead of the ray AC, we could have used the ray AF passing through F. This would be reflected from the mirror parallel to the principal axis OF and should also pass through B.

5.14 IMAGES IN CONCAVE MIRRORS

The type of image in a concave mirror depends on the distance of the object from the mirror.

1   A long way from the mirror, an object such as the Sun has a **small, inverted** and **real** image at the focus because practically parallel rays are incident on the mirror from a distant object.

2   As the object approaches the mirror, the image grows in size. Beyond C, the image is smaller than the object, inverted and real, as in Fig 5.10(*a*).

3   At C, the image is the **same size** as the object and is formed at C (see Fig 5.10(*b*)). This is because all the rays from C are reflected back along their original path.

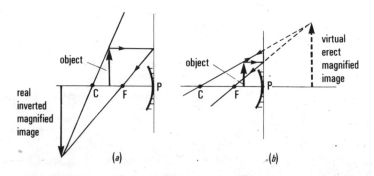

Fig 5.11 Magnified images. (*a*) Real (*b*) virtual

(a)   (b)

4   Between C and F, a magnified, inverted and real image is produced as in Fig 5.11(*a*)

5   Between F and P, that is, when the object distance is less than the focal length, **a magnified, upright and virtual** image is formed behind the mirror (see Fig 5.11(*b*)). This is the ray diagram which shows how the concave mirror is used as a magnifying mirror for shaving, or by a

dentist for examining teeth. The mirror must be placed close to the object, so that its distance away is *less* than the mirror's focal length.

5.15 MEASURING *r* OR *f* FOR A CONCAVE MIRROR

Figure 5.12 shows how the radius of curvature *r* or focal length *f* of a concave mirror M can be measured. An illuminated object O – such as crosswires with a lamp behind them – is moved until the sharpest image, I, in the mirror M is received beside O.

Fig 5.12 Measuring *r* for concave mirror

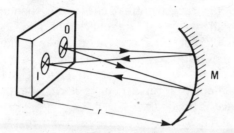

Since O and I are formed at the same place, the distance of O from M must be *r*, the radius of curvature (see Fig 5.10(*b*)). We have thus found *r*. The focal length $f = r/2$

CHECK LIST ▶

Make sure you can answer the following questions.

1   What is the advantage of a parabola shape for a mirror in place of a spherical shape? Name two uses of the parabolic reflector.
2   How does a concave mirror reflect rays
    (*a*)   parallel to the principal axis,
    (*b*)   passing through the centre of curvature,
    (*c*)   passing through the focus?
3   In a concave mirror, where is the object position when the image is the same size as the object? Where is the object position if an upright magnified image is seen? Draw ray diagrams in your answers.

5.16 EXAMPLES ON CONCAVE MIRROR

1

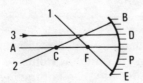

Fig 5.13 Reflected rays

Fig 5.13 shows three rays incident on a concave mirror at A, B and D respectively. In what directions are the three rays reflected?

Ray 1 – reflected at E **parallel** to the principal axis AP
Ray 2 – reflected at B along BC **back to C**, the centre of curvature
Ray 3 – reflected at D along DF to the **focus** F

2   In Fig 5.13, an object is placed
(a)   first at C and
(b)   then at F.
Where are the images in each case? Give brief reasons for your answer.
(a)   Object at C (centre of curvature), then image at C.
Reason – all rays from C are reflected back to C.
(b)   Object at F (principal focus), then image a very long way from mirror (at infinity).
Reason – all rays from F are reflected parallel to the principal axis AP.

3   A concave mirror forms an image 40 cm from the mirror at exactly the same place as the object.
(a)   What is the focal length of the mirror?
(b)   What do you know about the image compared to the object?
(c)   The object is now moved so that it is 30 cm from the mirror M. Draw a ray diagram showing how the image is formed and find its position from the mirror by a scale drawing.
(a)   Since the image is formed at the same place as the object, the object and image are both a distance r from the mirror, where r is the radius of curvature. So $r = 40$ cm. Then $f = r/2 = 20$ cm.
(b)   The image is inverted and the same size as the object.
(c)

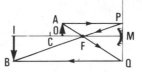

Fig 5.14 Image by drawing

Fig 5.14 shows the drawing. OA is the object, CF = FM = 20 cm to scale, and OM = 30 cm. Draw a ray AP – this is reflected through F. Draw another ray AF passing through F – it is reflected along QB. The image is therefore BI. Scale drawing shows that IM = 60 cm.

REFRACTION AT PLANE SURFACES

5.17 RAYS IN REFRACTION

Light rays generally change their direction when they pass into a medium of optical density different from the one in which they are travelling. This is because the speed of the light changes (see p.157). The phenomenon is called **refraction**.

Figure 5.15(a) shows that when a ray of light AP passes into an optically **denser** medium, it is refracted **towards** the normal POQ and travels in the direction OB. When it travels into an optically **less**

Fig 5.15 Refraction in (a) optically denser and (b) optically less dense medium

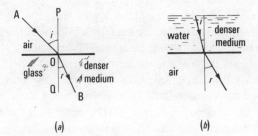

dense medium, it is refracted **away from** the normal as in Fig 5.15(b). So:

1 air to glass (or water) – refraction towards the normal;
2 glass (or water) to air – refraction away from the normal.

5.18 REFRACTION THROUGH RECTANGULAR BLOCK

Fig 5.16 shows a rectangular block of glass, so that the opposite sides HK and LM are parallel.

The ray OA incident normally (90°) on the side HK passes straight through the glass along AB and out into the air in the same direction along BC.

Fig 5.16 Refraction through rectangular block

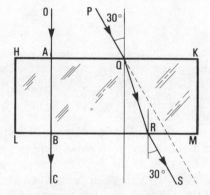

The ray PQ has an angle of incidence of 30° on the glass at Q, and is refracted along QR in the glass. Since LM is parallel to HK, QR makes the same angle with the normal at Q and at R. So QR comes out into the air along RS, where RS is **parallel** to PQ. You should remember that a **parallel-sided** block does not change the direction of a ray incident on it but only displaces or shifts it sideways as in Fig 5.16.

5.19 APPARENT DEPTH AND IMAGES DUE TO REFRACTION

Looking down, a pool of water appears to be shallower than is actually the case. You notice this in a swimming-bath – the bottom of the bath looks nearer the surface than it actually is.

Figure 5.17(*a*) shows how this phenomenon is explained by refraction of light. Suppose O is an object at the bottom of water. A ray OA is refracted away from the normal at A as it passes into the air and travels in the direction AB. The normal ray, OC, however, does not change direction and travels in the same direction CD.

Fig 5.17 Images in water-apparent depth

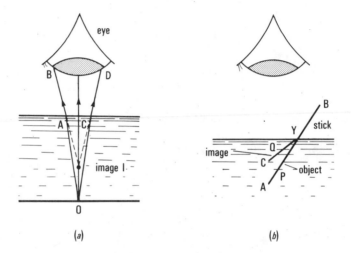

(a)   (b)

A person looking down at O sees the rays AB and CD as if they come from a point I where the rays intersect. So I is the image of O. I is **nearer** the surface than O and so, looking straight down at O, OC is the 'true' depth of the water and IC is what the depth appears to be, or the 'apparent' depth.

Figure 5.17(*b*) shows the appearance of a stick AB which is partly immersed in a pool of water. It looks 'bent' when it enters the water at Y. This effect is due to the apparent depth phenomenon just described. A point A on the stick appears at C, and a point P on the stick appears at Q. So the whole of the immersed part AY appears to be bent **upwards** along YC.

5.20 REFRACTION BY A PRISM

Figure 5.18 shows a solid triangular glass **prism** XYZ with equal angles of 60° and a pin at O. A ray OA is refracted towards the normal at A when it enters the glass and travels along AB. At B the ray is refracted away from the normal as it enters the air and travels along BC.

So the prism **deviates** (turns) the ray OA along the direction BC towards its base YZ.

In the same way, a ray OD is deviated along EF by the prism. The

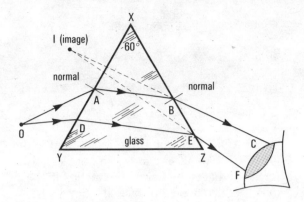

Fig 5.18 Refraction by prism

two refracted rays BC and EF enter the eye of an observer, who therefore sees the pin O at I, where the rays intersect.

5.21 LAWS OF REFRACTION

The angle of incidence, i, and angle of refraction, r, are the angles made with the **normal** (see Fig 5.15(a)). There are two laws of refraction:

1 The incident ray, refracted ray and the normal all lie in the same plane.
2 ✗ The ratio sin i/sin r is a constant for the two media (Snell's law).

5.22 REFRACTIVE INDEX The ratio sin i/sin r is called the **refractive index**, n, between two media, where i is the angle of incidence in one medium and r is the angle of refraction in the second medium.

From air to glass n may be about 1.5 or 3/2 (Fig 5.15(a)). Since light rays are reversible, the value of r, from **glass to air** is then 1/1.5 or 2/3, that is, we invert the value for air to glass.

5.23 EXAMPLES ON REFRACTION

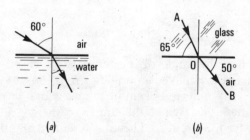

Fig 5.19 Calculations on refraction

1 The angle of incidence i on an air–water boundary is 60° (see Fig 5.19(a)). Calculate the angle of refraction r, if $n = 4/3$ for air–water.

We have $\quad \dfrac{\sin 60°(i)}{\sin r} = n = \dfrac{4}{3}$

So $\qquad 4 \sin r = 3 \sin 60°$

Thus $\qquad \sin r = \dfrac{3 \sin 60°}{4} = 0.6498$

So $\qquad r = 41°$ (approx)

2   A ray AO is incident at O in glass and is then refracted in air along OB. Fig 5.19(b). Using the angles of 65° and 50° shown in the diagram,
(a)   what is the angle of refraction in the air?
(b)   calculate the refractive index
        (i) from glass to air, and
        (ii) from air to glass.

(a)   The angle of refraction, r = the angle BO makes with the **normal** at O. So $r = 90° - 50° = 40°$.
(b)   (i) from **glass to air**, angle of incidence $i = 90° - 65° = 25°$

So   refractive index $= \dfrac{\sin 25°}{\sin 40°} = 0.66$

(ii) For **air to glass**, refractive index $= \dfrac{1}{0.66} = 1.5$

5.24 TOTAL INTERNAL REFLECTION AND THE CRITICAL ANGLE

When light travels from **glass to air** at a small angle of incidence i, a **weak** reflected beam is obtained in the glass and a strong refracted beam is obtained in the air, as in Fig 5.20(a). Note that the light in air is refracted **away** from the normal, so r is bigger than i.

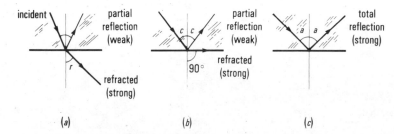

Fig 5.20 Critical angle and total internal reflection

When the angle of incidence is increased to some value C, the refracted ray makes an angle of refraction of 90° in air (Fig 5.20(b)). The weak reflected beam in the glass due to partial reflection is still obtained. But when the angle of incidence is only very slightly increased, **no** refracted beam is obtained and the reflected beam now appears **strong** (Fig 5.20(c)). Now we have 'total reflection'; before the angle of incidence reached the value C, 'partial reflection' was obtained.

C is called the **critical angle** for the glass–air boundary. It may be defined as **the angle of incidence in the dense medium when the angle of refraction in the less dense medium is 90°.**

5.25 CALCULATION OF C From air to crown glass, n is about 3/2. So from crown glass to air, n is 2/3. From $\sin i/\sin r = n$, using $i = C$ and $r = 90°$, we have

$$\frac{\sin C}{\sin 90°} = \frac{2}{3}$$

$$\sin C = \frac{2}{3} \times \sin 90° = \frac{2}{3} \times 1$$

$$= 0.6667$$

So $C = 42°$ (approx)

Generally, we can always calculate C from the formula

$$\sin C = \frac{1}{n}$$

where n is the refractive index of the material with incidence in air. So with glass of refractive index 1.5, $\sin C = 1/1.5 = 0.667$. Then $C = 42°$ as we have just found. With water of refractive index 4/3, $\sin C = 3/4$ from $\sin C = 1/n$, so $\sin C = 0.75$. Then $C = 49°$ approximately for water.

5.26 TOTAL REFLECTION PRISMS Mirrors silvered on the back produce several images of an object O. As shown in Fig 5.21(a), this is due to reflection–refraction at the silvering and the glass–air boundary. Hence the image of O cannot be focused with high accuracy if a mirror is used. The images in the mirror are often called **multiple images**.

Fig 5.21 Total reflecting prisms

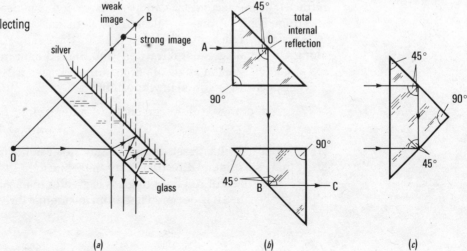

(a)   (b)   (c)

Glass prisms are used to reflect light in submarine periscopes and prism binoculars, where high precision is needed. The prisms, made of crown glass, have angles of 90°, 45° and 45° – they are right-angle isosceles prisms. The glass–air critical angle is about 42° for this glass, as shown before. Figure 5.21(*b*) shows a ray AO entering the prism normal to one side and incident **in the glass** at O. The angle of incidence in the glass is 45°. But the critical angle is 42° with air. So the light at O is **totally** reflected.

The reflected light at O is at 90° (45° + 45°) to AO. At B, in the lower prism, the angle of incidence in the glass is again 45°. So total reflection occurs. The light is reflected along BC parallel to AO. The two prisms together form a periscope, each prism deviating (turning) the incident light through 90°. Figure 7.18(*c*) shows how a 90°, 45°, 45° prism can deviate light through 180°, so reversing the light path. This is used in prism binoculars.

5.27 DISPERSION OF COLOURS IN WHITE LIGHT

A glass prism of angle 60° separates colours from a mixture. The name 'dispersion' is given to this separation. The colours travel in different directions in the glass because they have different speeds in glass. (In a vacuum, or air, all the colours have the same speed).

Fig 5.22 Dispersion by prism

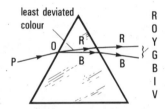

Figure 5.22 shows how a ray, PO, of **white light** is dispersed (separated into colours) at the first face of the prism. The colours are refracted at the second face and the dispersion is increased. You can see from Fig 5.22 that, in glass, blue light has a greater refractive index n than red light. The blue light in the beam PO is refracted along OB (small angle of refraction) and the red light in PO is refracted along OR (greater angle of refraction), and $n = \sin i/\sin r$.

The spectrum (colours) in white light are:

red, orange, yellow, green, blue, indigo, violet (ROYGBIV)

Remember that
(*a*)   red light has least deviation and violet light has most deviation from the original direction PO of the white light,
(*b*)   the speed of red light in glass is greater than that of violet or blue light because it is deviated less from its original direction PO.

CHECK LIST ▶

Make sure you can answer the following questions.

1 Draw ray diagrams showing how a ray of light is refracted from water to air and from air to water. Using a ray diagram, explain why a pool of water appears to be less deep to an observer.
2 What is meant by 'refractive index' of glass?
3 Draw a labelled diagram showing in it
   (a)   critical angle,
   (b)   total internal reflection at an air–glass boundary.
4 With the help of a diagram, explain how a 90° glass prism can act as a total reflector of light incident on it.
5 Draw a sketch showing how white light is dispersed by a glass prism. Label the colours obtained.

5.28 OPTICAL FIBRES. LIGHT PIPE

Optical fibres are long fine strands of glass which may be about one tenth of a millimetre in diameter. They have medical use as a 'light pipe' and they are now widely used in telecommunications for transmitting electrical signals. Optical fibre cables have now replaced the copper cables in the telephone system and carry hundreds of optical fibres inside them.

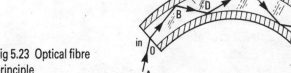

Fig 5.23 Optical fibre principle

Fig 5.23 shows the basic principle of transmitting light by an optical fibre. The central part or **core** has a greater refractive index than the outer coating or **cladding**. When an outside ray AO is refracted at O in a suitable direction OB, the angle of incidence on the core-cladding boundary at B is **greater than the critical angle** between the two media. All the light is therefore reflected at B. The reflected ray BD meets the boundary at D at an angle of incidence also greater than the critical angle. And so on along the fibre.

The light therefore travels from end to the other at X with practically no loss of intensity. So the fibre acts like a 'light pipe'. A bent or twisted fibre still 'pipes' the light from one end to the other. An optical fibre cable is therefore used to examine the throat or larynx areas of hospital patients with difficulties here. One end is placed in the throat and the areas are examined by looking at the other end with a magnifier.

5.29 OPTICAL FIBRES IN TELECOMMUNICATIONS

British Telecom, and telecommunication firms in other countries, have replaced copper cables for transmitting electrical signals. Many more messages can be sent using an optical fibre cable than a copper cable and the messages are clearer at the other end and can be transmitted more quickly.

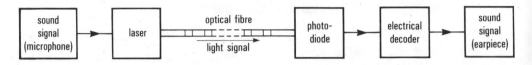

Fig 5.24 Transmission and reception of sound signals (diagrammatic)

Fig 5.24 shows the principle in diagrammatic form. The sound signal is changed to a light signal by a special form of laser and this is sent along the optical fibre in binary digits or bits. At the other end the light signals are incident on a photodiode which changes them to electrical signals and these are decoded and passed to a telephone earpiece. In this way messages are sent along the optical fibres from one end to the other. Very many signals can be sent along a single cable at one time by a technique called 'multiplexing'.

5.30 EXAMPLES ON CRITICAL ANGLE AND TOTAL INTERNAL REFLECTION

1   Fig 5.25 shows several rays in air entering the eye of a fish F in water.
(a)   Can the fish see an object at
        (i) P and
        (ii) Q?
(b)   What is the critical angle for air–water?
(c)   Find the refractive index of water.

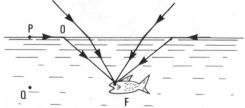

Fig 5.25 Example on refraction

(a)   (i) Yes; the ray from P is refracted in water to the eye.
        (ii) Yes; rays from Q are reflected at the water boundary to the eye.
(b)   By drawing the normal at O, the critical angle is 49°.
(c)   Refractive index n is given by $\sin C = 1/n$. So $n = 1/\sin C = 1/\sin 49° = 1.33$

2   Fig 5.26 shows a plastic cube. An incident ray AO is refracted along OB in the cube and comes out along BD in the air. Angle NOB is 40°.
(a)   What is the critical angle for the glass?
(b)   Is the light reflected back into the glass at B as bright as the incident light OB?
(c)   Using $\sin i/\sin r = n$, calculate angle i.

Fig 5.26 Example on critical angle

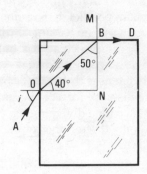

(a)   Critical angle C = angle OBN = 90° − 40° = 50°
(b)   No. Most of the light incident in the glass at B is refracted into the air along BD.
(c)   Refractive index of glass, n = 1/sin C = 1/sin 50° = 1.31

So $\dfrac{\sin i}{\sin r} = \dfrac{\sin i}{\sin 40°} = 1.31$

So $\sin i = 1.31 \times \sin 40° = 0.842$
giving $i = 57°$

LENSES

Lenses have been used for more than three hundred years. Today, they are used for spectacles, as magnifying glasses, in the lens camera and slide projector, and in telescopes.

In this section we shall show that the kind of image obtained with a lens depends on the type of lens used and the distance of the object from the lens.

5.31 CONVERGING AND DIVERGING LENSES. FOCUS AND FOCAL LENGTH

There are two types of lens. A **converging lens** is thicker in the middle than at the edges as shown in Fig 5.27(a). Its 'principal axis' is the line joining the middle of its opposite faces. When a narrow beam parallel to the principal axis is incident on the lens, it converges the beam to a point F on its axis called the **principal focus**. F is real.

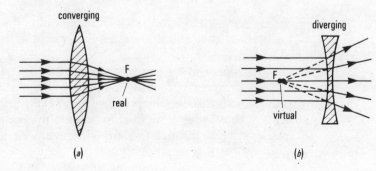

Fig 5.27 Converging and diverging lenses.

(a)   (b)

A **diverging lens** is thinner in the middle than the edges, as shown in Fig 5.27(*b*). When a beam parallel to the principal axis is incident on the lens, the beam diverges after passing through it and appears to come from a point F on the principal axis **behind** the lens. So the principal focus F of a diverging lens is **virtual**.

The **focal length**, *f*, of a lens is the distance from the principal focus to the lens. So *f* is a +ve distance for a converging lens (real is positive rule) and *f* is a −ve distance for a diverging lens.

In this book we need only discuss the converging (or convex) lens.

5.32 MEASURING FOCAL LENGTH OF CONVERGING LENS

1 PLANE MIRROR

Place a plane mirror M behind the lens as in Fig 5.28. Move an illuminated object O (e.g. crosswires) until a *clear* image I is formed beside O. Then OL = *f*, which can be measured.

Explanation When I is formed beside O, the rays from O have struck the mirror M normally and are reflected back along the same path (see Fig 5.28). So the light incident on the lens from M is a **parallel** beam. Hence I is at the focus of the lens.

Fig 5.28 Measuring focal length

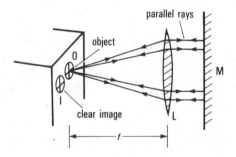

2 QUICK BUT NOT ACCURATE

At the back of the room opposite a window, move the lens until a **sharp** image of the window frame is formed on a wall or piece of paper. The distance from the paper to the lens is roughly the focal length because the window, a distant object, sends practically parallel rays to the lens.

5.33 DRAWING IMAGES IN LENSES

With thin lenses,

(*a*)   represent the lens by a straight line, as in Fig 5.29;

(*b*)   draw a ray from the top point of the object parallel to the axis – this passes through the principal focus F (Fig 5.29(*b*) or (*c*));

(*c*)   draw a ray from the top point to the middle of the lens – this passes straight through the lens without any change in direction. The two rays meet at the top point of the image, which is then drawn by a straight line to meet the axis.

Figure 5.29(*a*) shows the image when the object is a very long way from the lens. The top point then sends parallel rays, inclined to the axis, which meet at F. Fig 5.29(*b*) shows the real, inverted, small image produced as the object approaches the lens. When the object is at a distance 2*f* from the lens, the image as the **same size** as the object, a point which should be remembered (see Fig 5.29(*c*)).

When the object is nearer than 2*f*, the lens produces a **magnified** inverted image as in Fig 5.30 (*a*).

Fig 5.29 Images in converging lens

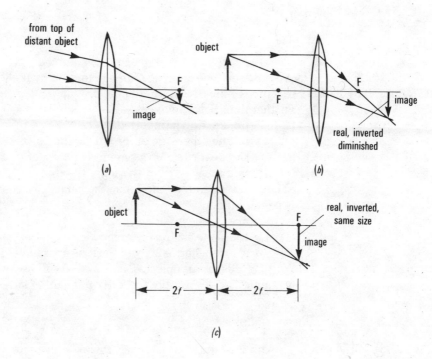

(*a*)

(*b*)

(*c*)

5.34 THE MAGNIFYING GLASS (A SIMPLE MICROSCOPE)

When the object is **nearer the lens than its focal length** *f* the image is **magnified**, **upright** and **virtual** (Fig 5.30(*b*)). Compare Fig 5.30(*a*) with Fig 5.30(*b*). **So the image is real and inverted when the object is farther than *f* from the lens; but virtual and upright when nearer the lens than *f*.**

Fig 5.30 Magnified images
– magnifying glass

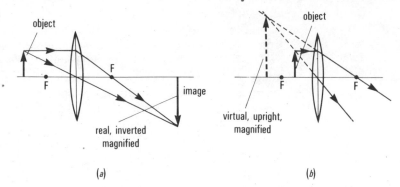

object

F
F
image

real, inverted
magnified

(a)

object

F
F

virtual, upright,
magnified

(b)

**5.35 HOW OBJECT
DISTANCE FROM FOCUS F
AFFECTS IMAGE**

We now see that the type of image formed by the lens depends on the **distance of the object from F**, the principal focus. Remember that:

1 **Further than F**, the image is
   (a)   upside down (inverted)
   (b)   on the other side of the lens to the object
   (c)   can be formed on a screen (real image).

2 Starting a long way from the lens, the image is formed at F. As the object gets nearer to the lens, the image moves away from F and becomes bigger.

3 **At distance 2f**, the inverted real image is
   (a)   the same size as the object
   (b)   also a distance 2f from the lens on the other side.
   So if f = 20 cm, an object 40 cm (2 × 20 cm) away forms an image of the same size 40 cm from the lens on the other side.

**5.36 LENS CAMERA AND
SLIDE PROJECTOR**

The camera (shown in Fig 5.31) is similar in action to the eye. It has
(a)   a converging lens;
(b)   an aperture or stop which limits the light passing through the lens;
(c)   a light-sensitive film on which the real, inverted image is formed. The image is small because the object is a long way from the lens.

Unlike the eye, the focal length of the lens cannot be altered. So the image is **focused** by moving the lens towards or away from the film. The amount of light passing through the lens is controlled by the diameter of the **aperture** and by the **speed** of the shutter, which opens and shuts over a particular time, depending on the lighting conditions and the type of film used.

For example, in poor lighting conditions, the aperture is opened wide. In photographing a fast-moving car, the speed of the shutter, opening and closing, must be fast, such as $\frac{1}{256}$ of a second, otherwise a blurred image is obtained.

Fig 5.31 Lens camera

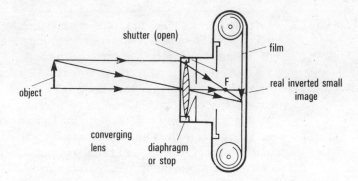

SLIDE PROJECTOR

This has

(a)   a powerful small lamp O to illuminate the slide S;

(b)   a 'condenser' or lens which collects the light from O and sends it through S;

(c)   a converging projection lens L;

(d)   a white screen A one which the clear magnified image of the slide is produced (see Fig 5.32).

Fig 5.32 Slide projector

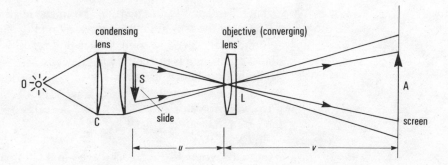

The slide must be slightly farther from L than its focal length so that a real inverted image is produced. The slide must be placed upside down, in which case the image is obtained the right way up to be seen, as shown. The nearer the slide is placed to the focus F of the projection lens, the larger will be the image on the screen.

CHECK LIST ▶ Make sure you can answer the following questions.

1   An object is 15 cm from a converging lens of focal length 12 cm. Draw a ray diagram showing how the image is formed. Describe the image.

2   Draw a ray diagram showing how a magnifying glass works.

3   Name as many differences, and as many similarities, as you can between the object and image when

(a)   a lens camera and

(b)   a slide projector are used.

5.37 EXAMPLES ON LENSES

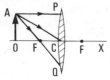

Fig 5.33 Refraction through lenses

1 An object OA is placed in front of a converging lens of principal focus F. Fig 5.33. State what happens to the three incident rays AP, AF and AC after they are refracted through the lens.

Give a reason for direction of the ray AC after refraction.

After refraction, ray AP travels along PF.

After refraction, ray AEQ travels parallel to CX.

After refraction, ray AC travels in the same direction.

AC travels in the same direction after refraction because the middle of the lens at C is a parallel-sided piece of glass and therefore does not change the direction of AC.

2 In Fig 5.34(a), a converging lens with focus F forms an image IA. Explain how you would find the object position in a ray diagram.

Fig 5.34 Drawing object from image

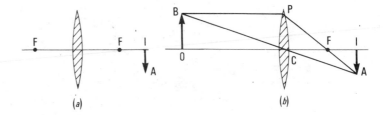

(a)   (b)

Fig 5.34(b) shows the method. From the head A of the image, draw AF to meet the lens at P. Then draw a line PQ parallel to CF. Now join AC and extend AC to meet PQ at B. Then B is the top point of the object and so OB is the complete object.

3 A converging lens is used for

(a)   a lens camera,

(b)   a projector and

(c)   a magnifying glass

In each case:

(i) where is the object placed in relation to the lens focus F?

(ii) how does the image look compared with the object?

(a)   (i) The object is usually a long way from the lens focus F

(ii) The image is inverted, real and much smaller than the object.

(b)   (i) The object is a short distance from F away from the lens.

(ii) The image is inverted, real and much bigger than the object.

(c)   (i) The object is between F and the lens.

(ii) The image is upright, virtual (same side as object) and much bigger than the object.

YOU SHOULD KNOW

1   Shadows and eclipses are formed by light travelling in a straight line.

2   A pin-hole camera forms a small inverted image on the film due to light passing through the pin-hole. A hole larger than normal, or a hole **very** small, produces blurring of the image.

3   **Reflection by plane mirror**
    (i) Angle of incidence = angle of reflection.
    (ii) The image has the same size as the object, is as far behind the mirror as the object is in front and is laterally (sideways) inverted.

4   **Reflection at curved mirror (concave type)**
    (i) Parabola shape (not spherical shape) preferred for motor headlamp or aerial receiver
    (ii) for drawing images in spherical concave mirror use a ray parallel to principal axis and a ray either through the centre of curvature or through the focus,
    (iii) image is the same size as object as a distance 2f from the mirror,
    (iv) a large upright virtual image is obtained for a distance less than f from mirror.

5   **Refraction at plane surface**
    (i) From air to glass or water, a ray is refracted towards the normal. From glass or water to air, the ray bends **away** from the normal.
    (ii) From a dense to a **less** dense medium, a critical angle and total internal reflection can be obtained. Used in total reflecting prisms and the optical fibre. Sin $C = 1/n$ to calculate critical angle C.

6   **Converging lens**
    (i) For ray diagrams, use a ray parallel to the principal axis and a ray through the centre of the lens.
    (ii) The image is inverted and the same size as the object at a distance 2f from the lens.
    (iii) At a distance **less** than f, the image is upright, magnified and virtual (behind the lens) – magnifying glass.

7   **Lens camera** has a converging lens and a small image. The amount of light passing in depends on the aperture and the shutter speed. **Slide projector** has a converging lens and forms a large image on the screen when the slide is near the focus.

8   **Dispersion** A glass prism, often 60°, disperses (separates the colours in) white light. The colours from red to violet have different speeds or refractive index in glass but the same speed in a vacuum or air.

YOU SHOULD UNDERSTAND

1   How to form the image in a pin-hole camera and how to calculate its height.

2 **Reflection**

(i) How to draw the image of an object in a plane mirror and in a concave mirror;

(ii) Why parabolic mirrors are used;

(iii) Why a curved mirror is used as a make-up mirror to produce a magnified image.

3 **Refraction**

(i) How rays are refracted from air to glass and from glass to air.

(ii) The meaning of refractive index.

(iii) How a critical angle and total internal reflection is obtained for air–glass, and how a total reflecting prism works in a periscope.

4 **Lenses**

(i) How images are drawn in ray diagrams.

(ii) The ray diagram for a magnifying glass.

5 The difference between the images obtained when using a lens camera, a slide projector and a magnifying glass.

6 How a glass prism produces dispersion of white light.

APPLICATIONS

You should be able to answer the following questions

1 A lamp of height 20 cm is placed 50 cm from the hole of a pin-hole camera, whose box has a length of 10 cm. Draw a ray diagram showing the image and calculate its height.

2 Draw a ray diagram showing how a periscope works using

(i) two plane mirrors,

(ii) two glass prisms.

Which gives the clearer image and why?

3 A converging lens of focal length 10 cm produces an image three times the height of the object. Where is the object position if the image is

(a)   inverted,

(b)   upright?

Draw a ray diagram of each case.

4 Show by ray diagrams how a slide projector and a magnifying glass each produces magnified images. Why is a lamp necessary for the projector?

5 A glass prism disperses white light. Draw a labelled diagram showing how dispersion occurs and give the colours obtained.

Which has the greater refractive index in glass – red or violet light?

QUESTIONS 5 OPTICS

MULTIPLE CHOICE QUESTIONS

1 In Fig 5A, a ray AB is reflected by mirror B to a parallel mirror C, and then reflected along CD parallel to AB. In this case

A   the angle of incidence of AB on mirror B is 60°
B   CD is not 90° to AB
C   the angle of incidence of BC on C is 45°
D   AB makes an angle of 120° with BC

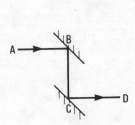

Fig 5A Question 1   Fig 5B Question 2

2   A ray XO is incident on one side of a rectangular glass block. Fig 5B.
    The ray emerging from the opposite side is
       A P   B Q   C R   D S

3   A ray PQ enters a rectangular glass block, is reflected and refracted at
    R, and finally emerges at T into the air. Fig 5C. The critical angle of
    the glass is
       A   20°   B   30°   C   40°   D   50°

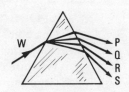

Fig 5C Question 3   Fig 5D Question 4

4   A ray W of white light is incident on a glass prism. Fig 5D. The beam
    of light coming out of the prism has four colours at P, Q, R and S. The
    violet colour is
       A P   B Q   C R   D S

5   A converging (convex) lens has a principal focus F and forms an
    image on a screen at T Fig 5E. In this case the object is at
       A P   B Q   C R   D S

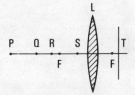

Fig 5E Question 5

6   In a lens camera, the lens used is
   A   converging and of variable focal length
   B   diverging and long focal length
   C   converging and short focal length
   D   converging and long focal length

SHORT ANSWER QUESTIONS

7   A ray AO makes an angle of 40° with a plane mirror X. Fig 5F. The reflected ray OB is then incident on a plane mirror Y and is reflected along BC.
       As shown, the mirrors X and Y make an angle of 60° with each other.
       Calculate the angle θ which BC makes with mirror Y.

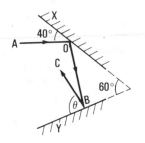   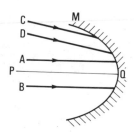

Fig 5F Question 7   Fig 5G Question 8

8   In Fig 5G, M is a curved mirror of a parabola shape with a principal axis PQ.
       Copy the sketch and show on it the incident parallel rays A,B and C,D and their reflected paths.
       Why are curved mirrors of this shape used for headlamp reflectors or large astronomical telescopes and not mirrors of spherical shape?

9   Fig 5H shows part of an **optical fibre**. This has a glass core (inside) which is optically denser than the glass cladding (coating) Y. A ray of light AO in the core X makes a small angle of incidence i with the boundary off the cladding.

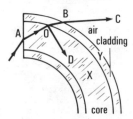

Fig 5H Question 9

(*a*)   Explain why only a snall amount of light is reflected along OD and the rest of the light is refracted along OB and BC in the directions shown.

(*b*)   In a new drawing, show how a ray of light can travel along a fibre without losing its intensity and explain why this occurs.

State **two** applications of optical fibres.

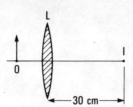

Fig 5I Question 10

10 A luminous object 0 is 3 cm high. Fig 5I. It forms an image I which is 30 cm from the converging (convex) lens L as shown.

(*a*)   In a diagram, show three rays from the top of the object which are refracted to the image.

(*b*)   By a scale drawing, find the focal length of the lens.

11 A luminous object is placed in front of a converging (convex) lens of focal length 20 cm. Fig 5J. An image is formed 30 cm from the lens,

(*a*)   on the opposite side to the object

(*b*)   on the same side as the object.

Find by drawing (or otherwise) the distance of the object from the lens in (*a*) and in (*b*).

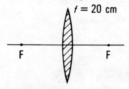

Fig 5J Question 11

12 A **lens camera** and a **slide projector** both use a converging (convex) lens. In these optical instruments what is the difference between

(*a*)   the size of the images formed,

(*b*)   the position of the objects from the lens,

(*c*)   the way in which a bright image is obtained?

Draw sketches to illustrate your answers in (*a*), (*b*) and (*c*).

ELECTRICITY

CONTENTS

Contents

6.1 ELECTRICAL NATURE OF MATTER

As we shall see later (p.297), an atom is made up of a small central **nucleus** surrounded by tiny particles called **electrons** (see p.289). The nucleus and the electrons carry electric charges. There are two kinds of charge, **positive** (+ve) and **negative** (−ve). The nucleus has most of the mass of the atom and is positively charged. **The electrons are negatively charged.** The positive charge on the nucleus exactly balances the negative charge on the electrons. So the atom is electrically **neutral**.

6.2 INSULATORS AND CONDUCTORS

In some materials the electrons are held tightly to the atoms. They are not free to wander about in the material. Such materials will not allow electric charge to flow through them, and are called **insulators**. The plastic covering on mains cables is made from an insulator to protect us from electric shock.

Metals are **conductors** of electricity. Electric charge can flow through them because the metal contains electrons which are free to wander. The human body is also a conductor of electricity.

6.3 CHARGES PRODUCED BY RUBBING

Electric charges appear on insulators when they are rubbed. An acetate rod rubbed with a duster becomes positively charged. The acetate rod will then pick up small pieces of paper which are near to it.

When the acetate is rubbed, some electrons from the atoms in the acetate move over to the duster. This means that there is now **less** negative charge in the acetate than positive charge. So the acetate has an unbalanced **positive** charge. The duster, however, has extra electrons and so this is **negatively** charged.

When a piece of polythene is rubbed electrons move from the duster to the polythene. Here the polythene becomes negatively charged. The duster has a positive charge.

If an electric charge is produced by rubbing a metal, electrons will leak through the metal and the body. Metals must be held with an insulating handle if they are to be charged by rubbing them.

6.4 FORCES BETWEEN CHARGES

Fig 6.1 shows a simple experiment to investigate the forces between charges. Strips X and Y are both made of polythene and rubbed all along their length. Whichever end of X is brought close to Y it is found that Y is always pushed away. The same thing happens if two acetate rods are used, so

LIKE CHARGES REPEL.

If X is made of acetate and Y is made of polythene then the rods attract when they are rubbed, so

UNLIKE CHARGES ATTRACT.

Fig 6.1 Force between charges

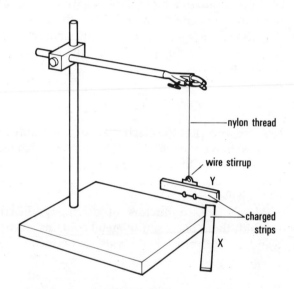

Forces between charges causes dust to build up on television screens and on black plastic records. In a TV the picture is produced by a beam of electrons hitting the inside of the screen. Electrons are negatively charged, and so there is a build-up of this charge on the screen. This attracts particles of dust which stick to the screen. A plastic record becomes charged when it rubs on the inner cover, or when the stylus causes friction in the groove as its plays. Again the charged record collects dust.

▼ REASONS FOR ATTRACTION OF DUST

When a positively charged acetate rod is brought near to a piece of paper the electrons in the atoms of the paper are attracted, and move away slightly from the positive nuclei in the atoms. This causes a build-up of negative charge on the paper near to the acetate rod, and a build-up of positive charge away from the rod.

Since the negative charge on the paper is nearer the acetate than ▲ the positive charge, the force of attraction on the paper is greater than the force of repulsion. So the paper is attracted to the acetate. This is also why the particles of dust near a television screen, or any small particles near a charged object, are attracted.

6.5 DUST REMOVERS

Not all effects of charges are a nuisance. In a factory chimney the dust particles from the fire are charged. Dust removers inside the chimney consist of two metal grids which are charged, one positively and one negatively. This is done by connecting the grids to the positive and negative terminals of a high voltage supply. The negative dust particles are attracted to the positive grid, and the positive ones are attracted to the negative grid. In this way a lot of dust can be removed and so prevents air pollution.

Fig 6.2 Dust removers

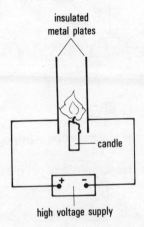

insulated metal plates

candle

high voltage supply

Fig 6.2 illustrates a laboratory experiment to show this effect. As the high voltage supply is turned up the candle flame broadens because the charged particles in the flame are attracted towards the plates.

6.6 CHARGING BY INDUCTION

A metal sphere can be charged from a charged rod without the rod touching the sphere. The way this is done is called **induction**, and the charges obtained are called **induced charges**. Fig 6.3 shows the stages in charging by induction.

In Fig 6.3(a) the negative rod repels electrons to the left side of the metal sphere. This leaves an excess positive charge on the right of the sphere. In Fig 6.3(b) a hand momentarily touches the sphere. The charged rod then repels electrons away from the sphere through the body to earth. In Fig 6.3(c) the finger is taken away, making it impossible for electrons to return to the sphere. There is therefore a deficiency of electrons on the sphere. Finally, in Fig 6.3(d), the charged rod is removed. The electrons remaining then distribute themselves evenly over the sphere. Note that

1   it is essential to remove the finger **before** the charged rod is finally taken away; and

Fig 6.3 Charging by
induction

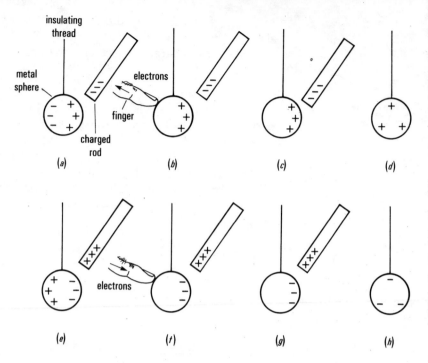

2   the charge acquired by the electroscope is **opposite** in sign to that of the
     charging rod.
         Fig 6.3(e) to (h) show the sequence of events if a positive rod is used.
     The readers should work out what is happening in each diagram.

CHECK LIST ▶ Make sure you can answer the following questions.

1   What is the difference between a conductor and an insulator?
2   Explain why a metal held in the hand cannot be charged by rubbing.
3   What happens to some of the electrons in polythene when rubbed by a duster?

6.7 ELECTRIC CURRENT   A metal, such as copper, contains electrons which are **free to move**.
     This is why copper is a good conductor of electricity. The filament of a
     lamp is made of tungsten metal. Fig 6.4 shows a battery connected to a
     lamp by means of two metal wires. We now have a complete path of
     metal from the positive terminal of the battery to the negative terminal.
     The battery pushes the free electrons in the metal around the circuit.
         This flow of electric charge is called an **electric current**. The unit of
     electric current is the **ampere** (A). A circuit will flow only if there is a
     complete conducting path from one terminal of the battery to the
     other. The battery provides the energy to the circuit as the current
     flows through it.

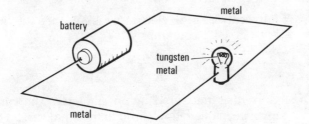

Fig 6.4 Complete circuit

Electrons are negatively charged. So they flow round the circuit from the negative terminal of the battery to the positive terminal. Before electrons were discovered, scientists did not know what was flowing in the wires. At this time, everyone agreed to suppose that the current was a flow of positive charge going from the positive of the battery to the negative. This is called the **conventional** current direction. It is still generally used, even though we know that the electrons flow the other way.

6.8 CIRCUIT SYMBOLS

You should know the meaning of the circuit symbols shown in Fig 6.5, as they are used often.

Fig 6.5 Circuit symbols

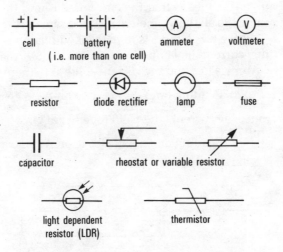

6.9 ELECTRIC CHARGE

Electric charge is measured in units called **coulombs** (C). The charge on a single electron is the tiny value of -1.6×10^{-19} coulombs. A current of 1 ampere means that 1 coulomb of charge flows each second. So

1 ampere = 1 coulomb per second

If a current of I amperes flows for t seconds, then the number of coulombs of charge, Q, flowing in the time t is given by,

$Q = I \times t$.

If the current in an electric fire is 4 A, then the charge Q flowing in 30 s is $4\times30 = 120$ coulombs.

6.10 MEASUREMENT OF CURRENT

Current is measured by an **ammeter**. The current to be measured must be made to flow through the ammeter. So the ammeter, A, must be placed in **series** as shown in Fig 6.6. Electric current is not 'used

Fig 6.6 Current in a series circuit

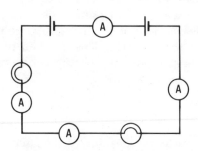

up'. This means that the current all round the circuit in Fig 6.6 is the same. So all the ammeters read the same value.

In Fig 6.7, lamp 1 is in parallel with lamp 2. Ammeter A_1 measures the current in lamp 1, and ammeter A_2 that in lamp 2. Since no current is lost and the current splits at P, then:

Reading on A_3 = Reading on A_1 + Reading on A_2

Since the currents then join together at Q:

Reading on A_1 + Reading on A_2 = Reading on A_4

Fig 6.7 Currents in parallel circuits

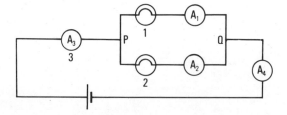

CHECK LIST ▶

Make sure you can answer the following questions.

1 Why is a metal a conductor of electricity?
2 Why is the current the same all round a series circuit?
3 What happens to an electric current when it splits into two or more branches in a parallel circuit?

6.11 POTENTIAL DIFFERENCES

Batteries can make an electric current flow around a circuit. Potential difference (p.d.) is the name we give to the electrical 'push' of the battery trying to make the current flow. The bigger the p.d. of the battery the harder it will push and more current is likely to flow. This is not an exact meaning of p.d. but it is a helpful way to think about it. Potential difference is measured in **volts**. A **voltmeter** is used to measure p.d. It is always connected in **parallel** between the two points where the p.d. is required.

6.12 DEFINITION OF P.D.

The electrons flowing in a circuit carry energy provided by the battery. This is transformed to other forms of energy in other parts of the circuit. The potential difference (in volts) between two points in a circuit is a measure of the energy transformed in joules for each coulomb of charge flowing between the points. 1 volt is defined as the p.d. between two points if 1 joule of energy is transformed when 1 coulomb flows.

From this definition it follows that if V volts is the p.d. between two points and W joules of energy are transformed when Q coulombs flow, then

$$W = QV$$

WORKED EXAMPLES

1 What charge flows when a current of 4 A flows through an electric fire for 1 hour?
   1 hour = $60 \times 60 = 3600$ s. So using charge, $Q = I \times t$

   $Q = 4 \times 3600$
   $= 14\,400$ coulombs (C).

2 In the last example if the p.d. of the supply is 240 V, what energy is transformed by the fire in 1 hour?

   $W = QV$
   $= 14\,400 \times 240$
   $= 3\,456\,000$ joules (J)
   $= 3.456$ MJ   (1 MJ = 1 megajoule = $1\,000\,000$ J)

6.13 VOLTAGES IN A SERIES CIRCUIT

In the circuit shown in Fig 6.8, a resistor R is connected in series with a motor, to a battery. Voltmeters are connected to measure the p.d. across each component. It will be found that p.d.s across the resistor and the motor, 4 V and 7 V, add up to the p.d. of the battery. The 'push' of the battery is shared between the two components – though not necessarily equally. Generally, **potential differences add up around a series circuit**.

Fig 6.8 Voltages in a series circuit

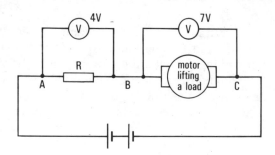

The reading of 4 V across R means that 4 joules of energy are transformed to heat in R for each coulomb flowing. The 7 V across the motor which is lifting a load means that when one coulomb flows through the motor, 7 joules of energy are transformed to increase the potential energy of the load and to produce some heat inside the wires of the motor. The total energy transformed is 11 joules and this must be supplied by the battery. So the p.d. across the battery is 11 volts. The statement that voltages add in a series circuit therefore follows from the conservation of energy.

CHECK LIST ▶ Make sure you can answer the following questions.

1 If there are three 1.5 V cells in series, what is the p.d. across all three of them?
2 How is (a) an ammeter, (b) a voltmeter connected in a circuit?

6.14 RESISTANCE

We have described a battery as a source of electrical 'push' trying to make a current flow. The current which does flow depends also on the electrical resistance between the terminals of the battery. For a battery sitting on a shelf only air connects the terminals. Air has an enormous resistance and so practically no current flows. The battery does not run down. When the terminals are joined by a filament lamp the resistance is much less. A larger current now flows to light the lamp.

The resistance, R, of a resistor is defined by

$$R = V/I$$

where V is the p.d. across the resdistor, and I is the current flowing through it. The unit of resistance is the ohm (Ω).

From $R = V/I$ we see that $V = IR$, and $I = V/R$. These formulae are used in a lot of circuit calculations. For example, for a p.d. of 10 V across a resistor of 5 Ω, the current I is given by

$$I = V/R = 10/5 = 2A$$

For a resistor of 20 Ω, and the same p.d. of 10 V,

$$I = V/R = 10/20 = 0.5\,A$$

The higher resistor allows only a smaller current to flow. This agrees with what we expect by common sense.

6.15 OHM'S LAW

Resistors can be made of a length of metal wire or a small piece of carbon material. For these materials the resistance can remain the same even if the voltage and current change, so the ratio V/I is constant. This means that doubling the p.d. produces double the current, three times the p.d. produces three times the current, and so on.

Temperature and other physical conditions, however, can affect resistance, so these conditions must be kept constant if resistance is not to change. This relation was first discovered by Ohm, and a full statement of Ohm's law reads:

The resistance of a conductor is the ratio p.d./current and is always constant provided that the physical conditions, such as temperature, remain unaltered.

Metals and carbon obey Ohm's law and are called 'ohmic' materials. Other materials such as semiconductors and diodes for example, do not and are called 'non-ohmic'.

Fixed value resistors are made of a length of a wire wound on a small insulating cylinder (wire-wound resistors), or of a small piece of a carbon mixture (carbon resistors). Variable resistors are called **rheostats**. These are made so that a connection can be made at various points along the length of a resistor by a moving contact.

6.16 MEASUREMENT OF RESISTANCE

Fig 6.9 shows a circuit to measure the resistance of a resistor R. Different values of V and I are measured for various positions of the rheostat. R = V/I can be calculated for each position and the average found.

Fig 6.9 Measurement of resistance

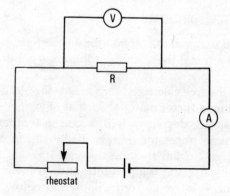

Care should be taken to see that the resistor does not warm up during the experiment, otherwise its resistance would change. To ensure this the current must be small enough not to produce much heat in R. Also, the current should not be left on longer than needed.

Fig 6.10 Graphical treatment of results

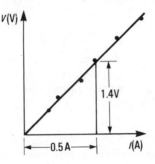

The results can also be plotted on a graph. Fig 6.10 shows the graph obtained when V is plotted against I. We can find the resistance from the slope (or gradient) of the graph. With the figures shown on the diagram the slope = $R = 1.4/0.5 = 2.8\,\Omega$.

WORKED EXAMPLE

Calculate the resistance of the filament of a mains lamp which draws a current of 0.2 A when connected to 240 V mains.

Resistance $R = V/I = 240/0.2 = 1\,200$ ohm (Ω).

6.17 EFFECT OF TEMPERATURE ON MATERIALS

1 For **pure metals**, such as copper or tungsten, the resistance **increases as the temperature rises**. This can be demonstrated experimentally by using a filament lamp instead of the fixed resistor in the circuit of Fig 6.9. It will then be found that values of V/I get larger as the lamp gets hotter. So as the current gets larger and the tungsten warms up, the resistance becomes higher. Fig 6.11 shows the graph of V against I. As the current gets bigger the slope of the graph increases.

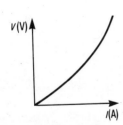

EXPLANATION FOR METALS

In a solid material the atoms vibrate more strongly as the temperature rises. In a metal these atomic vibrations get in the way of the move-

Fig 6.11 Graph of p.d. against current for a filament lamp

ment of the free electrons. This makes the electrical resistance rise.

2 In a **semiconductor** material such as silicon or germanium, however, the resistance **decreases with a rise in temperature**. This can cause problems in transistor circuits. If the silicon material of a transistor has a large current flowing through it, then heat will be produced. This will raise the temperature and so lower the resistance of the transistor. A larger current will therefore flow, producing more heat,

and so on. This effect, called 'thermal runaway', can damage the transistor. Transistor circuits need to be designed carefully so that large currents are prevented from flowing.

▼ EXPLANATION FOR SEMICONDUCTORS

Unlike a metal, in a semiconductor only a few of the atoms have lost electrons, which then become free. As the temperature rises the atomic vibrations get larger and more atoms can shake an electron loose. So the number of electrons available to carry current rises with temperature, and so the resistance of the material falls.

CHECK LIST ▶

Make sure you can answer the following questions.

1 Draw a circuit diagram of an experiment to measure the resistance of a resistor.
2 Name one material which increases its resistance with temperature rise, and one which decreases its resistance.
3 A current of 1 A flows through a resistor when the p.d. is 4 V. If the resistor obeys Ohm's law, what current flows for a p.d. of 12 V?

6.18 THERMISTORS AND LDRs

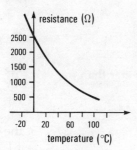

A **thermistor** is a semiconductor device whose resistance **decreases greatly with temperature**. This can be used in electronic circuits to help detect changes of temperature (p.272). A graph of resistance against temperature for one type of thermistor is shown in Fig 6.12.

An **LDR** (**Light Dependent Resistor**) is a device whose resistance **decreases greatly as the intensity of light shining on it rises**. This has uses in electronic circuits which help detect changes in light levels, for example, from daytime to evening.

Fig 6.12 Graph of resistance against temperature for a thermistor

---

6.19 SEMICONDUCTOR DIODE

A semiconductor **diode** has a resistance which depends on which way round it is connected in a circuit. With a battery connected as in

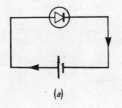

(a)

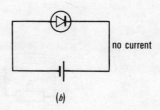

no current

(b)

Fig 6.13 Semiconductor diode

Fig 6.13(*a*) the resistance is very low. A large current would flow. With the battery connected the other way round as in Fig 6.13(*b*), the resistance is very high and so practically no current flows. So the diode acts as a one-way device – it only allows current to pass in one direction.

A graph of current against potential difference or voltage for a semiconductor diode is shown in Fig 6.14. Note that we have plotted *I* upwards and *V* horizontally. 'Negative' p.d.s show that the power supply has had its positive and negative terminals reversed, and the current is then very low.

Fig 6.14 Current against p.d. for a semiconductor diode

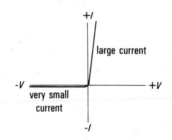

6.20 RESISTORS IN SERIES

If two resistors R_1 and R_2 are wired in **series**, as shown in Fig 6.15, their combined resistance R is the sum of their separate resistances. So in Fig 6.15

$$R = R_1 + R_2$$

Fig 6.15 Resistors in series

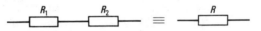

Note that the combined resistance is always **greater than the value of the larger resistor.**

6.21 RESISTORS IN PARALLEL

If two resistors R_1 and R_2 are wired in **parallel**, as shown in Fig 6.16, their combined resistance is **less than the resistance of the smaller one**. This is because there are two paths for the current to flow. For two equal resistors in parallel their equivalent resistance, R, is halved. In general the formula for calculating the equivalent resistance (Fig 6.15) is

$$1/R = 1/R_1 + 1/R_2$$

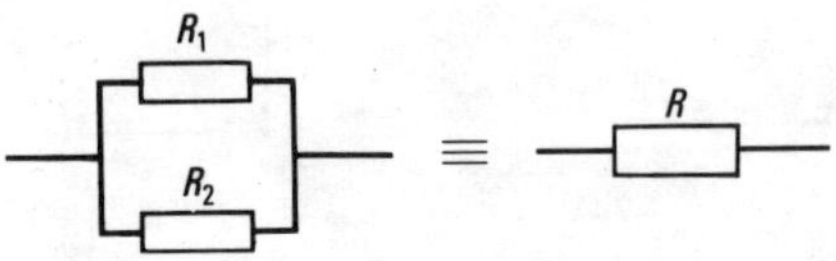

Fig 6.16 Resistors in parallel

WORKED EXAMPLE

Two resistors of $10\,\Omega$ and $15\,\Omega$ are connected (a) in series, (b) in parallel. What is their combined resistance in each case?

(a)   in series $R = R_1 + R_2 = 10 + 15 = 25\,\Omega$

(b)   in parallel $1/R = 1/R_1 + 1/R_2$

$$\frac{1}{R} = \frac{1}{10} + \frac{1}{15}$$

$$= \frac{3+2}{30} = \frac{5}{30}$$

so $R = 30/5 = 6\,\Omega$

6.22 RESISTANCE OF WIRES

The resistance of a metal wire at a fixed temperature depends on

1 the material of which the wire is made,
2 the length of the wire, and
3 the cross-sectional area of the wire.

Some materials, like copper, are very good conductors of electricity and are unsuitable for making resistors. Alloys, such as Nichrome, are not such good conductors and wire wound resistors can be made of these materials.

For a given material the resistance of a wire is **proportional to its length**, l. This is because a wire 2 m long is equivalent to two 1 m wires in series, Fig 6.17(a). So the resistance of a 2 m wire is double that of a 1 m wire. A 3 m wire has three times the resistance, and so on.

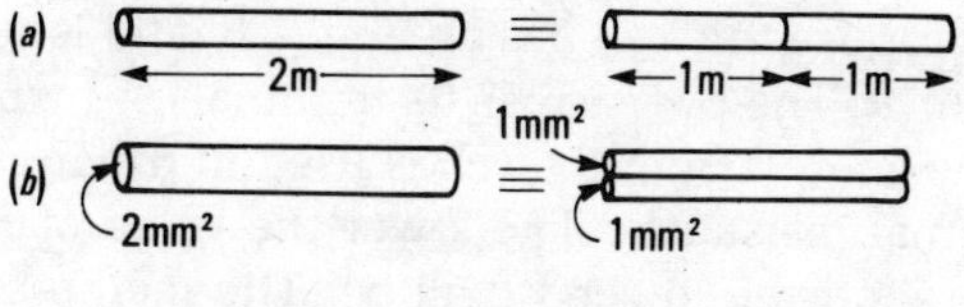

Fig 6.17 Resistance of wires

The resistance of a given material is also **inversely proportional to the cross-sectional area** of the wire. This is because a wire of $2\,mm^2$ cross-section is equivalent to two $1\,mm^2$ wires in parallel, Fig 6.17(b). So the resistance of a $2\,mm^2$ cross-section wire is half that of a $1\,mm^2$ wire. A $3\,mm^2$ wire has one third of the resistance, and so on.

WORKED EXAMPLE

Three wires A, B and C, are made of the same material. B has three times the length of A, but the same cross-sectional area. C has double the diameter of A but the same length. The resistance of A is $10\,\Omega$. What are the resistances of B and C?

Resistance is directly proportional to length, so the resistance of B is three times that of A, that is, $30\,\Omega$.

The diameter of C is double that of A, so its cross-sectional area is **four** times that of A. Resistance is inversely proportional to cross-sectional area, so the resistance of C is one quarter that of A, that is, $2.5\,\Omega$.

6.23 E.M.F. AND INTERNAL RESISTANCE

The **e.m.f. (electromotive force)** of a cell, battery or power supply is the potential difference across the supply when it is supplying a very small current. (We shall see later that it is a measure of the total energy produced from the supply for each coulomb of charge flowing right round the circuit.) The e.m.f. is measured in **volts**, and for a battery its value depends on the chemicals used. The e.m.f. is usually written on the battery, e.g. 9 V.

A high resistance voltmeter connected across a cell will give practically the value of the e.m.f. since the voltmeter will draw very little current. When a cell provides a lot of current, the p.d. across its terminals may be less than the e.m.f. of the cell because of the **internal resistance** of the cell, which we now discuss.

A cell has resistance inside it between its terminals. This is caused by the chemicals of which it is made. The internal resistance, r, is shown by the symbol in Fig 6.18. The dotted line is taken to indicate that r is really between the terminals of the battery.

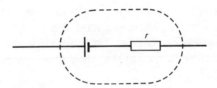

Fig 6.18 Symbol for internal resistance

Suppose this cell has an e.m.f. E, and is connected to a resistor R, Fig 6.19. The p.d. across its terminals, V, will now be less than E, as some energy from the cell is used in driving the current through the internal resistance. The lower the value of R, the more current will flow, and the lower V will be. The method of calculating V is illustrated in the following worked example.

Fig 6.19 E.m.f. and internal resistance

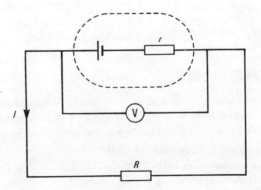

▼ WORKED EXAMPLE

In Fig 6.19, the e.m.f. of the cell is 10 V, and the internal resistance is 2 Ω Find the p.d. across the terminals of the cell when it is connected to a 3 Ω resistor.

The e.m.f. supplies energy to the **whole** circuit so,

$$E = \text{p.d. across } R + \text{p.d. across } r$$
$$= IR + Ir$$
$$= I(R+r)$$

In this case,

$$10 = I(2+3) = I \times 5$$

So $I = 2$ A.

The p.d. across the terminals of the cell is also the p.d. across R (see Fig 6.19).

So
$$V = \text{p.d. across } R$$
$$= IR$$
$$= 2 \times 3 = 6\text{ V}.$$

6.2 ELECTRICAL ENERGY

Electrical energy, like all forms of energy, is measured in **joules** (J). The electrical energy produced by a current I amperes flowing through a p.d. V volts for a time t seconds can be calculated from

$$\text{Energy} = VIt \text{ joules}.$$

The energy produced in one second is the **power**. This can be found by putting $t = 1$ s in the last formula, so

$$\text{Power} = VI \times 1 = VI$$

Remember that power is measured in joules per second, also called watts, symbol W. So if the p.d. across a working electrical motor is 50 V and the current is 2 A,

$$\text{power} = VI = 50 \times 2 = 100\text{ W}$$

▼ PROOF OF POWER = VI

We saw on p.206 that V volts meant that V joules of energy were transformed for each coulomb of electricity flowing. I amperes means that I coulombs flow each second.

$$\text{Power} = \text{Number of J per s}$$
$$= \text{Number of J per coulomb} \times \text{number of coulombs per second}$$
$$= V \times I = VI$$

▲ This verifies the last formula.

6.25 HEAT PRODUCED IN A RESISTOR

A resistor converts all the electrical energy supplied to heat. The power produced $= VI = IR \times I = I^2R$. So for a resistor,

$$\text{heat produced per second} = \text{power} = I^2R.$$

If V and R are given then power $= VI = V \times V/R = V^2/R$.

WORKED EXAMPLE

Two heating coils A and B produce heat at a rate of 1 kW and 2 kW respectively when connected to 250 V mains.

(a)   Calculate the resistance of each resistor.

(b)   Find the power they would produce when connected in series to the mains.

(a)   For the first resistor:

$$\text{Power} = VI$$
$$1000 = 250 \times I, \text{ so } I = 1000/250 = 4 \text{ A}.$$
So $\qquad R = V/I = 250/4$
$$= 62.5\,\Omega$$

For the second resistor:

$$\text{Power} = VI$$
$$2000 = 250 \times I, \text{ so } I = 2000/250 = 8 \text{ A}.$$
So $\qquad R = V/I = 250/8$
$$= 31.25\,\Omega$$

(b)   If the resistors are wired in series, their total resistance is $R_1 + R_2 = 62.5 + 31.25 = 93.75\,\Omega$.

using $\qquad R = V/I$
$$93.75 = 250/I, \text{ giving } I = 250/93.75 = 2.67 \text{ A}.$$
So $\qquad \text{power} = VI = 250 \times 2.67 = 666 \text{ W}$

Notice that this is **less** than the power produced when either resistor is connected to the mains separately. Can you see why?

CHECK LIST ▶

Make sure you can answer the following questions.

1   Name an electrical device used for detecting changes of (a) light intensity, (b) temperature.

2   What is the resistance of two $6\,\Omega$ resistors (a) in series, (b) in parallel?

3   What is the power of an electric fire which draws a current of 4 A when connected to 240 V mains?

4   Why is the p.d. across a battery different from its e.m.f. when the battery is providing current.

6.26 DOMESTIC ELECTRICAL ENERGY

Domestic and commercial electrical energy is measured in units called **kilowatt-hours (kWh)**. A kilowatt-hour is the electrical energy transformed by a 1 kilowatt appliance working for 1 hour.

To calculate the energy in kilowatt-hours, the power of the appliance in kilowatts is multiplied by the time in hours it is switched on. For example, a 3 kW electric fire left on for 2 hours uses $3 \times 2 = 6$ kWh. A 100 W light bulb switched on for 15 hours uses $0.1 \times 15 = 1.5$ kWh. Note that the power of the bulb must be put in kW (100 W = 0.1 kW).

The meter provided by the electricity board measures the total kWh used by all the appliances in the house. There are two types of dial used on meters. Fig 6.20 shows the two types.

Fig 6.20 Electricity meters

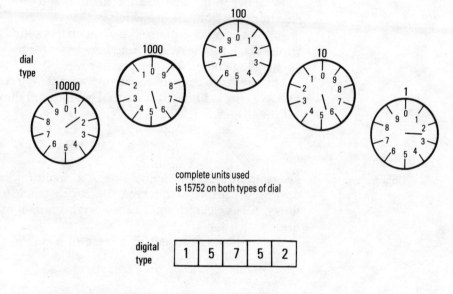

complete units used
is 15752 on both types of dial

The total electricity bill is calculated by multiplying the number of units used by the price per unit. The number of units used is found by subtracting the meter reading at the start of a three-month period (a quarter) from the reading at the end of the quarter.

WORKED EXAMPLES

1 How many joules are there in 1 kWh?

$$\text{One kWh} = \text{energy transformed by 1 kW (1000 W) for 1 hour (3600 s)}$$
$$= \text{energy when 1000 J are transformed each second for 3600 s}$$
$$= 1000 \times 3600 = 3\,600\,000 \text{ J} = 3.6 \text{ MJ}$$

2   A 3 kW electric fire is accidentally left on overnight for 9 hours. The cost of a unit of electrical energy is 5.2 p. How much money has been wasted?

$$\text{The number of units (kWh)} = \text{power in kW} \times \text{time in hours}$$
$$= 3 \times 9 = 27\,\text{kWh}$$

$$\text{The total cost} = 27 \times \text{cost of each unit}$$
$$= 27 \times 5.2$$
$$= 140\text{p} = £1.40$$

6.27 MAINS WIRING

In the wiring of a house and appliances, three cables are used: the **live, neutral** and **earth**. The neutral and earth are connected together by the electricity board at the nearest sub-station. There is never a high p.d. between neutral and earth. There is, however, a p.d. of 240 V between the live and the neutral, and so there is a danger of electric shock from the live wire.

In the wiring of a house the electricians use **red** cables for the live wires, **black** for the neutral, and **bare** wires for the earth. These wires are held together in a strong plastic cover.

For appliance connections to plugs a different colour code is used. The **live** wire is **brown**, the **neutral** is **blue**, and the **earth** is **green and yellow stripes**.

6.28 FUSES

Fuses are fitted into the live side of a circuit for safety reasons. The purpose of a fuse is to break the circuit when too large a current flows. A large current may cause overheating of cables and so start a fire.

A simple fuse consists of a piece of metal lead alloy wire which

Fig 6.21 Fuse

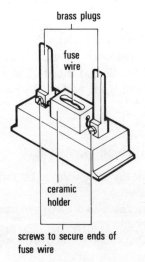
brass plugs
fuse wire
ceramic holder
screws to secure ends of fuse wire

melts when too large a current flows. The current at which a fuse 'blows' depends on how thick the wire is and what metal it is made of. In a fuse box the fuse wire must be replaced after it has blown and the faulty appliance repaired. Fig 6.21 shows a typical fuse from a fuse box. In a three-pin mains plug the fuse is contained in a glass tube. The whole glass tube and the fine wire inside it are replaced if the fuse blows.

6.29 SAFETY

To increase safety a combination of fuses and **earthing** is used. The metal case of an appliance is always connected to the earth wire. If a fault develops where the live wire touches the case, then a large current will flow to earth. This causes the fuse to blow so disconnecting the live wire.

For this to work correctly:

1 The correct value of fuse should be fitted. The fuse value should be high enough to take the normal current used by the appliance. It should not, however, allow too large a current to flow as this could cause overheating in the cables. The following table gives some suitable values.

> 3 A fuse: Television, hi-fi, table lamps.
>
> 7 A fuse: Iron, 1 bar electric fire, most power tools.
>
> 13 A fuse: Washing machine, most electric fires, dryer.

2 The plug must be wired correctly with three core cable. The yellow and green wire must be connected to the earth pin at the top of the plug. The brown live wire must be connected to the pin near the fuse. The blue neutral wire must be connected to the remaining terminal. Enough insulation should be removed from each wire to make good electrical contact, as shown in Fig 6.22(a). Removing too much wire,

Fig 6.22 Wiring of plugs

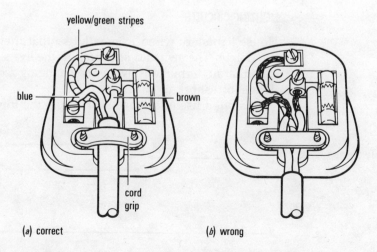

yellow/green stripes

blue   brown

cord grip

(a) correct   (b) wrong

however, can allow the metal wires to touch which would be dangerous (Fig 6.22(*b*)).

The cord grips should also be tightened on to the cable so that the wires cannot be pulled loose. These should grip the outer cable as in Fig 6.18(*a*).

6.30 HOUSE WIRING

In a house, various sections of wiring are connected to separate fuses in the fuse box – also called the '**consumer unit**'. A house may have five circuits:

     1 Upstairs lighting.
     2 Downstairs lighting.
     3 Upstairs power.
     4 Downstairs power.
     5 Cooker power.

Fig 6.23 shows the basic wiring diagram for such a system.

Fig 6.23 Wiring of consumer unit

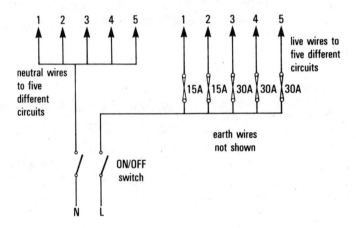

LIGHTING CIRCUITS

House lights are wired in **parallel** so that they can be switched on separately. The switches are wired in the live side of the circuit. This is so that no terminal is live when changing a bulb, so removing the danger of a shock.

It is often useful to have switches at the top and bottom of stairs

Fig 6.24 Two-way switches

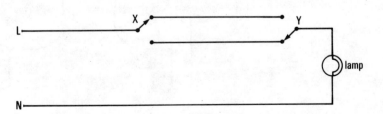

controlling a single lamp. The switches used are double throw, or two-way switches. A circuit using them is shown in Fig 6.24. X is the switch at the bottom of the stairs and Y is at the top.

In the position shown the lamp is off because there is no complete circuit. If either X or Y is moved to the other position the circuit will be completed and the lamp will light. Similarly if the lamp is on, then switching either X or Y will break the circuit.

POWER CIRCUITS

Power circuits are normally wired as a **ring main**. A three core cable is laid in a ring around the house with the ends connected at the consumer unit. Three pin sockets are wired in at various points around the ring. Fig 6.25. A ring main has a number of advantages.

1 It uses less wire than wiring each socket back separately to the consumer unit.
2 It is comparatively easy to add extra sockets.

Fig 6.25 Ring main

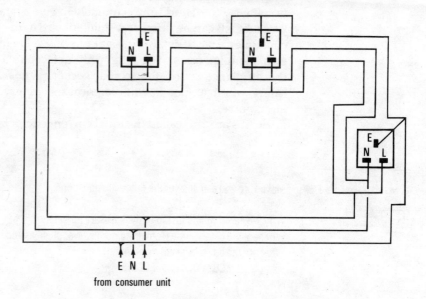

from consumer unit

CABLES

It is important to use the correct cable for wiring the various sections of a house. Power cable carries more current than lighting cable and must be thicker. The cross-sectional area of the metal wire in a cable is given in mm^2. Cable with live, neutral and earth wires is generally known as '**twin and earth**'. As a guide:

1.0 mm^2 twin and earth is suitable for lighting circuits.
2.5 mm^2 twin and earth is suitable for power circuits.
6.0 mm^2 twin and earth is suitable for wiring cookers.

6.31 MODERN DEVICES

Miniature circuit breakers (MCB) can be used to replace fuses in consumer units. These work magnetically and cut off the current when it exceeds a certain value. They can be reset simply by pressing a small button once the fault has been rectified. They have an advantage over fuses because it is easier to reset them than to rewire a fuse holder with the correct fuse wire. They are, however, quite expensive.

Earth circuit leakage breakers (ECLB) are devices which cut off the current very quickly if someone gets an electric shock, or if certain faults develop. Normally exactly the same current flows along the neutral and live wires. If someone accidentally touches the live wire a current flows through their body to earth. Less current then flows back along the neutral wire. The currents along the live and neutral wire are now **unequal**. An ECLB detects this fact and immediately breaks the live and neutral connections.

An ECLB will be able to detect a small difference of 30 mA. It will then cut off the supply in 25 ms ($\frac{1}{40}$th of a second). This current flowing for this short time is unlikely to give a fatal shock.

An ECLB can be fitted as a single device in the power supply to the consumer unit. It is also possible to buy a small ECLBs which plug into a single socket. The latter only detects a dangerous situation in the appliance connected to that socket. It does, however, improve safety when working with electrical machinery, such as an electric lawnmower.

ECLBs are also called 'residual current circuit breakers' (r.c.c.b.).

CHECK LIST ▶	Make sure you can answer the following questions.

1 Why are earthing and fusing both necessary for safety?
2 What are the colour codes for wiring domestic appliances and in house wiring?
3 What are the advantages of a ring main?
4 What is an MCB? What is an ECLB?

SUMMARY

(a) YOU SHOULD KNOW

1 Materials can be charged by rubbing them.
2 This is caused by the transfer of electrons.
3 Unlike charges attract – like charges repel.
4 Materials which allow a flow of charge are called conductors. Insulators do not allow a flow of charge through them.
5 Small objects are attracted to a charged material.
6 Conductors can be charged by induction.
7 An electric current in a metal is due to a flow of electrons.
8 A complete circuit is needed for an electric current to flow.

9　The meaning of symbols for common circuit components.
10　Current is measured in amperes on an ammeter wired in series.
11　Charge is measured in coulombs.
12　Current is not lost in a circuit. It is the same all round a series circuit. Currents add in parallel circuits.
13　The potential difference (electrical 'push') trying to send a current through a component is measured in volts on a voltmeter. The voltmeter is wired in parallel with the component.
14　In a series circuit the p.d. across the battery is the sum of the separate p.d.s across each component.
15　Resistance = V/I and has the unit ohm (Ω).
16　At a fixed temperature, metals and some other materials have a constant resistance. This is Ohm's law.
17　The resistance of a pure metal increases with temperature, but for a semiconductor resistance decreases with temperature.
18　A thermistor decreases in resistance when heated.
19　An LDR decreases in resistance when light falls on it.
20　A semiconductor diode lets a large current flow one way only.
21　Electrical energy is measured in joules (J).
22　The electrical energy transformed per second = VI = power.
23　For domestic electrical energy consumption the kilowatt-hour is the unit of energy used.

(b) YOU SHOULD UNDERSTAND

1　Why small objects are attracted by a charged object.
2　The relationship between current and charge summarized by $Q = It$.
3　How the definition of p.d. leads to $W = QV$.
4　The reasons for the change of resistance with temperature for metals and semiconductors.
5　The idea of the electromotive force.
6　The idea of internal resistance.
7　The reasons for the relations: Power = $VI = I^2R = V^2/R$.
8　The safety precautions connected with earthing and fusing.

(c) APPLICATIONS.

You should be able to:
1　apply the equation $Q = It$ for charge;
2　apply the equation $W = QV$ for electrical energy;
3　apply the formula $R = V/I$ for a resistor;
4　describe an experiment to measure resistance;
5　sketch graphs of V against I for a metal at fixed temperature, a filament lamp, and a semiconductor diode;
6　calculate equivalent resistors in series and in parallel;
7　apply the equations power = $VI = I^2R = V^2/R$;
8　calculate domestic electricity consumption and the cost of bills;
9　describe the wiring of a three-pin plug;
10　describe the main features of house wiring including a ring main and its advantages.

MULTIPLE CHOICE QUESTIONS

1　A positively charged rod is placed near to an insulated metal sphere. Which of the diagrams in Fig 6A correctly shows the arrangement of charge on the sphere?

Fig 6A

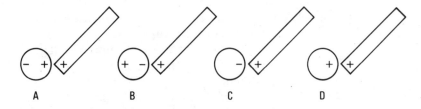

A　　　　B　　　　C　　　　D

2　An insulating rod is charged negatively. This is due to
    A　A deficiency of electrons
    B　An excess of electrons
    C　A deficiency of protons
    D　An excess of protons

The following are four electrical devices:
    A　Variable resistor
    B　LDR
    C　Thermistor
    D　Semiconductor diode
    Which of these

3　varies in resistance according to the light intensity falling on it?
4　allows current to flow one way only?

Two resistors of 20 Ω and 30 Ω are combined. These are possible values for the combined resistance.
    A　12 Ω　　　B　15 Ω　　　C　25 Ω　　　D　50 Ω
    Which gives the correct resistance when they are wired in

5　parallel?
6　series?

7　Which of the circuits shown in Fig 6B can be used to determine the resistance of R?

Fig 6B

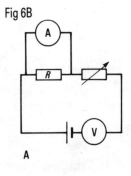
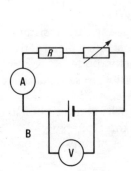
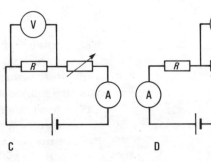

A　　　　　　B　　　　　　C　　　　　　D

A 240 V lamp is rated at 60 W.

8 When it is working correctly the current flowing is

    A ¼ A   B ½ A   C 2 A   D 4 A

9 The resistance of the lamp is

    A 4 Ω   B 60 Ω   C 480 Ω   D 960 Ω

The graphs in Fig 6C show current plotted against voltage for four electrical devices.

Fig 6C
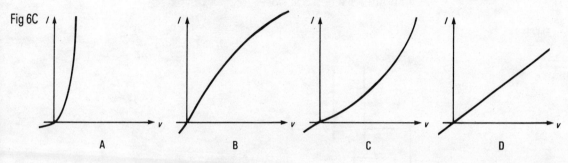

    A   B   C   D

Which gives the correct graph for

10 a fixed resistor?

11 a filament lamp?

12 A 3 kW electric fire is switched on for 20 hours a week. The cost of electrical energy is 5p per unit. What is the cost of the fire in a 3 month period?

    A £12   B £24   C £36   D £48

SHORT ANSWER QUESTIONS

13 Fig 6D shows a thunder cloud near a tall church steeple. The base of the thundercloud is charged negatively. The lightning conductor is broken at the base and is not connected to earth.

Fig 6D
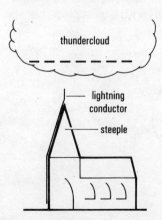

thundercloud

lightning conductor

steeple

(a)   What effect will the cloud have on the free electrons in the metal of the lightning conductor?

(*b*)   Add to the sketch the position of any positive and negative charges on the lightning conductor.
(*c*)   The conductor is repaired and is correctly connected to earth at the base of the steeple. What difference does this make to your answers to (*a*) and (*b*)?

14   In the circuit of Fig 6E the candle is unlit and switch S is closed. No current flows. If the candle is lit, a current is observed on the galvanometer when S is closed.

Fig 6E

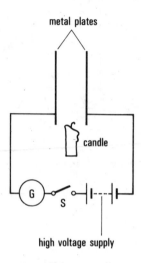

metal plates

candle

high voltage supply

(*a*)   Why does no current flow when the candle is unlit?
(*b*)   Why is there a current when the candle is lit?
    The candle is now lit for 5 minutes with S open. At the end of this time the plates are examined and found to be clean. This experiment is repeated with S closed. At the end of 5 minutes the plates are found to be sooty.
(*c*)   Explain these observations.

15   Fig 6F shows a circuit with a battery, a rheostat and a lamp.

Fig 6F

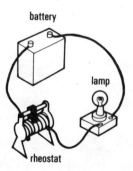

battery

lamp

rheostat

(*a*)   Draw a circuit diagram of this arrangement.
(*b*)   Redraw the circuit diagram adding an ammeter to measure the current in the circuit, and a voltmeter to measure the p.d. across the lamp.

(c)   Explain how you would use this circuit to measure the current through the lamp for various p.d.s across it.

(d)   Sketch the graph of p.d. against current you would expect to obtain.

16 In the circuit of Fig 6G the battery has negligible internal resistance. Calculate:

(a)   the total resistance in the circuit;

(b)   the current flowing in the circuit;

(c)   the p.d. across the 100 Ω resistor.

(d)   The 100 Ω resistor is replaced by a thermistor, and the p.d. across this thermistor becomes 3 V. What is the value of the resistance of the thermistor?

(e)   If the thermistor is heated, what happens to the value of the p.d. across it? Explain your answer.

Fig 6G

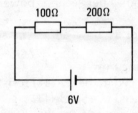

17 A candidate for a GCSE examination sets up the circuit of Fig 6H in order to try to test Ohm's law for the 500 Ω resistor.

Fig 6H

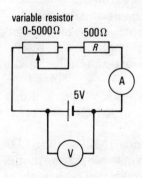

(a)   What is wrong with this circuit?

(b)   The student takes readings of the ammeter and voltmeter for various positions of the rheostat. Sketch a graph of p.d. against current for the results obtained.

(c)   Draw the circuit diagram the student should have used.

(d)   The student now connects up the correct circuit but replaces R with another device X. The readings on the ammeter now vary as the experiment is performed, particularly as the student moves to adjust the rheostat. All the connections are secure, and the battery is not running down. What is X most likely to be? Explain your answer.

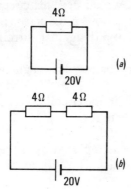

Fig 6I

In the circuit of Fig 6I(*a*) calculate:
(*a*)   the current flowing.
(*b*)   the number of joules per second (power) of heat produced in the 4 Ω resistor.

Another equal resistor is now added in series as in Fig 6I(*b*). Calculate
(*c*)   the current flowing now.
(*d*)   the power produced in the two 4 Ω resistors together.
(*e*)   the power produced in a single 4 Ω resistor.
(*f*)   Comment on the reasons for the difference in the heat produced in a 4 Ω resistor in the two circuits.

19   For safety the circuit for a 3 kW electric kettle which has a metal case is both earthed and contains a fuse.
(*a*)   Why is the kettle earthed?
(*b*)   Why does the circuit contain a fuse?
(*c*)   What may happen if a fault developed and the kettle was earthed but the circuit did not contain a fuse?
(*d*)   What rating of fuse should be fitted in the 3 pin plug of the kettle?
(*e*)   During a week a 2 kW electric fire is used for a total of 30 hours. What is the cost of the electrical energy used if 1 'unit' costs 6p?

20   In a house you might find (i) MCBs, (ii) an LDR, and (iii) an ECLB.
(*a*)   Say where each of these may be found.
(*b*)   Explain the purpose that each might be serving.

MAGNETISM AND ELECTROMAGNETISM

CONTENTS

7.1 MAGNETS

Magnets can be made from alloys of iron, nickel and cobalt. Soft iron is pure iron. It is easy to magnetize but very easily loses its magnetism. This makes it suitable for use in **electromagnets**, which are only magnetic when switched on (p.234). Steel is produced when a small percentage of carbon is added to iron. Steel is much harder to magnetize than soft iron, but keeps its magnetism better. It is therefore more suitable for making permanent magnets. It is possible to make even better permanent magnets using alloys of iron, nickel and cobalt.

When a permanent magnet is suspended as in Fig 7.1, it will swing so that it points approximately north–south. The end which points N is called the 'N–pole'. The other end is the S–pole. Experiments show that

LIKE POLES REPEL and UNLIKE POLES ATTRACT.

Fig 7.1 Suspended magnet

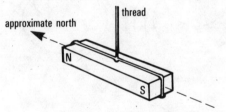

A compass is a small pivoted magnet used for direction finding. A plotting compass is an even smaller pivoted magnet for studying magnetic fields.

7.2 MAGNETIC FIELDS

A magnet produces a **magnetic field** in the space around it. This field can affect other magnets or magnetic materials, as we shall see.

Field lines can be drawn to illustrate the magnetic field. They show the direction in which a small plotting compass would point. Arrows are put on the field lines to show the direction in which the N–pole of the compass points. Fig 7.2 shows the field lines in three cases, and illustrates the direction of small plotting compasses placed in the field.

Iron filings can be quickly used to show the pattern of field lines. A compass is still needed to put arrows on the lines.

Fig 7.2 Magnetic fields of magnets

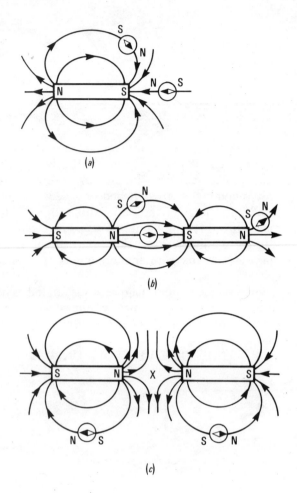

CHECK LIST ▶   Make sure you can answer the following questions.

1   Why is soft iron suitable for electromagnets and steel for permanent magnets?
2   Using a plotting compass, how would you identify which end of a magnet was an N–pole?
3   Sketch the field lines of a bar magnet.

7.3 FIELDS PRODUCED BY CURRENTS

A plotting compass is affected when it is placed near a wire carrying a current. This shows that a magnetic field is produced by the current. The shape of the field lines produced by a wire carrying a current depends on the shape of the wire. Small compasses placed near a straight wire show that the field lines are circular, as shown in Fig 7.3.

Fig 7.3 Field of a straight wire: (a) compass around a straight wire; (b) pattern of field lines; (c) right-hand thumb rule

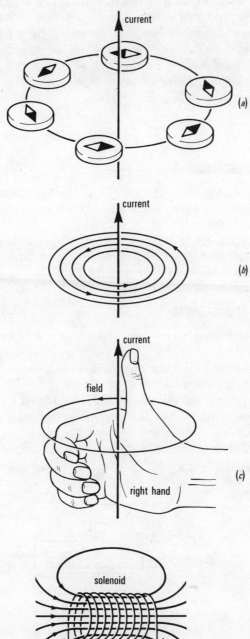

current

current

current

field

right hand

(a)

(b)

(c)

Fig 7.4 Field of a solenoid

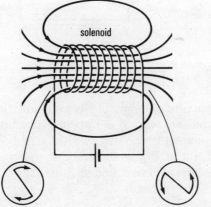

solenoid

A **solenoid** is a long coil of wire. When a current flows through it a field is produced as shown in Fig 7.4. Notice that outside the solenoid the field is rather like that produced by a bar magnet. Inside the solenoid the field lines are straight. The direction of the field lines can be remembered by noting that, when viewed from the end a clockwise current behaves like an S–pole. An anticlockwise current behaves like an N–pole.

7.4 USES OF A SOLENOID

1 MAKING MAGNETS

A permanent magnet can be made by putting the unmagnetized material inside a solenoid. A very large current is then passed through the solenoid for a short time. The very large magnetic field produced inside the solenoid now magnetizes the material. If the material is steel, or a suitable alloy, it remains magnetized when the current in the solenoid is switched off.

2 ELECTROMAGNETS

An electromagnet consists of a solenoid wound on to a **soft iron core**. Soft iron is used as it is very easily magnetized, but loses nearly all its magnetism when the current is switched off. Large electromagnets are used in some cranes, as shown in Fig 7.5. When the current is switched on the electromagnet is energized and an iron or steel load can be lifted. When the current is switched off the electromagnet loses its magnetism and the load is released.

Fig 7.5 Electromagnet in a crane

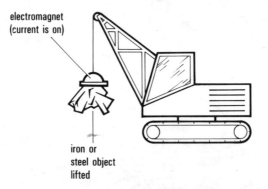

electromagnet
(current is on)

iron or
steel object
lifted

The structure of a simple electromagnet is shown in Fig 7.6. Note that the coils are wound in opposite directions around the two sides of the U-shaped core. This produces an N–pole at one end and an S–pole at the other, as shown. The pattern of field lines produced when the current is switched on is also shown.

Fig 7.6 Electromagnet

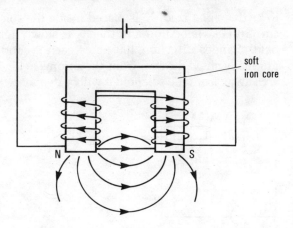

3 RELAYS

A **relay** is used whenever a current in one circuit is required to make a current flow in another circuit. Often this is used in electronic circuits when a small current flowing in a transistor can be used to operate a relay. The relay can then switch on a much bigger current. For a practical example of this sort see p.271.

The structure of a relay is shown in Fig 7.7(*a*). When the switch K is closed, the electromagnet becomes magnetized. This attracts the soft iron strip D so that it touches C. A current can then flow in the circuit connected to X and Y. When K is opened the electromagnet ceases to be magnetized. The springy strip B pulls D away from C. This breaks the circuit between X and Y.

Fig 7.7 Relay

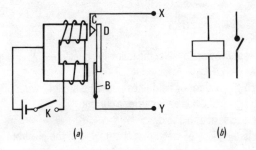

(*a*)   (*b*)

The circuit symbol for a relay is shown in Fig 7.7(*b*).

4 DEMAGNETIZING MATERIALS

It is sometimes required to demagnetize materials. For example if the tape head in a tape recorder becomes magnetized the quality of the sound reproduction is not so good. Materials can be demagnetized by magnetizing them rapidly in alternating directions while the strength of the magnetizing field is gradually reduced. This can be done by using a solenoid carrying **alternating current**. In Fig 7.8 the material to be demagnetized, X, is placed inside the solenoid. The alternating current is switched on and then X is slowly removed. The magnetic field changes direction 100 times each second, and the material is gradually moved away from the strong field. When the material is well away from the solenoid it will be demagnetized.

Fig 7.8 Demagnetizing

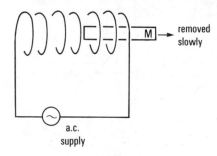

A tape demagnetizer is shown in Fig 7.9. The tip, T, of the core of the solenoid is placed near the tape head. The demagnetizer is now gradually moved away so that the alternating field near the tape head gets gradually weaker.

Fig 7.9 Tape head demagnetizer

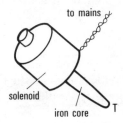

CHECK LIST ▶ Make sure you can answer the following questions.

1 Sketch the pattern of field lines near (i) a straight wire, (ii) a solenoid, (iii) a U-shaped electromagnet when each carries a current.
2 List the uses of a solenoid.
3 Why is the piece of metal that is attracted to the electromagnet in a relay made of soft iron?
4 How can a material be demagnetized?

FORCE ON A CONDUCTOR

7.5 FORCE ON A CURRENT IN A MAGNETIC FIELD

Electric motors work because a force is exerted on a wire carrying a current when it is placed in a magnetic field. A simple experiment to demonstrate this effect is shown in Fig 7.10.

Fig 7.10 Force on a
conductor

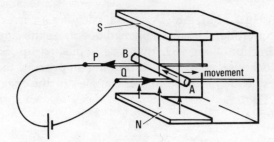

Fig 7.10 Force on a
conductor

The current-carrying movable wire AB is pushed to the right over the fixed wires P and Q. Note carefully that in the diagram PQ is placed at **right angles** to the field. In this case the force is a maximum. There would be no force if the wire were placed parallel to the field. Note that:

1 The force is perpendicular to the field and the current.
2 Reversing either the direction of the current OR the direction of the field makes the force reverse in direction. If both current and field are reversed, then the force is in the same direction as before.
3 The size of the force increases if the current increases.
4 The size of the force increases if the strength of the magnetic field increases.
5 The force is greatest if the wire is at right angles to the magnetic field. It is zero if the wire is parallel to the magnetic field.

The direction of the force can best be remembered using **Fleming's Left-hand Rule**. It states that if the first three fingers of the left hand are held at right angles to each other with the First finger pointing along the Field and the seCond finger along the Current, then the thuMb points in the direction of Motion or force. This is illustrated in Fig 7.11.

Fig 7.11 Fleming's left-hand rule

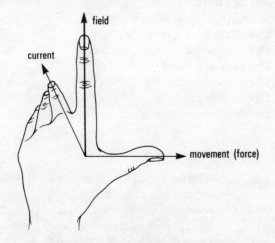

Examples of apparatus which use this effect are moving coil meters and motors. In both instruments there is a coil carrying a current situated in a magnetic field, which we now consider.

7.6 COIL IN A MAGNETIC FIELD

In Fig 7.12(a), ABCD is a coil carrying a current. By Fleming's Left-hand Rule, AB will be pushed down. As the current is in the opposite direction along CD, that side is pushed up. So the coil **turns anti-clockwise**, as shown. If nothing stopped it, the coil would come to rest with its plane at right angles to the magnetic field, as in Fig 7.12(b).

Fig 7.12 Coil in a magnetic field

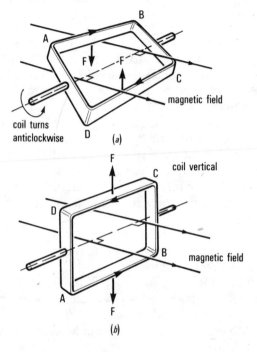

The strength of the turning effect on the coil can be increased by increasing any or all of:

1. The strength of the field.
2. The number of turns on the coil.
3. The area of the coil.
4. The current in the coil.

Modifications can be made to a moving coil to make it work as a meter or as a motor, which we can now discuss.

7.7 MOVING COIL METER

Fig 7.13(a) shows a diagram of the meter. It has

(a)   a rectangular coil abcd
(b)   a powerful magnet with curved poles N and S
(c)   a fixed soft-iron cylindrical core E about which the coil turns
(d)   an axle PQ in jewelled bearings
(e)   springs X and Y
(f)   a pointer and a scale

Fig 7.13 Moving coil meter

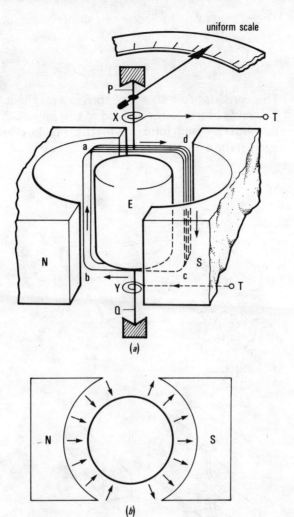

(a)

(b)

The field between the poles, shown in Fig 7.13(b), is called a **radial field** because the field lines point along radii. The coil abcd rotates as explained in the last section. Note that

1 The turning effect remains the same while the coil turns as the coil remains parallel to the field. This is only true because the field is radial.

2 The turning effect is opposed by the springs. This means that the greater the current, the more the coil will turn before the turning effect of the current is cancelled by that of the springs. The angle of rotation is proportional to the current, so the scale is **uniform** – that is the graduations are equally spaced.

   To get a more sensitive instrument, that is to obtain a larger deflection for the same current:

1 The number of turns on the coil can be increased.

2 The magnetic field can be made stronger.

3 The springs can be made of thinner wire so that they twist more easily.

7.8 THE MOTOR

This consists of a coil of wire abcd in a magnetic field, as in Fig 7.14(a). The ends of the coil are joined to two halves, P and Q, of a **split-ring commutator**, which turns with the coil. Two **brushes**, X and Y, press against the commutator as it turns.

Fig 7.14 The motor

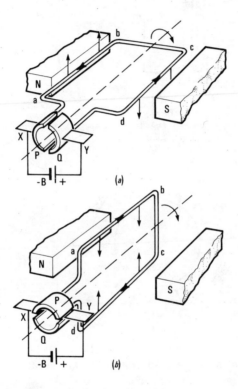

(a)

(b)

Suppose the current flows round the coil in the direction dcba. By Fleming's Left-hand Rule, dc is pushed downwards and ab upwards. The coil therefore turns clockwise. When the coil's momentum takes it just past the vertical, the two halves of the commutator switch brushes. So P now touches Y, and Q touches X, as in Fig 7.14(b). This means the current is **reversed** in the coil. So the forces reverse, as shown, and the coil **continues to turn** clockwise.

The speed and power of a motor can be increased by

1 using a larger current;
2 increasing the strength of the magnetic field;
3 using more turns of wire;
4 increasing the area of the coil.

In most cases the field is made larger by winding the coil on a soft iron core called an **armature**.

7.9 CHARACTERISTICS OF A MOTOR

It is often useful to know how a motor behaves as the load on it changes. Fig 7.15 shows an apparatus for investigating this. A friction belt passes over the shaft of the motor. The difference in reading between the two spring balances is a measure of the load on the motor. This can be increased by tightening the friction belt.

Fig 7.15 Characteristics of a motor

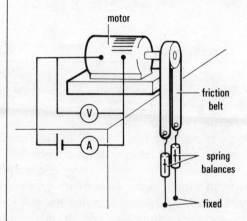

Using this apparatus it is possible to investigate the following:

1   The variation of speed with load. Use a rev counter and stop watch to measure speed. Do this at different loads and plot a graph of speed against load.

2   The variation of power with load. The power is the energy produced per second. This can be found by multiplying the load, by the speed of the edge of the shaft where it rubs on the friction belt. A graph of power against load can be plotted.

3   The variation of efficiency with load. Efficiency is given by

$$\text{Efficiency} = \frac{\text{Mechanical power out}}{\text{Electrical power supplied}} \times 100\%$$

The mechanical power out is measured as in 2. The electrical power supplied is measured by connecting an ammeter in series with the motor and a voltmeter in parallel. The electrical power supplied is then $I \times V$ (p.215). This can be done at various loads and a graph of efficiency against load plotted.

Make sure you can answer the following questions.

1　How can you demonstrate that a wire carrying a current in a magnetic field experiences a force?
2　How can the direction of this force be predicted?
3　What factors govern the size of the force?
4　Why does a coil carrying a current **turn** in a magnetic field?
5　How can a moving coil meter be made more sensitive?
6　What, in the construction of a motor, allows the coil to turn continuously?
7　What factors control the power generated by a motor?

ELECTROMAGNETIC INDUCTION

7.10　EXPERIMENTAL OBSERVATIONS

In Fig 7.16(a), when the magnet X is pushed into the coil, a current flows in the galvanometer G. This illustrates the important fact that when the magnetic field through a coil changes, a potential difference or voltage is produced in the coil. In Fig 7.16(a) it is this p.d. which produces the current flowing in the circuit.

This process is called **electromagnetic induction**, and mechanical energy from the movement of the magnet is transferred to electrical energy. The p.d. produced is called the **induced electromotive force (e.m.f.)**, and the current which results is called the **induced current**.

Fig 7.16 Experimental observations

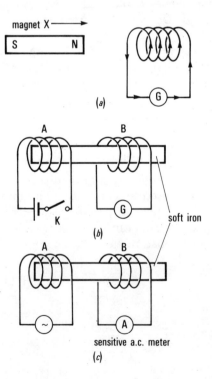

(a)

(b)

soft iron

K

sensitive a.c. meter

(c)

In Fig 7.16(*a*) a current is produced only when the magnet moves relative to the coil. To get an induced current the magnetic field through the coil **must be changing**. Figs 7.16(*b*) and (*c*) show other ways of making the field through coil B change. In Fig 7.16(*b*) the coil, A, produces a changing field whenever the battery switch, S, is closed or opened. When this is done a current flows in B. If a **steady** current flows in A, **no** deflection is seen in G.

In Fig 7.16(*c*), alternating current is now used in coil A. The magnetic field produced in coil B is now always changing, and so there is an alternating current induced. This registers continuously on the a.c. meter.

Soft iron is used in these experiments because it greatly increases the size of the magnetic field (p.231). This increases the size of the induced e.m.f.

7.11 LAWS OF INDUCTION

1 LENZ'S LAW

This states: 'The induced current flows in such a way as to **oppose** the motion or change producing it.'

This may be demonstrated using the apparatus of Fig 7.16(*a*). It will be noticed that the induced current flows so that the left hand end of the coil behaves as an N–pole (p.234). So the current flows in such a direction that the coil **repels** the inwards motion of the magnet. If the N–pole of the magnet were then moved away from the coil, the current direction would be reversed. Now the left hand end of the coil behaves as an S–pole. This attracts the magnet, again opposing its motion.

In general the direction of the induced current is reversed if either the direction of the field **or** the direction of motion is reversed.

2 FARADAY'S LAW

Faraday gave the name **magnetic flux** to the magnetic field lines passing through a coil. Faraday's law states: The size of the induced e.m.f. is proportional to the **rate of change of magnetic flux** linking (i.e. passing through) the coil.

Faraday's Law shows that the following factors help to produce a large induced e.m.f.

(*a*)   rapid change or movement;
(*b*)   large values of field;
(*c*)   large area of coil;
(*d*)   since the e.m.f. is induced in each turn of the coil, a large number of turns also helps to produce a large e.m.f.

7.12 INDUCED E.M.F. IN A STRAIGHT WIRE

An induced e.m.f. can be obtained when a straight wire is moved in a magnetic field. The greatest e.m.f. is produced when the wire is at right angles to the field and moves at right angles to the field. There is no e.m.f. when the wire is moved parallel to the field.

Fig 7.17 E.m.f. in a straight wire

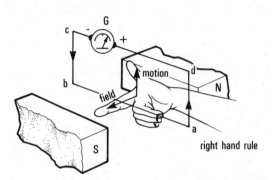

right hand rule

Fig 7.17 shows an apparatus for illustrating this. As the wire ab is moved upwards, it 'cuts' the field lines of the magnet. So there is a change in the field lines linking the circuit abcd. The current direction can be found from Lenz's Law, or more directly, from Fleming's **Right-hand rule**. This is shown in Fig 7.17. The First finger is in the direction of the Field, the thuMb in the direction of the Motion, and the seCond finger in the direction of the induce Current.

| CHECK LIST ▶ | Make sure you can answer the following questions. |

1   Why is there no induced current in a coil situated near to a powerful magnet?
2   Give three ways in which a changing magnetic field can be produced in a coil.
3   What factors could be changed to reverse the direction of the induced current?
4   What factors affect the size of the induced e.m.f.?
5   What is the best way to position and move a straight wire near a magnet to get the greatest induced e.m.f.?

7.13 THE A.C. DYNAMO OR ALTERNATOR

A **dynamo** is a machine for producing electrical energy from mechanical energy. This is the opposite of a motor which produces mechanical energy from electrical energy. Basically, a dynamo consists of a coil rotating in a magnetic field.

In Fig 7.18 the coil abcd is made to rotate clockwise. As it does so, the sides ab and cd of the coil move across the field lines. In the position shown, ab moves up and cd down. Fleming's Right-hand rule shows that the currents induced in ab and cd flow as shown. The ends of the coil are connected to two rings R_1 and R_2 which rub against carbon brushes P and Q. These connect the coil to the outside circuit

Fig 7.18 A.c. dynamo

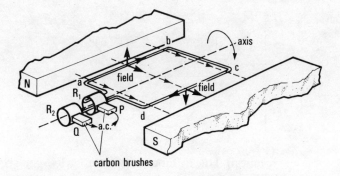

in which the current is required. Fig 7.19 shows a simpler diagram showing just the coil.

Fig 7.19 Action of a.c. dynamo

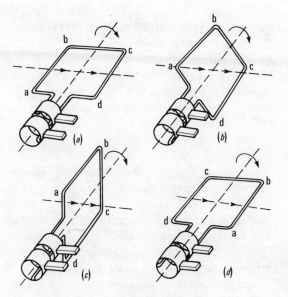

As the coil rotates to the position shown in Fig 7.19(b), the sides ab and cd are no longer moving at right angles to the field. This means that the size of the e.m.f. is less (p.244). In Fig 7.19(c) the sides of the coil are moving **parallel** to the field and so the e.m.f. is zero. After this ab starts to move down through the field and cd moves upwards. The e.m.f. now reverses. In Fig 7.19(d) the e.m.f. is numerically the same as in Fig 7.19(a), but is in the reverse direction.

This means that **alternating e.m.f.** and **alternating current** (a.c.) are produced by the dynamo, as illustrated in Fig 7.20. The points marked (a) to (d) show the e.m.f.s produced in the positions corresponding to Fig 7.19 (a) to (d).

The greatest e.m.f. produced is called the **peak** e.m.f. Similarly the greatest current which flows as a result is called the **peak** current. The time for one complete cycle of the a.c. is called the **time period**. This is the same as the time taken for the coil to turn through one complete

Fig 7.20 E.m.f. from a.c.
dynamo

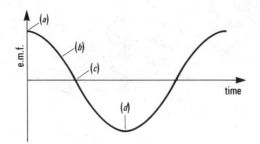

rotation. The number of whole cycles per second is called the **frequency** of the a.c. and is measured in hertz (p.147). Time period and frequency are related by:

Time period = 1/Frequency.

For domestic mains electricity the peak e.m.f. is 340 volts, the frequency is 50 Hz, and the time period is $\frac{1}{50}$th second.

The e.m.f. or voltage produced by a dynamo may be increased by ·
(a)   increasing the rate of rotation;
(b)   increasing the strength of the magnetic field. For example by winding the coil on a soft iron armature;
(c)   increasing the number of turns on the coil.

7.14 TAPE RECORDER HEADS

In a tape recorder the recording head relies on the fact that an electric current produces a magnetic field. Fig 7.21 shows a record head with the tape moving across it. The record head is a small electromagnet and as a current flows through it a magnetic field is produced, as shown. This magnetizes a layer of magnetic material on the tape.

If a microphone is providing the current to the tape head, the current varies as the sound pressure on the microphone. So the magnetic signal on the tape stores these variations of sound pressure as variations of magnetization.

Fig 7.21 Tape recorder
'record' head

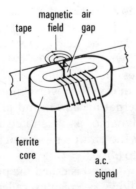

The playback head works on the principle of electromagnetic induction. The structure of the head is very similar to the record head

– in some tape recorders the same head serves both purposes. When the tape moves past the head the changes in magnetization produce a changing magnetic field. This induces a current in the coil of the head. This current is then amplified and fed to the loudspeaker.

| CHECK LIST ▶ | Make sure you can answer the following questions. |

1 Why does the current from a dynamo change direction with each half turn of the coil?
2 List the factors which increase the voltage produced by a dynamo.
3 What is alternating current, and what is meant by its frequency?
4 What principle is used by (a) the record head, (b) the playback head in a tape recorder?

7.15 THE TRANSFORMER

The purpose of a transformer is to change the **voltage** of an alternating current supply. A **step-up** transformer increases the alternating voltage; a **step-down** transformer decreases it. The transformer consists of two coils wound on a soft iron core, as in Fig 7.22. The supply voltage V_{in} is connected to the **primary** coil, and the voltage produced V_{out}, is obtained from the **secondary** coil.

Fig 7.22 The transformer

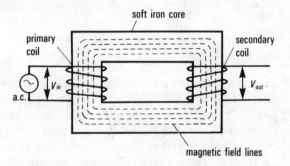

If there are n_p turns on the primary and n_s turns on the secondary then for an ideal transformer,

$$\frac{V_{out}}{V_{in}} = \frac{n_s}{n_p}$$

n_s/n_p is called the **turns ratio**. If n_s is greater than n_p, then V_{out} is greater than V_{in} and the transformer steps up the voltage. For a step-down transformer n_s is less than n_p.

7.16 ENERGY IN A TRANSFORMER

Most of the energy supplied to the primary of a transformer is transferred to the secondary. Only a small amount of energy is wasted as heat in the transformer itself. This means the **efficiency** of the transformer is high. The efficiency of any machine (p.52) is defined by,

$$\text{efficiency} = \frac{\text{output power}}{\text{input power}} \times 100\%$$

Now, electrically power $= IV$. So if I_p is the current flowing in the primary, and I_s is the current in the secondary, then the input power is $I_p V_{in}$, and the output power is $I_s V_{out}$. So for a transformer,

$$\text{efficiency} = \frac{I_s V_{out}}{I_p V_{in}} \times 100\%$$

Note carefully that the transformer cannot create energy. The output power must always be less, or equal to, the input power. If the transformer steps up the voltage, then although the secondary produces a higher voltage than the primary, the current it can supply is less than in the primary.

7.17 ENERGY LOSS IN A TRANSFORMER

In practice energy losses in a transformer are caused by
(a)   heat produced in the primary and secondary coils. This can be reduced by making the resistance of these coils as low as possible.
(b)   heat produced by currents induced in the soft iron core. These are called **eddy currents** and can be reduced by making the electrical resistance of the core as high as possible. This is done by making the iron core of thin laminations, separated by insulating paint.

7.18 HOW A TRANSFORMER WORKS

The alternating current in the primary of a transformer produces an alternating magnetic flux in the soft iron core. Fig. 7.22. This flux passes through the secondary coil. Since the flux is alternating, an induced voltage will be produced in the secondary coil.

Note carefully that there is **no** electrical connection between the primary and secondary coils – the coils are insulated from each other and from the soft iron core.

WORKED EXAMPLE

A transformer working from 240 V mains has 20 turns on the secondary and gives an output voltage of 12 V. The efficiency of the transformer is 90% and it is used to light a 12 V lamp which draws a current of 4 A. Calculate
(a)   the number of turns on the primary, and
(b)   the primary current.
(a) $\dfrac{V_{out}}{V_{in}} = \dfrac{n_s}{n_p}$

So $\qquad \dfrac{12}{240} = \dfrac{20}{n_p}$

and $\qquad n_p = 400$ turns.

(b) $\qquad \dfrac{I_s V_{out}}{I_p V_{in}} = 90\% = 0.9$

So $\qquad \dfrac{4 \times 12}{I_p \times 240} = 0.9$

and $\qquad I_p = 0.22$ A

7.19 GENERATION OF ELECTRICITY

An alternating current generator or alternator was discussed on p.244. Generators in power stations use the same principles. The generator can be turned in a variety of ways. In coal- and oil-powered stations the fuel is first burned to produce heat. The heat is used to boil water and produce steam at high pressure. The steam is passed through a **turbine**. This has a complicated system of fan blades on a central shaft. As the steam forces its way through the turbine the shaft is made to rotate. This shaft is coupled to the alternator which generates the electricity. Fig 7.23 shows a block diagram of such a power station.

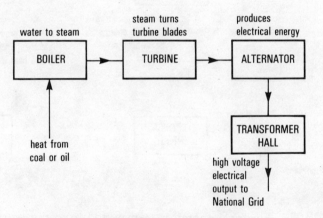

Fig 7.23 Block diagram of power station

In a nuclear power station the arrangement is basically similar, but a nuclear reactor is used to generate the heat. This process is dealt with in more detail on p.302.

In a hydroelectric power station, the turbines are not turned by steam, but by water. Water in a high lake is allowed to fall through pipes. The water pressure on the blades of the turbine causes it to rotate as the water flows through.

The energy flow in these types of power station is illustrated in Fig 7.24.

Fig 7.24 Energy flow in
power stations

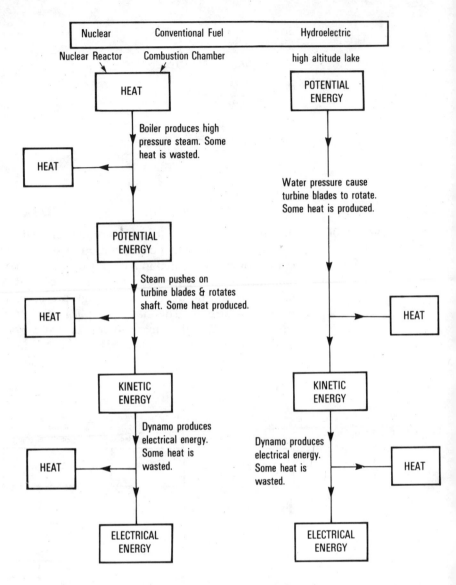

7.20 TRANSMISSION OF ELECTRICAL ENERGY

Electrical energy is transmitted from the power station along cables called a **transmission line**. These cables are generally supported on pylons which can be seen stretching across the countryside. Occasionally special underground cables are used.

The cables have some small resistance R, and so heat will be produced in them when a current flows. This heat will be energy wasted. The heat produced per second is I^2R and so for the heat loss to be as small as possible, I must be small. Now power $P = VI$. So to transmit a large power, the voltage V must be **large** in order that I can remain small. In this way the power transmitted (VI) can be high, whilst keeping the heat loss in the cables (I^2R) to a minimum.

To achieve this, **transformers** are used. The electrical energy from the alternator, at about 11 000 volts, is stepped up to a very high voltage (e.g. 400 000 volts) by means of a transformer. This is then transmitted over the large distances all over the country. It is then transformed down, in stages, to usable safe voltages near the consumer.

Transformers will not operate on direct current (d.c.). To be able to transmit at high voltages and so reduce energy wastage, alternating current (a.c.) must be used.

7.21 THE NATIONAL GRID SYSTEM

The electrical energy from a power station feeds the **National Grid System**. This is a system of transmission cables linking all the power stations. This enables the Central Electricity Generating Board (CEGB) to cope with faults in any power station. If a particular generator becomes faulty the energy it would normally produce can be replaced by increasing the power output from other power stations. Without the grid system each power station would supply energy to a particular area. A power station fault would then leave that area without electricity.

The main 'super-grid' system operates at very high voltages, nearly 400 000 volts, for long distance transmission of energy. For consumption by large factories and industry this is transformed down to about 11 000 volts. For consumption in the home this is further reduced to 240 volts.

CHECK LIST ▶

Make sure you can answer the following questions.

1 Draw a diagram of a transformer and name the main parts.
2 What is the difference between a step-up and a step-down transformer?
3 A transformer operates from 240 V mains and produces a p.d. of 24 V. What can you say about the number of turns on the primary compared with the number of turns on the secondary?
4 What are the reasons for energy loss in a transformer?
5 What are (a) the differences, (b) the similarities between a coal and a nuclear power station?
6 Why must a.c. be used for transmission of electrical power?

SUMMARY

(a) YOU SHOULD KNOW

1 Iron, steel, cobalt and nickel are magnetic materials.
2 Iron is easily magnetized and demagnetized. Steel and other alloys are harder to magnetize and demagnetize.
3 Like poles repel, unlike poles attract.

4 A suspended magnet points N–S.
5 A magnet produces a magnetic field.
6 An electric current produces a magnetic field.
7 A wire carrying a current in a magnetic field experiences a force.
8 The factors which affect the size of the force on a current-carrying conductor.
9 A coil carrying a current in a magnetic field experiences a turning effect.
10 The factors which govern the size of the turning effect on a current carrying coil in a magnetic field.
11 The factors governing the sensitivity of a moving coil meter.
12 A changing magnetic flux through a coil produces an induced e.m.f.
13 The factors which affect the size of the induced e.m.f. in a coil.
14 A straight wire moving across a magnetic field produces an induced e.m.f.
15 The factors which affect the size of the induced e.m.f. produced by an alternator.
16 A transformer can be used to step up or step down an alternating voltage.
17 The names of the main parts of nuclear, conventional and hydro-electric power stations, together with their function.
18 Electrical energy is transmitted at high voltage to minimize energy wastage.

(b) YOU SHOULD UNDERSTAND

1 How to identify the poles of a magnet using a plotting compass.
2 Why a current carrying coil in a magnetic field experiences a turning effect.
3 The action of a split-ring commutator in a motor.
4 How to use Lenz's law to find the direction of the induced current.
5 How the size of the induced e.m.f. in a straight wire is affected by the direction of motion of the wire.
6 Why an alternator produces an alternating e.m.f.
7 The principles of tape recorder 'record' and 'replay' heads.
8 The operation of a transformer.
9 Why high voltage transmission reduces energy loss.
10 The purpose of the National Grid system.

(c) APPLICATIONS.

You should be able to
1 sketch the field pattern of a bar magnet.
2 sketch the field pattern of a straight wire and a solenoid.
3 describe the uses of a solenoid – making magnets, electromagnets, relays, demagnetizing.
4 find the direction of the force on a wire carrying a current in a magnetic field.
5 describe the structure of a moving coil meter.

6 describe the structure of a motor.
7 describe the structure of an alternator.
8 describe the structure of a transformer.
9 use the formula $V_{out}/V_{in} = n_s/n_p$.
10 use the formula efficiency $= (I_s V_{out}/I_p V_{in}) \times 100\%$.

QUESTIONS 7. MAGNETISM AND ELECTROMAGNETISM

MULTIPLE CHOICE QUESTIONS

The following are electrical devices.
    A motor   B moving coil meter   C dynamo
D relay
    Which of these
1 works on the principle of electromagnetic induction?
2 has a split-ring commutator?

3 Fig 7A shows a wire carrying a current in a magnetic field.

Fig 7A

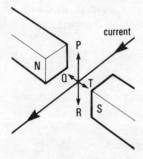

The wire will experience a force in the direction
    A P   B Q   C R   D T
4 Fig 7B shows a straight wire carrying a current.

Fig 7B

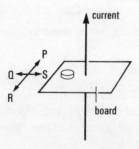

The small compass shown will point in the direction
    A P   B Q   C R   D S
5 In which of the following applications is a solenoid **not** used?
    A tape head demagnetizer   B electromagnet
    C moving coil meter   D relay

The following are four principles concerned with electro-magnetism.

    A A wire carrying a current produces a magnetic field.

    B A wire moving in a magnetic field has an e.m.f. induced in it.

    C A wire carrying a current in a magnetic field experiences a force.

    D A changing magnetic field through a coil produces an induced e.m.f. in the coil.

Which of these is most closely associated with

6   an electromagnet?

7   a motor?

8   Which of the following facts does **not** help explain why a moving coil meter has a uniform scale?

    A The pointer is made of a very light material.

    B The turning forces on the coil are proportional to the current.

    C The coil moves in a radial magnetic field.

    D The turning forces due to the springs are proportional to the angle turned through.

9   A transformer has a primary p.d. of 240 V and a secondary p.d. of 12 V. The number of turns on the primary is 200. The number of turns on the secondary is

    A 10   B 20   C 2000   D 4000

The following are parts of a power station.

    A combustion chamber   B turbine

    C dynamo   D transformer

Which of these converts

10 electrical energy into electrical energy?

11 chemical energy to heat energy?

12 Which of the following statements about the National Grid System is **not** true?

    A Electrical energy is transmitted at high voltage.

    B The system uses d.c.

    C Transformers are used at the power station.

    D Underground cables can be used to transmit electrical energy.

SHORT ANSWER QUESTIONS

13 (*a*)   Fig 7C(*a*) shows a magnet and some plotting compasses near to it. One compass is marked with the direction it points. Complete the diagram showing the direction of the other compasses, and mark in the poles of the magnet.

      (*b*)   In Figs 7C(*b*) and (*c*) mark in the compass directions similarly. Also show the direction of the current flowing in the straight wire and solenoid respectively.

Fig 7C

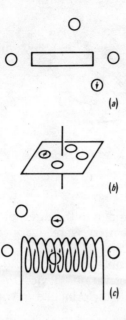

(a)

(b)

(c)

14 Fig 7D shows a relay connected to a motor circuit.

Fig 7D

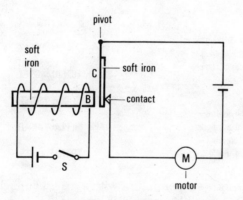

(a)   When S is closed what happens to the soft iron core B?
(b)   What now happens to the soft iron piece C?
(c)   Why does the motor now stop?
(d)   How could the structure of the relay be modified so that when S is closed the motor starts rather than stops?
(e)   Why would a relay not work properly if B were made of steel rather than soft iron?

15 Fig 7E shows a simple d.c. motor.
(a)   State 3 ways of improving the performance of such a motor.
(b)   Add arrows at each point marked X showing the direction of current flow.
(c)   In the position shown the side ab of the coil is pushed upwards. Why is the side cd pushed downwards?

Fig 7E

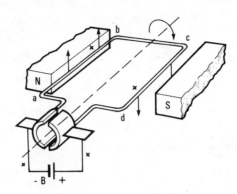

(d)   What would happen to the direction of rotation of the motor if the terminals of the battery were swapped over, and the poles of the magnet interchanged?

16   Fig 7F shows three principles concerned with electromagnetism. Also shown are the names of various devices. Add to the diagram lines connecting each device to the principle on which it operates.

Fig 7F

A current-carrying
wire produces a
magnetic field

a current-carrying wire
in a magnetic field
experiences a force

a wire moving in
relation to a magnetic
field has an e.m.f.
induced in it

ALTERNATOR

TAPE "RECORD" HEAD

MOTOR

RELAY

ELECTROMAGNET

MOVING-COIL METER

TAPE "REPLAY" HEAD

TRANSFORMER

17   Fig 7G shows a pendulum with a magnet attached to its ends. At the instant shown the magnet is moving upwards towards the coil, and the centre zero galvanometer G deflects to the right.

Fig 7G

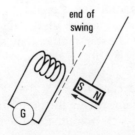

end of
swing

(a)   What will be the reading on G when the magnet reaches the end of its swing?

(*b*)   What happens to the reading on G as the magnet swings downwards away from the coil?

(*c*)   Suggest two ways of modifying the apparatus so as to increase the greatest deflection on G.

(*d*)   If the coil and G are removed, the swings of the pendulum do not die away as quickly as when the coil and G are present. Explain why this is so.

18   Fig 7H shows a transformer.

Fig 7H

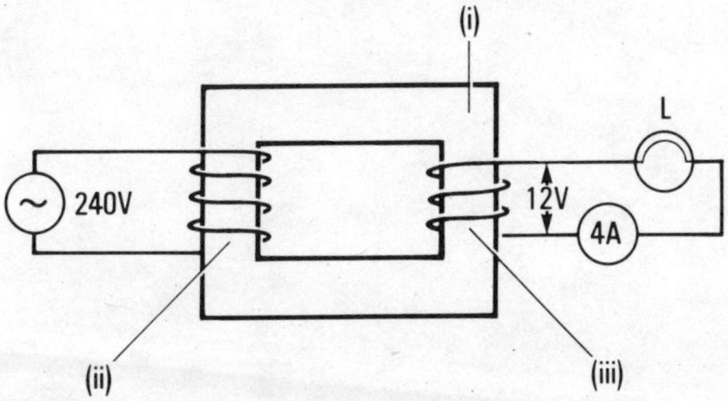

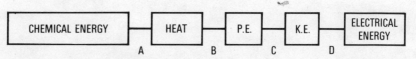

(*a*)   State the name of part (i) of the transformer, and of the two coils (ii) and (iii).

(*b*)   There are 20 turns on coil (iii). Use the data marked on the diagram and calculate the number of turns on coil (ii).

(*c*)   Calculate the power consumption of the 12 V lamp L.

(*d*)   What power is supplied by the mains if the transformer were 100% efficient?

(*e*)   Give two reasons why practical transformers are not 100% efficient.

19   In the transmission of electrical energy over the National Grid:

(*a*)   Why is a very high voltage used for long distance transmission?

(*b*)   Why cannot such high voltages be used in the home?

(*c*)   How are safe voltages obtained for domestic use?

(*d*)   Why must alternating current be used for power transmission?

(*e*)   What advantages has the National Grid over a system where local power stations supply power to the nearby area?

20   Fig 7I shows a simplified energy flow diagram for a conventional power station.

Fig 7I

CHEMICAL ENERGY		HEAT		P.E.		K.E.		ELECTRICAL ENERGY
	A		B		C		D	

(*a*)   State the names of the components A, B, C and D in the power station which are responsible for the energy changes shown.

(*b*)   A power station wastes energy at various points in this sequence. Redraw the diagram showing where energy is wasted.

(*c*)   Give the reason for each loss of energy you have shown.

ELECTRONICS

CONTENTS

In this chapter we look at how a cathode ray **oscilloscope** works. This uses electron streams moving in a vacuum. The rest of the chapter will deal with **solid state** devices. We shall first consider the **semiconductor diode** and its uses in a power supply. Then the **transistor** and how it is used as a switch in control or alarm circuits. Finally we shall consider the uses and functions of **logic gates**.

PRODUCTION OF ELECTRON STREAMS AND THE OSCILLOSCOPE

8.1 THERMIONIC EMISSION

A metal contains electrons which are free to move. It is the one-way movement of these electrons which carries the current in a metal (p.204).

If a metal is heated, some of the free electrons may gain sufficient energy to escape from the metal. This is rather like heating water to 'boil off' some of the water molecules as vapour. The process of emission of electrons from a hot metal is called **thermionic emission**. Electrons are more easily emitted if the metal is coated with an oxide of barium or strontium.

This effect is used in the production of an electron beam in a cathode ray oscilloscope, as we now see.

8.2 STRUCTURE OF CATHODE RAY TUBE

The cathode ray tube used in an oscilloscope is shown in Fig 8.1.

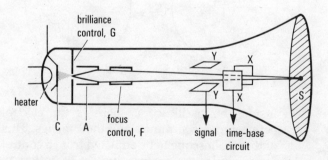

Fig 8.1 Cathode ray tube

It contains:

1 A **heater** heating a metal **cathode** C. The heater 'boils off' electrons from the cathode by thermionic emission.

2 An **anode** A. There is a high positive p.d. between the anode and

cathode so that the electrons emitted from the cathode are strongly attracted to the anode. There is also a small hole in the anode through which the accelerated electrons can pass.

3   An electrode G, used as a **brightness control**. It is positioned between A and C and has a negative potential applied to it which can be varied by turning the brightness control knob. The greater the negative potential of G, the fewer electrons will pass through it and the fainter the spot on the oscilloscope face will appear.

4   An electrode F, which together with A, acts as an electron lens. The p.d. between A and F is varied to **focus** the electrons to give a sharp spot on the screen.

5   Two pairs of plates, XX and YY. Voltages applied to the X-plates are used to deflect the electron beam sideways, whereas voltages connected to the Y-plates deflect the beam vertically.

6   A **screen** S, coated with a fluorescent material which glows when struck by high-energy electrons. S is connected to the anode by painting the inside of the tube with conducting paint. This ensures that electrons lose no energy after passing through the anode, and prevents a build up of static charge on the screen.

8.3 THE Y-PLATES

The Y-plates are connected to the Y-terminals on the front panel of the oscilloscope. Suppose that a p.d. from a battery is connected to these terminals, so that the top Y-plate is positive and the bottom one negative. The electrons in the beam will experience an upward force as they pass through the plates – remember that electrons are negatively charged. This will cause the spot on the screen to deflect upwards, as in Fig 8.2(a). If the battery connections are reversed the spot will be deflected downwards as in Fig 8.2(b).

Fig 8.2 Use of Y-plates

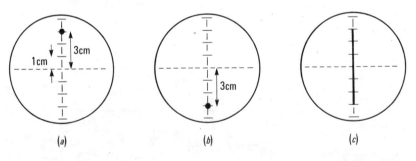

(a)   (b)   (c)

Inside the oscilloscope there is an electronic circuit connected between the Y-terminals and the Y-plates. This allows the **sensitivity** of the oscilloscope to be adjusted from a control on the front panel. If, for example, the control was set at 2 V/cm then an input of 2 V is needed to deflect the spot vertically by 1 cm. In Fig 8.2(a) and (b) the spot is deflected by 3 cm. So the potential difference supplied by the battery must be $3 \times 2 = 6$ V. The oscilloscope can therefore be used as a **voltmeter**. If we had a much higher p.d. to measure of about 50 V, then the sensitivity control would be altered to perhaps 20 V/cm. In this case we would obtain a deflection of 2.5 cm for a 50 V input.

If an a.c. signal of 50 Hz is connected to the Y-terminals the spot moves up and down very rapidly. A straight line is seen on the screen as shown in Fig 8.2(c).

8.4 THE TIME-BASE

An oscilloscope has an internal circuit which causes a special varying voltage to be applied to the X-plates. This has the effect of making the spot 'sweep' across the screen from left to right at a uniform speed and then 'fly back' very quickly. The speed at which the spot crosses the screen can be controlled from the front panel of the instrument. When the time-base is on, the oscilloscope will display a graph of the signal voltages applied to the Y-terminals against time. Fig 8.3(a), (b) and (c) show how the traces of Fig 8.2 appear when the time-base is switched on.

Fig 8.3 Use of time-base

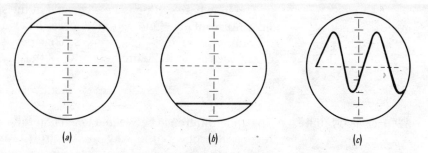

(a)   (b)   (c)

The time-base control on the front panel is calibrated to show the time taken by the spot to cross each cm of screen. For example, 1 ms/cm means that the spot moves horizontally 1 cm in a time of 1 ms (1 millisecond = $\frac{1}{1000}$th of a second). Fig 8.4 shows how this can be used to measure time intervals. Here A is a sonar signal (p.155) emitted by a ship, and B is the trace from the echo. The time base is set at 0.1 s/cm. The distance between the emitted signal trace A, and the reflected trace is 4.5 cm. So the time between signal and reflection is $0.1 \times 4.5 = 0.45$ s. This can then be used to find the distance of the reflecting object from the ship as described on p.155.

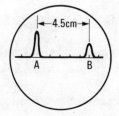

Fig 8.4 Sonar signals

WORKED EXAMPLE

The trace seen on an oscilloscope is shown in Fig 8.5. The sensitivity of the oscilloscope is set as 5 V/cm, and the time base setting is 1 ms/cm. Find the peak voltage and frequency of the a.c. signal.

Fig 8.5 Worked example

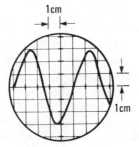

The peak vertical displacement is 3 cm, and each cm vertically corresponds to 5 V. So the peak voltage is $5 \times 3 = 15$ V.

The time base setting is 1 ms/cm so that the spot takes 1 ms to move 1 cm horizontally. One complete cycle takes up to 5 cm, so the time for one cycle is $5 \text{ ms} = \frac{5}{1000}\text{ s} = \frac{1}{200}\text{ s}$. This means that there must be 200 cycles each second. So the frequency of the a.c. signal is 200 Hz.

8.5 TELEVISION TUBES

The chief difference between a television tube and a tube in a cathode ray oscilloscope is the way the electron beam is deflected. In the oscilloscope the electron beam is deflected by the **electric field** set up when a p.d. is applied to the X- or Y-plate.

In a television tube, coils around the neck of the tube set up a **magnetic field**. Since electrons carry negative charge they will be deflected by this magnetic field in the opposite direction to that predicted by Fleming's Left-hand Rule. The advantage of using magnetic deflection for a TV tube is that the electron beam can be deflected through much bigger angles. So the tube can be made much shorter than would be possible with electric deflection.

CHECK LIST ▶   Make sure you can answer the following questions.

1   In an oscilloscope tube what is the purpose of (a) the heater, (b) the cathode, (c) the anode and (d) the X- and Y-plates?

2   A battery is connected to the Y terminals of an oscilloscope and the spot deflects 3 cm vertically. The sensitivity of the oscilloscope is set at 0.5 V/cm. What is the p.d. across the battery?

3   Explain what it means if the time-base of an oscilloscope is set at 2 ms/cm. (1 ms = 1/1000 s.)

SEMICONDUCTOR DIODES AND POWER SUPPLIES

8.6 THE SEMICONDUCTOR DIODE

As we saw on p.211 a semiconductor diode has a very high resistance to the flow of electricity in one direction, but a very low resistance to the flow in the other direction. Effectively this means that it acts like a 'valve' and will allow the flow of an electric current one way only. As a reminder the circuit symbol for a diode is shown in Fig 8.6. The arrow shows how conventional current (positive charge) would flow.

Fig 8.6 Circuit symbol of a diode

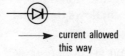

current allowed this way

When a voltage is applied to a diode to produce a current in the allowed direction this is called a 'forward' voltage. If the voltage is reversed in direction so that no current flows it is called a 'reverse' voltage. Although a diode has a low forward resistance, it will not conduct unless the forward voltage is greater than about 0.6 V. This fact is sometimes important in circuit design.

In the next few sections we shall consider how diodes can be used to produce a steady d.c. supply from a.c. mains. A device to do this is called a d.c. **power supply**. Power supplies are needed in all radio, hi-fi and television equipment to give the steady d.c. needed to operate the transistor circuits.

8.7 HALF-WAVE RECTIFICATION

The process of producing a d.c. supply from an a.c. supply is called **rectification**. The simplest circuit to achieve this is shown in Fig 8.7(a). Note how a transformer is represented in circuit diagrams.

Fig 8.7 Half-wave rectification

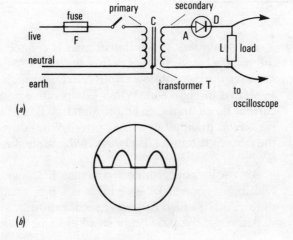

(a)

(b)

The circuit consists of:

1 A transformer T to change the mains voltage to the required value. Note that the switch to the transformer is in the live wire. This ensures that no part of the circuit can become live when the power is switched off. Also note that the soft iron core of the transformer, C, is earthed. This ensures that if a fault developed in the insulation of the primary coil so that the core became live, then a current would flow to earth blowing the fuse F. (See p.219 for a discussion of mains safety.)

3 A single diode D. When the terminal A of the secondary is positive then a current can flow through D and the load, L. The load represents the circuit requiring the d.c. supply. When A is negative no current flows. So the current flows through L one way only.

DISADVANTAGES OF HALF-WAVE RECTIFICATION

An oscilloscope can be used to show the variation of p.d. across the load with time. The trace produced is shown in Fig 8.7(*b*). Note that although the p.d. is never negative, it is not steady. Most electronic devices require a steady p.d. A way of improving the situation is to use a **bridge rectifier**, which we now consider.

8.8 THE BRIDGE RECTIFIER

A circuit containing a bridge rectifier is shown in Fig 8.8(*a*).

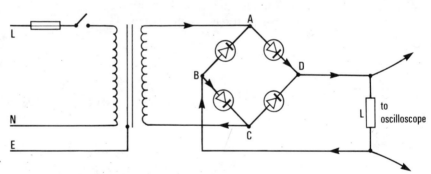

Fig 8.8(*a*) Bridge rectifier

The secondary of the transformer is connected to A and C and so the voltage between these points alternates. When A is positive and C negative the current flows from A to D, through L to B, and then to C, as shown in Fig 8.8(*a*). When C is positive and A negative then the current flows from C to D, through L to B, and then to A as shown in Fig 8.8(*b*). In either case the current flows downwards though L. So the current through L is always in the same direction and is therefore d.c.

An oscilloscope connected across L shows the variation of p.d. with time. Fig 8.8(*c*). Since there is a p.d. during both half cycles of the a.c. this is called **full-wave rectification**.

Although the p.d. has a steadier value than with a single diode,

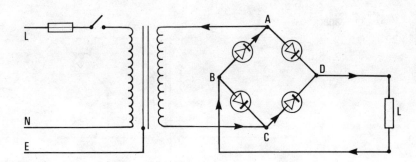

Fig 8.8(b)

Fig 8.8(c)

there is still not a steady p.d. The situation can be improved by adding a capacitor as we now see.

USE OF A CAPACITOR IN A POWER SUPPLY

A capacitor is a device which can store charge and so store energy. It consists of two conducting plates separated by an insulator. Its symbol is shown in Fig 8.9.

Fig 8.9 Circuit symbol of a capacitor

A power supply circuit using a capacitor is shown in Fig 8.10(a). The capacitor can store charge during the time when the current from the bridge rectifier is at its greatest. It can then supply current to the load when the output from the bridge rectifier falls. This process is illustrated in Fig 8.10(b). The voltage across the load now fluctuates much less, as shown. If the load takes a large current, then it is harder for the capacitor to supply the extra current when the output from the rectifier falls. So in this case there are greater variations of p.d.

Fig 8.10 Use of a capacitor
for 'smoothing'

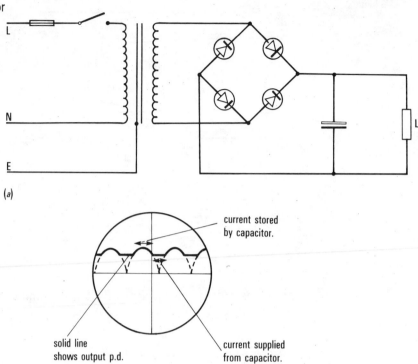

(a)

(b)

CHECK LIST ▶   Make sure you can answer the following questions.

1   Draw the circuit symbol of a diode and a capacitor.
2   State briefly the important properties of (a) a diode and (b) a capacitor which make them useful in circuits.
3   Draw a diagram of a bridge rectifier circuit which includes a capacitor.
4   Sketch a graph of p.d. against time for the output of the power supply of question 3, (a) with the capacitor present, and (b) if the capacitor were removed.

THE TRANSISTOR

8.9 THE TRANSISTOR AS A SWITCH

Fig 8.11 shows the circuit symbol of a transistor. It has three electrodes, the emitter, collector and base, as shown.

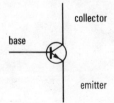

Fig 8.11 Circuit symbol of a transistor

The applications we consider later use the transistor as a **switch**. Fig 8.12(*a*) shows a circuit containing a transistor. Note that the emitter is connected to the negative of the battery, and the collector is connected to the positive via a lamp L. As the circuit stands, the lamp would not be lit. The transistor is behaving as a switch in the **OFF** position. To make the lamp light, the p.d. between the base and the emitter must be greater than about 0.6 V.

Fig 8.12 Transistor as a switch

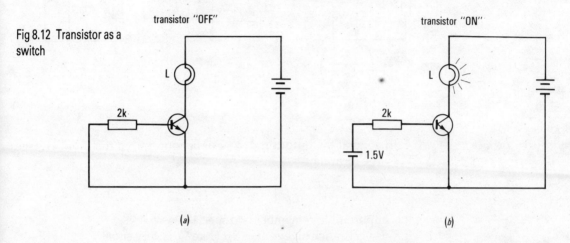

transistor "OFF"

transistor "ON"

L

2k

L

2k

1.5V

(*a*)

(*b*)

The circuit of Fig 8.12(*b*) shows a battery connected between base and emitter. This has a p.d. of 1.5 V and so the transistor will act like a switch in the **ON** position. The lamp L will light.

The 2 kΩ (= 2 000 Ω) resistor is to protect the transistor. Without the resistor the current flowing into the base from the battery would be large and damage the transistor.

To make use of this switching property of the transistor we must first consider the potential divider circuit.

8.10 THE POTENTIAL DIVIDER

Fig 8.13(*a*) shows a potential divider circuit. It consists of two resistors in series across a supply. It produces an output p.d. across one of the resistors, as shown. The purpose is to divide the applied potential by a given amount.

Consider for example the case when $R_1 = R_2$, Fig 8.13(*b*). The current through each resistor is the same since they are in series. So the p.d. across each must be the same. If the supply has a p.d. of 6 V, then the p.d. across each resistor will be 3 V. So the output voltage across R_2 is 3 V, which is half the applied p.d.

Now think of the case where $R_1 = 2R_2$, Fig 8.12(*c*). In this case the p.d. across R_1 will be double that across R_2 as it has the same current and twice the resistance ($V=IR$). So here the p.d. across R_1 is 4 V and the p.d. across R_2 is 2 V. Note that the p.d.s have to add up to the 6 V of the supply. In this instance the output voltage is one third of the applied p.d.

Fig 8.13 Potential dividers

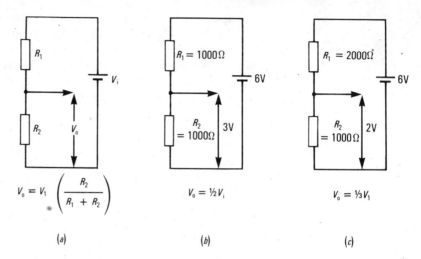

$$V_0 = V_1 \left(\frac{R_2}{R_1 + R_2} \right)$$

(a)

$$V_0 = \frac{1}{2} V_i$$

(b)

$$V_0 = \frac{1}{3} V_1$$

(c)

In general the output p.d. V_0 can be found from the input voltage V_i by the formula

$$V_0 = V_i \left(\frac{R_2}{R_1 + R_2} \right)$$

It is important to remember two special cases:

1   If R_1 is very much bigger than R_2. Here V_0 is very small.
2   If R_1 is very much less that R_2. Here V_0 is practically the same as V_i.

8.11 POTENTIAL DIVIDER WITH A TRANSISTOR

Fig 8.14 shows a potential divider circuit connected to a transistor. R_2 is a variable resistor.

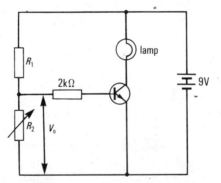

Fig 8.14 Potential divider with a transistor

When R_2 is set to be very small, R_1 is much greater than R_2, and so V_0 is practically zero. The p.d. between base and emitter is therefore very small and the transistor is in the OFF state. As R_2 is increased, V_0 becomes bigger. There will come a point when the base emitter voltage exceeds 0.6 V, and the transistor will be in the ON state. The lamp will now light.

This idea may be used to construct a variety of alarms, as we now see.

8.12 USE OF TRANSISTOR IN A LIGHT ALARM CIRCUIT

Fig 8.15 shows a circuit where the lamp L comes on when the light falling on the LDR (p.211) is cut off.

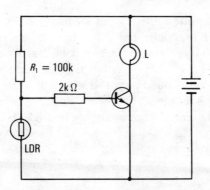

Fig 8.15 A light alarm switch

When the LDR is illuminated its resistance R_2 is about $1000\,\Omega$. R_1 is much greater than this, so V_0 is very small. The transistor is therefore off and L does not light. When the LDR is in the dark its resistance rises to some millions of ohms. R_1 is now much less than R_2, so V_0 is near the p.d. of the supply. This switches the transistor ON, and L lights.

This circuit forms the basis of an alarm to switch on house lights automatically as its gets dark. House lights work from a.c. and use too great a current to work directly from a transistor. To switch on the house lights a relay circuit must be incorporated as in Fig 8.16.

Fig 8.16 Circuit to switch lights on at evening

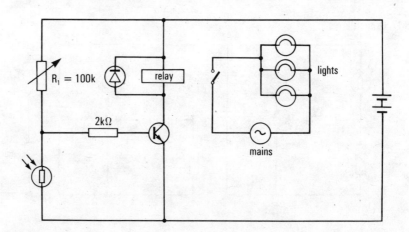

Note:

1 When the transistor switches ON a current flows through the relay. This closes switch S which switches on the house lights.

2   R_1 is a variable resistor. This can be used to adjust the precise level of light at which the relay operates.

3   There is a diode connected across the relay which protects the transistor from damage when the current through the relay is switched off.

▼ REASON WHY DIODE IS NEEDED

When the current in the relay is switched off by the transistor, there is a change of magnetic field through the relay and so there is an induced voltage. This voltage can be large enough to damage the transistor. The diode prevents this. The induced p.d. is opposite in direction to the applied p.d. and so can produce a current through the diode. At this moment the diode acts like a short circuit and prevents the induced voltage from being big enough to damage the transistor. Under normal circumstance the diode has a reverse p.d. across it and ▲ so no current flows through it.

8.13   OTHER ALARM CIRCUITS

Similar circuits to that just discussed can be made to operate other types of alarm. For example:

1   A circuit where a light L comes on when the illumination falling on a LDR increases, Fig 8.17(a). This is the opposite of the alarm we have just discussed.

2   A temperature alarm which comes on when the temperature of a thermistor (p.211) gets too high, Fig 8.17(b).

3   A frost alarm which comes on when the temperature of a thermistor gets too low, Fig 8.17(c).

Alarms 2 and 3 use the fact that the resistance of a thermistor decreases greatly as its temperature rises.

Fig 8.17 Other alarms

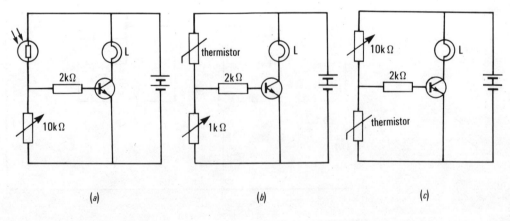

(a)   (b)   (c)

CHECK LIST ▶ Make sure you can answer the following questions.

1 The p.d. between the base and emitter of a transistor is 0.1 V. Is the transistor on or off?
2 The p.d. between base and emitter of a transistor is 1 V. Is the transistor on or off?
3 A 1 kΩ resistor is in series with a 4 kΩ resistor. The p.d. across the two resistors is 10 V. What is the p.d. across the 1 kΩ resistor?
4 In a circuit to switch on lights when it gets dark:
  (a)   Why is a resistor placed in series with the base of the transistor?
  (b)   Why is a diode placed across the relay coil?
  (c)   What is the name of the device which is sensitive to the changes of light intensity?
5 Sketch a circuit diagram of an alarm which might operate a motor to open the windows of a greenhouse when it gets too hot in the greenhouse. How could the temperature at which the motor operated be adjusted?

LOGIC GATES

8.14 DIGITAL CIRCUITS – LOGIC STATES

A traffic light control system must make the red, orange and green lights go on or off in the correct order at the correct times. The electronic signals in the control system need only be voltages which go ON and OFF. An electronic system of this type is called a **digital system**. An amplifier in a hi-fi unit produces a voltage which alternates in a complicated way and which represents the sound signal it is reproducing. This is called an **analogue system**. We shall consider only digital systems in the rest of this chapter.

Since a voltage is either on or off it is usual to represent the full ON voltage by '1'. Zero voltage or OFF is represented by '0'. The full voltage is also said to be 'high', and zero voltage is called 'low'.

Fig 8.18 A gate circuit using relays

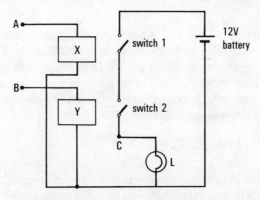

A logic circuit is shown in Fig 8.18. Two relays X and Y each have one terminal connected to the negative of the battery. The other terminals are connected to A and B respectively. When A is connected to 12 V, switch 1 closes. When B is connected to 12 V, switch 2

closes. If both A and B are connected to 12 V then both switches close. In this case C is connected to the 12 V supply and the lamp L lights up. The behaviour of the circuit can be summarized by the following table:

Voltage at A	Voltage at B	Voltage at C
0	0	0
12	0	0
0	12	0
12	12	12

Using the notation of '1' to represent the full 12 V, and '0' to represent zero voltage the table can also be written:

A	B	C
0	0	0
1	0	0
0	1	0
1	1	1

A table like this is called a **truth table**.

An arrangement where one or more inputs control an output is called a **gate**. Here two inputs A and B control the voltage at C. This arrangement is called an **AND** gate since A and B both need to be high to make C high. Most gates in electronic circuits use **integrated circuits** which operate electronically, rather than using relays. We now discuss such devices.

8.15 GATES

There are five gates commonly used in circuits. The **NOT, AND, OR, NAND** and **NOR** gates. The **NOT** gate simply converts a high (on) input into a low (off) output and vice versa. It is also called an **INVERTER**.

As we have just seen an **AND** gate only gives an output if both inputs are on.

An **OR** gate gives an output if either input is on.

A **NAND** gate gives an output which is exactly the opposite of an **AND** gate. It is exactly like an **AND** gate followed by a **NOT** gate.

A **NOR** gate gives an output which is exactly the opposite of an **OR** gate. It is exactly like an **OR** gate followed by a **NOT** gate.

These facts are summarized in Fig 8.19 which gives the circuit symbols for the gates and their truth tables.

Fig 8.19 Types of gate

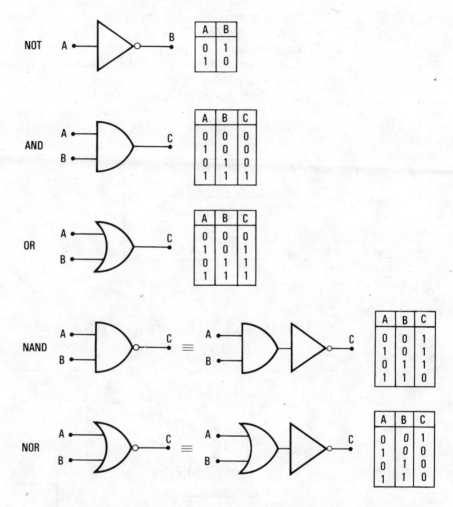

NOT

A	B
0	1
1	0

AND

A	B	C
0	0	0
1	0	0
0	1	0
1	1	1

OR

A	B	C
0	0	0
1	0	1
0	1	1
1	1	1

NAND

A	B	C
0	0	1
1	0	1
0	1	1
1	1	0

NOR

A	B	C
0	0	1
1	0	0
0	1	0
1	1	0

8.16 LIGHT EMITTING DIODES

To show whether the output of a gate is on or off a light emitting diode (LED) may be used. This behaves as a semiconductor diode but light is emitted when a current flows through it. It is possible to manufacture LEDs to emit red, green or yellow light. The circuit symbol for an LED is shown in Fig 8.20(*a*). It is usual in any circuit to include a resistor in series with the LED to prevent too large a current flowing which may damage it. This is shown in Fig 8.20(*b*).

Fig 8.20 Light emitting
diode (LED)

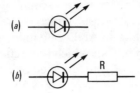

(a)

(b)

8.17   LATCHES

If a burglar sets off an alarm by opening a window we would want the alarm to continue to ring even if the burglar promptly shuts the window again. An electronic device for doing this is called a latch. Fig 8.21 shows a block diagram of a latch. Input B is connected to 0 V. The output is OFF. If input A is momentarily touched to the 5 V supply, the output will go ON and stay on even when A is removed from the 5 V supply. Lamp L will then stay alight. To reset the latch to off, B must be momentarily touched on to the 5 V supply.

Fig 8.21 Electronic latch

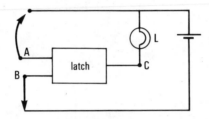

8.18   APPLICATIONS OF GATES

1 HEATING CONTROL FOR AN ELECTRIC KETTLE

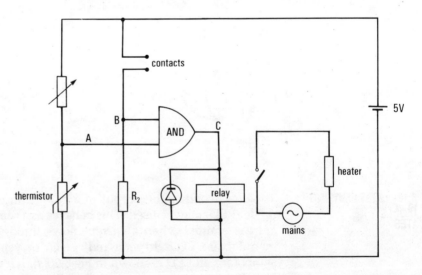

Fig 8.22 Heater control on a kettle

Fig 8.22 shows a suitable circuit. The two contacts protrude into the kettle above the heating element. If there is water in the kettle there will be a fairly low resistance between these contacts, much less than R_2. Input B of the **AND** gate will be high. So if input A is high, the output of the gate will be high and the heating element will switch on. If there is no water in the kettle, the resistance between the contacts is higher than R_2 and the input B of the gate will be low. So the output of the gate is bound to be off whatever the value of A. This ensures that the heater cannot come on if there is no water in it.

Input A is used to switch the heater off when it reaches the required temperature. The thermistor is placed so that it has the same temperature as the water. As the water heats up the resistance of the thermistor will fall and the voltage at input A of the **AND** gate will fall. The output at C will fall and the heater will be switched off.

Note carefully why the **AND** gate is helpful. The heater will come on only if there is water in the kettle **AND** the water is not too hot.

2 A BURGLAR ALARM

Fig 8.23 shows a circuit of a burglar alarm using a latch. The switches 1, 2 and 3 are on windows or doors. There may be any number of switches in series. Normally all switches are closed and so input A of the latch is low.

If a burglar enters and causes a switch to open, even for a split second, then the output of the latch will go high and the alarm will sound.

Fig 8.23 A burglar alarm

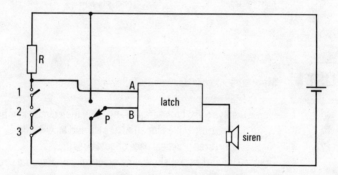

The latch can be reset so that the alarm stops sounding by pressing button P. This momentarily connects input B of the latch to the 5 V supply and causes the output to switch over to the 'off' state.

8.19 COMBINATIONS OF GATES

Fig 8.24 shows two gates interconnected. There are three inputs A, B and C and one output E. We can work out the behaviour of this circuit as follows.

Fig 8.24 Combination of gates

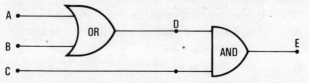

E will be high only if C and D are both high, since the second gate is an **AND** gate. D will be high if either A or B is high, since the first gate is an **OR** gate. So E is high if C is high, and either A or B (or both) is high.

A practical use of this could be in an alarm to warn a car driver that a door is open. A and B would be connected to switches in the doors. These would be arranged to make the input go high if the door was open. C would be connected to a switch under the driver's seat. The driver's weight would operate the switch and cause C to go high.

If the driver was not seated, doors could be opened without the alarm going off. With the driver seated ready to drive off, the alarm would sound if either door (or both) were open. A circuit with switches arranged to achieve this is shown in 8.25.

Fig 8.25 Car door alarm

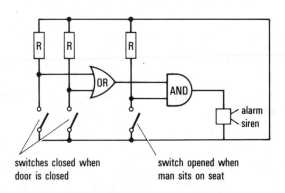

switches closed when
door is closed

switch opened when
man sits on seat

CHECK LIST ▶

Make sure you can answer the following questions.

1   Name the five main types of gate and draw their circuit symbols.
2   Write out the truth tables for an AND gate and an OR gate.
3   State clearly three practical uses of gate circuits.
4   Draw a circuit diagram showing a practical use of a gate circuit. Give a brief explanation of how it works.

SUMMARY

(a) YOU SHOULD KNOW

1   The names of the main parts of the cathode ray tube.
2   What is meant by half-wave rectification.
3   The disadvantages of half-wave rectification.
4   The arrangement of diodes in a bridge rectifier.
5   What is meant by full-wave rectification.
6   The output of a bridge rectifier can be smoothed by adding a capacitor across the output.

7   The circuit symbol for a transistor and the names of the three electrodes.
8   A transistor can be used as an electronic switch.
9   The base of transistor needs a series resistor to prevent damage to the transistor.
10 A relay used in a transistor circuit has a reverse diode placed in parallel with the relay coil. This prevents damage to the transistor.
11 In digital circuit a high (ON) voltage is represented by '1' and a low (OFF) voltage is represented by '0'.
12 The names of the five main types of gate and their circuit symbols.
13 An LED is a diode which emits light. It is useful in indicating the state of a logic output (on or off).

(b) YOU SHOULD UNDERSTAND

1   What is meant by thermionic emission and how it occurs.
2   How a C.R.O. can be used to measure p.d. by using the Y-plates and the sensitivity control.
3   The purpose of a time-base on an oscilloscope.
4   Why, in a power supply,
    (a)   a transformer is needed.
    (b)   the live side of the primary has a switch and a fuse.
    (c)   the core of the transformer is earthed.
5   Why a bridge rectifier produces full-wave rectification.
6   Why a capacitor across the output produces a smoother d.c. from a power supply, and why the smoothness is not so good if the load takes a large current.
7   How a potential divider circuit operates.
8   How an LDR can be used with a transistor to produce light-activated switches.
9   Why a diode connected across a relay coil in transistor circuits protects the transistor from damage.
10 How a thermistor can be used with a transistor to produce temperature activated switches.
11 How a truth table describes the behaviour of a gate.
12 How combinations of gates can be used for a wide variety of purposes.

(c) APPLICATIONS

You should be able to:
1   describe the function of the main parts of a cathode ray tube.
2   calculate p.d.s applied to an oscilloscope from the screen deflection and the number of V/cm read from the sensitivity control.
3   calculate frequency and time intervals using screen waveforms together with the time-base setting.
4   calculate the output voltage from a potential divider given the input voltage and the value of the resistors.
5   explain the action of a light operated switch.
6   explain the action of a temperature operated switch.

7   describe some practical uses of gate circuits.
8   work out the behaviour of circuits containing more than one gate.

QUESTIONS 8 ELECTRONICS

MULTIPLE CHOICE QUESTIONS

The following are parts of a cathode ray tube:
    A X-plates   B anode   C heater   D cathode
    Which of these
1   accelerates the electrons?
2   deflects the electron beam horizontally?

The following graphs show waveforms displayed on an oscilloscope:

Fig 8A

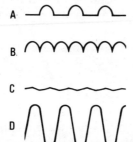

Fig 8B shows a bridge rectifier circuit.

Fig 8B

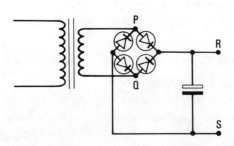

Which of the graphs best indicates the p.d.
3   across PQ?
4   across RS?

Fig 8C shows four transistor circuits.

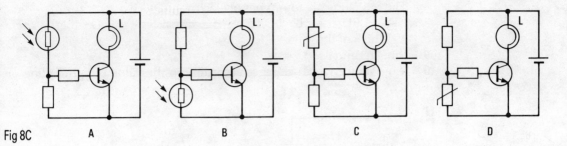

Fig 8C   A   B   C   D

Which of the circuits causes lamp L to light when

5 a temperature gets too low?

6 a light intensity gets too low?

Fig 8D shows the circuit symbols for four types of gate.

Fig 8D

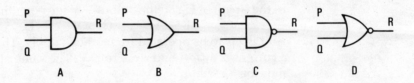

A   B   C   D

Which of these has the following truth tables?

7

P	Q	R
0	0	1
1	0	1
0	1	1
1	1	0

8

P	Q	R
0	0	0
1	0	1
0	1	1
1	1	1

The following are four types of electronic device.

A LED   B LDR   C transistor   D thermistor

Which of these has

9 three terminals?

10 a resistance which changes according to the value of light falling on it?

11

Fig 8E

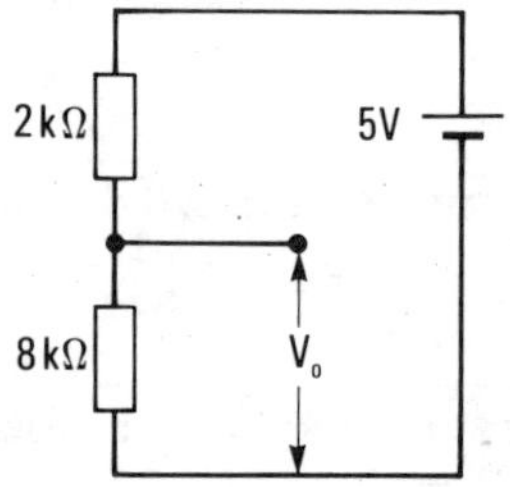

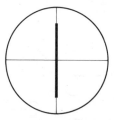

In the circuit of Fig 8E the output V of the potential divider is

A 0 V   B 1 V   C 4 V   D 5 V

12 An LED is to be operated from a 12 V supply. The LED operates with a current of 10 mA and a p.d. of 2 V. The value of the series resistor R must be

A 10 Ω   B 100 Ω   C 1000 Ω   D 10000 Ω

SHORT ANSWER QUESTIONS

13 (a) Draw a diagram of a cathode ray tube labelling the main parts.

(b) Explain the purpose of the X- and Y-plates.

(c) Fig 8F shows a trace on an oscilloscope screen. Explain why a line is seen, when the electrons strike the screen at a single point.

Fig 8F

14 Fig 8G(a) shows a trace seen on an oscilloscope screen, and Fig 8G(b) shows the position of the sensitivity and time-base controls on the front panel.

(a) What is the peak voltage of the signal?

(b) What is the frequency of the signal?

State and explain the effect on the trace of

(c) turning the sensitivity control one place to the right.

(d) turning the time-base control one place to the left.

Fig 8G

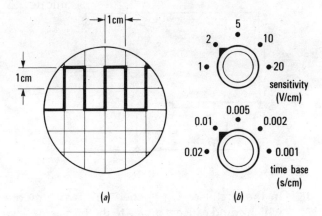

(a) (b)

15 Fig 8H shows a bridge rectifier circuit using four diodes P, Q, R and S.

Fig 8H

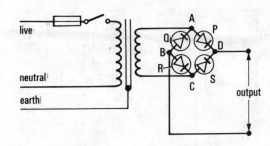

(a) When A is positive with respect to C, through which two diodes does the current flow?

(b) When A is negative with respect to C, through which two diodes does the current flow?

(c) Sketch a graph showing the output waveform.

(d) Where should a capacitor be connected to 'smooth' the output waveform?

(e) Why does the output still fluctuate slightly if the load takes a large current?

16 In the power supply circuit of Fig 8H

(a) Why is the on/off switch put in the live side of the primary coil?

(b) The primary circuit is also fused, and the transformer core is earthed. Why are both of these precautions needed?

17 Fig 8I shows a circuit for investigating the behaviour of a transistor as a switch.

(a) Describe what happens to the reading on the voltmeter as R_2 is increased from zero to a value much greater than R_1.

(b) Describe what happens to the lamp L during this process.

Fig 8I

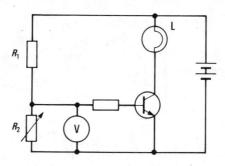

18   In the circuit of Fig 8J there are two components missing, each of which could cause damage to the transistor.

Fig 8J

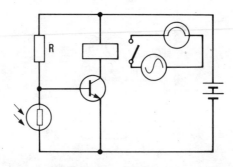

(a)   Redraw the circuit adding the two components.
(b)   Given that the relay switch is normally open, state and explain whether the lamp is lit when the LDR is in the dark or light.
(c)   How could the circuit further be modified so that the level of illumination at which the lamp operates could be adjusted?

19   Fig 8K shows two **NOT** gates connected to the input of an **AND** gate.

Fig 8K

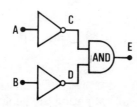

(*a*) Complete the truth table for this circuit.

A	B	C	D	E
0	0	1		
1	0	0		
0	1	1		
1	1	0		

(*b*) Write down the truth table for an **OR** gate.

(*c*) Explain why the circuit of Fig 8K is exactly equivalent to a **NOR** gate.

20 In a traffic light sequence the green light only comes on when the red and orange lights are both off.

(*a*) Complete the following truth table for the signals. Use '0' to mean off, and '1' to mean on.

	R	0	G
1	0	0	
2	0	1	
3	1	0	
4	1	1	

(*b*) Which line of the truth table represents:
(i) STOP?
(ii) GET READY TO GO?
(iii) GO?

(*c*) To control the green light, the red and orange signals could be connected to the inputs of a gate, and the green to the output. State and explain which type of gate is suitable for this purpose.

ATOMIC STRUCTURE AND RADIOACTIVITY

CONTENTS

INTRODUCTION

In this chapter we shall describe the structure of the atom. Radioactivity, which comes from the nucleus of the atom, will also be discussed. Finally we shall consider the way nuclear reactors work, and look at some of the problems of generating electricity from nuclear power.

9.1 ATOMIC STRUCTURE

There are three types of particle which form atoms; electrons which move in most of the space of the atom, and protons and neutrons which are confined to a tiny nucleus.

1 ELECTRONS

These are particles carrying a **negative charge** of 1.6×10^{-19}C, and which have a mass of about $\frac{1}{2000}$th of the mass of a hydrogen atom. Electrons move throughout the space inside atoms.

2 PROTONS

These are particles carrying a **positive charge** of 1.6×10^{-19}C, numerically equal to the charge on the electron. Their mass is about 2000 times greater than that of an electron. Protons are confined to the nucleus of the atom, and for hydrogen the nucleus is a single proton. Protons exist in the nucleus of all atoms.

3 NEUTRONS

These are particles which have very nearly the same mass as a proton, but which carry **no charge**. They exist in the nuclei of all atoms except hydrogen. The table below shows a summary of these facts.

Particle	Charge	Mass (electron=1)	Where found
Electron	-1.6×10^{-19}C	1	In all space around nucleus
Proton	$+1.6 \times 10^{-19}$C	~2000	In the nucleus
Neutron	0	~2000	In the nucleus

9.2 PROTON AND MASS NUMBERS

Two numbers are used to describe the number of the various particles in the atom.

(a) THE PROTON NUMBER, Z

This is also know as the **atomic number**. It is equal to the number of protons in the nucleus. An atom is electrically neutral, so the number of positive protons is equal to the number of negative electrons. So the proton number is also the number of electrons in a neutral atom.

The number of electrons decides how the atom behaves chemically. So it is the proton number which decides the element to which the atom belongs. For example, all atoms having Z=8 are oxygen atoms; all atoms for which Z=17 are chlorine atoms.

(b) THE MASS OR NUCLEON NUMBER, A

This is the **total** number of particles, protons and neutrons, in the nucleus. Any particle in the nucleus is called a nucleon, so A is the number of nucleons. Since the electrons are very light, nearly all of the mass of an atom is in the nucleus. A therefore gives an approximate indication of the mass of atom.

The number of neutrons in the nucleus is A–Z, since the number of protons is Z.

The information about an atom X is written $^{A}_{Z}X$. So $^{234}_{90}Th$ shows that the element Th – thorium – has 90 protons in the nucleus, and 234 protons and neutrons altogether. So the number of neutrons is 144. Note that if Z were **not** 90, then the element would **not** be thorium.

9.3 IONS

An atom is electrically neutral, but often an atom can gain, or lose an electron. In sodium chloride (common salt), each sodium atom gives up an electron which is gained by a chlorine atom. The atoms are no longer neutral and are called **ions**. The chlorine ions are negative, since they have gained an electron. The sodium ions are positive since they have one too few electrons to balance exactly the positive charge of the protons in the nucleus. The electrical attractive forces between these positive and negative ions hold the ions together to form the solid sodium chloride.

CHECK LIST ▶   Make sure you can answer the following questions.

1   Which particle has nearly the same mass as a proton?
2   Which particle has an equal but opposite charge to a proton?
3   Which particle moves in most of the space of the atom, but has only a tiny fraction of the mass of the atom?

4   In the element protoactinium $^{234}_{91}$Pr, how many electrons are there moving around the nucleus in a neutral atom? How many protons and how many neutrons are there in the nucleus?

9.4 ISOTOPES

Isotopes are atoms with the same number of protons but different numbers of neutrons. Chlorine, for example, exists with two naturally occuring isotopes. One isotope has 17 protons and 18 neutrons, and can be written as $^{35}_{17}$Cl. The other isotope has 17 protons and 20 neutrons and so can be written $^{37}_{17}$Cl. Note that each isotope must have 17 protons in order to be chlorine.

The average chemical relative atomic mass of chlorine is about 35.5, nearer to 35 than 37. This is because there are more atoms of $^{35}_{17}$Cl than of $^{37}_{17}$Cl in naturally occurring chlorine.

As we shall see later some isotopes emit radioactive particles. These are called **radioactive isotopes**.

RADIOACTIVITY

9.5 RADIOACTIVE SOURCES

A radioactive source is one which emits high energy particles or radiation. These emissions

(a)   come from the nuclei of atoms in the source, and

(b)   can have enough energy to knock electrons out of atoms which they meet on their path. Atoms which receive this treatment therefore become ions, and we say that the radioactive particles produce **ionization**.

The particles emitted are alpha (α) and beta (β) particles, and the radiation emitted is gamma (γ) radiation. Their nature is discussed later. Sources may emit α, β, or γ-rays singly, or in a mixture.

The fact that radioactive sources ionize atoms means that they can damage cells in the human body. In school laboratories the sources are weak and will not produce any ill effects unless mishandled. Some simple laboratory rules include:

1   Always handle sources with special tongs. These are long handled to keep the hands and body as far from the source as possible. The radiation from radioactive sources gets weaker with increasing distance.

2   During an experiment keep as far as is reasonable from the source – for the same reason as above.

3   As soon as the experiment is finished, the source should be replaced in its lead box. Lead is a material which is an effective absorber of radioactivity as we shall see later.

Stronger sources used in research or handled in the nuclear waste industry need much greater precautions, including the use of remote handling devices.

Radioactivity is unaffected by changes of temperature or pressure or chemical combination of the atoms because such changes do not affect the nucleus of an atom. There is no way of stopping a source being radioactive other than by waiting until the radioactivity dies down – often a very long time. This is the main reason for the problem in dealing with the radioactive waste from power stations (p.302).

9.6 RADIATION DETECTORS

1. GEIGER-MULLER (GM) TUBE

This consists of a metal tube with an inner wire electrode insulated from it, as in Fig 9.1. The tube which is sealed by a thin mica 'window', contains gas at low pressure. A p.d. of a few hundred volts is maintained across the terminals T.

Fig 9.1 Geiger-Muller tube

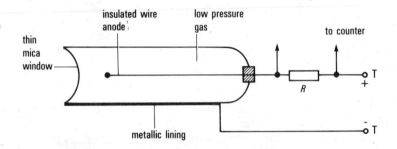

The GM tube relies on the ionizing property of the radioactivity in order to work. When an ionizing particle enters the GM tube a short 'pulse' of current flows through R. This sets up a voltage 'pulse' across R which can be counted on a suitable instrument (p.293).

2. SOLID STATE DETECTOR

This is a semiconductor device which produces short pulses of current when struck by an ionizing particle. These pulses can be amplified and fed to a counter.

3. DIFFUSION CLOUD CHAMBER

This allows the tracks of single α- and β-particles to be made visible. It consists (Fig 9.2) of a Perspex box and lid D, with a metal plate P dividing it into two compartments. A small quantity of alcohol is poured into the upper compartment and dry ice (solid carbon dioxide) is packed into the lower lagged compartment L. The source N is mounted as shown.

The alcohol vapour near P is cooled to a very low temperature by the dry ice and becomes 'supersaturated'. Ions are produced along the track of the radioactive particle and these attract alcohol molecules making them cluster together and so form droplets. A light

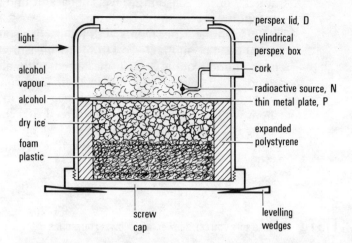

light

perspex lid, D

cylindrical
perspex box

alcohol
vapour

cork

alcohol

radioactive source, N

thin metal plate, P

dry ice

expanded
polystyrene

foam
plastic

screw
cap

levelling
wedges

Fig 9.2 Diffusion cloud
chamber

illuminates the top compartment so that trails of cloud droplets are
seen along the path of the radioactive particle.

9.7 COUNTERS AND RATEMETERS

1. SCALER

This is an electronic device which counts the number of voltage
pulses from a GM tube or solid state detector. To find the count rate it
is necessary to divide the count shown on the scaler by the time taken
for the count. This gives the number of counts per second, which is a
measure of the intensity or activity of the radiation received by the
GM tube or solid state detector.

2. RATEMETER

This gives a direct reading on a meter of the intensity of the radiation.
The meter is calibrated directly to read the number of counts per
second.

9.8 BACKGROUND RADIATION

A GM tube connected to a ratemeter will give a reading (a few counts
per second on average), even with no radioactive source present. This
is called **background** radiation. It has a number of origins;

1 Cosmic rays which come from outer space.
2 Naturally occuring radioactive material found in the Earth's surface.
3 Man-made radiation released from the testing of nuclear weapons or
from disasters such as occurred at the Chernobyl power station
explosion in 1986.

Under normal circumstances the background radiation is harmless,
but can reach dangerous levels in accident situations such as Cher-

nobyl. For this reason the levels of background radiation are carefully monitored.

In scientific experiments with radioactive sources, the background count must be subtracted off from any measured count. To do this the background count is first measured with all radioactive sources removed to a good distance in their lead containers. Suppose the background count is 3 per second measured in this way. The experiment with the source is now performed. If a count rate in the experiment is 26 per second, then this must be corrected to 26−3 = 23 counts per second. This gives the true count rate from the source alone.

CHECK LIST ▶

Make sure you can answer the following questions.

1 What is meant by an isotope?
2 Name the three different types of radiation.
3 List the safety precautions needed when using radioactive sources in a school laboratory.
4 Name two detectors which can be used to count radioactive particles.
5 Can you see individual radioactive particles in a cloud chamber? What actually is visible in a cloud chamber?
6 Why is it important to monitor the background count?
7 Why must the background count be measured in laboratory experiments with radioactive sources?

9.9 PROPERTIES OF α- AND β-PARTICLES AND γ-RAYS

1. α-PARTICLES

These need a solid state detector or special GM tubes with thin mica windows to detect them. This is because they are absorbed by thin thicknesses of material. A piece of paper placed between an α-source and a detector is found to absorb most of the α-particles. Moving a source gradually away from a detector shows that the particles have a definite range of a few centimetres in air.

α-particles are the most strongly ionizing of the three types of radiation. A single α-particle can ionize many thousands of air molecules along each millimetre of its path. For this reason they do not travel very far in air before they have lost all their kinetic energy. Similarly they are quickly absorbed in solid materials.

α-particles can also be detected in a diffusion cloud chamber. Thousands of ions are produced along the track of a single particle, and this enables droplets of cloud to form easily along their path.

2. β-PARTICLES

These can easily be detected in a GM tube. β-particles do not produce such strong ionization as α-particles and are therefore not so easily absorbed. They can be stopped by a few millimetres of aluminium, but are not significantly affected by a single sheet of paper. Because they only produce weak ionization they are much harder to observe in a cloud chamber. β-particles have no definite range in air, but the number received by a GM tube gets gradually less as the source is moved away from the tube.

3. γ-RADIATION

These rays can be most easily detected with a GM tube. The radiation is very weakly ionizing and cannot be detected in a diffusion cloud chamber.

γ-rays need a considerable thickness of lead (about 1m) to stop the radiation completely.

A γ-source obeys an inverse-square law in air, that is, moving the source twice as far from the detector reduces the intensity to one quarter; moving it three times as far away reduces the intensity to one ninth. This suggests that γ-rays spread in all directions round the source and are not absorbed by air.

9.10 NATURE OF α- AND β-PARTICLES AND γ-RAYS

Experiments have shown that α-particles consist of a stream of relatively heavy particles of positive charge 2e, where e is the numerical value of the charge on the electron. They are nuclei of helium, that is, atoms of helium which have been stripped of two electrons. A helium nucleus consists of 2 protons and 2 neutrons – 4 neuclons in total. So with the notation discussed on p.290, an α-particle could be written as $_2^4\alpha$, or $_2^4He$.

β-particles are fast moving electrons. They are very light, having a mass of about $\frac{1}{2000}$th the mass of a proton. They are negatively charged and carry a charge of $-e$, where $e = 1.6 \times 10^{-19}C$.

γ-rays are not particles, but are electromagnetic waves of extremely short wavelength, less than 10^{-10} m (p.158).

9.11 EFFECT OF A MAGNETIC FIELD

α-particles are heavy and move at high speeds such as 10^6 m/s. They are therefore difficult to deflect in a magnetic field. If a strong magnetic field is applied at right angles to the path of α-particles they are deflected slightly in a direction predicted by Fleming's Left-hand Rule, (p.237). The second finger points along the direction of movement of positive charge, that is, along the path of the α-particles. Since Fleming's Left-hand Rule correctly predicts the way they are deflected, the α-particles must be positively charged.

Although β-particles are fast moving, they are so much lighter than α-particles that they are easy to deflect in a magnetic field. A magnetic field, directed at right angles to a stream of β-particles, gives a direction of deflection opposite to Fleming's Left-hand Rule, showing that β-particles carry a negative charge. Fig 9.3 shows an experiment illustrating the magnetic deflection of β-particles.

Fig 9.3 Deflection of β-particles in a magnetic field

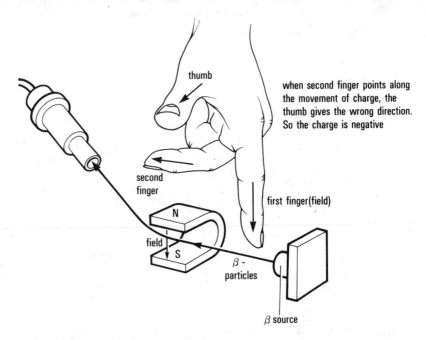

when second finger points along the movement of charge, the thumb gives the wrong direction. So the charge is negative

thumb

second finger

first finger(field)

N

field

S

β - particles

β source

Since γ-rays are uncharged they are not affected by a magnetic field.

9.12 HEALTH HAZARDS

We have already mentioned the safety precautions needed when using radioactive sources in the laboratory. Most of the health hazards are because of the danger of damaging internal organs. α-particles which only penetrate small distances in solid materials are likely to be less dangerous than β-particles or γ-rays. If, however, any α-source finds it way into the body, for example by eating contaminated food or breathing radioactive dust, then the α-particles can be very dangerous. Sources of β-particles and γ-rays are always dangerous.

It is therefore important to make sure the environment does not become contaminated with radioactive material. Problems related to this are dealt with in the section on nuclear reactors (p.302). Workers in laboratories and nuclear processing plants such as Sellafield must also be protected from radiation. To protect against γ-rays thick blocks of lead, iron or high density concrete are used to reduce the intensity of the rays. Such blocks will easily absorb α- and β-particles. Workers also wear small badges which contain photographic material which is sensitive to the radiations. The film is regularly developed to check whether the worker has been exposed to a level of radiation which might be dangerous.

9.13 SUMMARY OF PROPERTIES

Fig 9.4 summarizes the properties of the three types of radiation.

Radiation	α	β	γ
Ionizing power	large	medium	small
Penetrating power	thin sheets of paper	several mm of aluminium	many cm of lead
Effect of magnetic field	small, in direction expected for +ve charge	large, in direction expected for -ve charge	no deflection
Charge	$+2e$	$-e$	zero
Mass (electron mass =1)	about 8000	1	zero
Nature	Helium nuclei	electrons	electromagnetic waves

Fig 9.4 Properties of radiations

CHECK LIST ▶ Make sure you can answer the following questions:

1 Write out a table such as Fig 9.4 from memory.
2 What experiment shows that β-particles are negatively charged?
3 Why are α-particles relatively harmless when the source is outside the body?

9.14 THE NUCLEAR ATOM

We have said that the atom consists of a tiny nucleus consisting of protons and neutrons, with a cloud of electrons moving in the bulk of the space of the atom. Evidence for this first came from an experiment performed (1909) by Geiger and Marsden who were students of Lord Rutherford. The apparatus is shown in Fig 9.5. α-particles from the

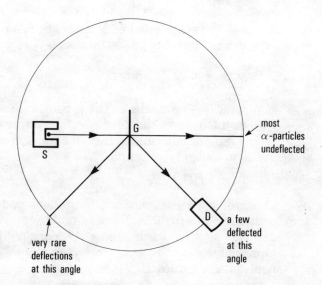

Fig 9.5 Geiger's and Marsden's experiment on α-particle scattering

source S were fired at a very thin sheet of gold foil G. A detector D was used to find out how many α-particles were deflected at various angles. The whole apparatus was kept in a vacuum, as α-particles only have a short range in air.

Two important facts emerged from the experiment.

1 Most of the α-particles went straight through the gold foil with very little deflection. This means that most of the atom must be empty, and atoms could **not** be thought of as hard spheres (like snooker balls).

2 A small number of α-particles were deflected by large angles, and some even bounced back from the gold foil.
These observations can be explained by the nuclear idea of the atom. Most α-particles only pass near electrons in the bulk of the atom. Electrons are too light to deflect the α-particles from their path. This explains observation 1. Occasionally, however, the α-particle which is positively charged would come near to the heavy positively charged nucleus. The positive charges repel and the α-particle is pushed out of its path by the heavy gold nucleus. This explains observation 2.

9.15 NUCLEAR CHANGES IN RADIOACTIVE EMISSION

1. α-EMISSION

An α-particle is a helium nucleus, ^4_2He. It thus contains 2 protons and 2 neutrons. When an α-particle is emitted from the nucleus of an atom the proton number decreases by 2 and the nucleon number decreases by 4. So.

$$Z \rightarrow Z-2 \text{ and } A \rightarrow A-4$$

An example is the emission of an α-particle from the nucleus of $^{238}_{92}\text{U}$:

$$^{238}_{92}\text{U} \rightarrow ^4_2\alpha + ^{234}_{90}\text{Th}$$

Because the proton number decreases by 2, a new element, thorium, (Th), is formed whose proton number is 90.

2. β-EMISSION

A β-particle is an electron. The β-particle has little mass compared with a proton, and a charge of −1e. So it can be written $^0_{-1}e$.

The β-particle is emitted from the nucleus by a neutron changing into a proton and an electron:

$$^1_0n \rightarrow ^1_1H + ^0_{-1}e$$

The proton (^1_1H) remains in the nucleus and the electron ($^0_{-1}e$) is emitted as a β-particle. There is no change in the total number of particles in the nucleus, and so A remains the same. The proton number increases by 1 as there is one more proton (and one less neutron) in the nucleus. So

$$Z \rightarrow Z+1 \text{ and } A \rightarrow A$$

An example of β-emission can be written:

$$^{234}_{90}\text{Th} \rightarrow ^{\ 0}_{-1}\text{e} + ^{234}_{91}\text{Pr}$$

The proton number increases by 1, so a new element Pr, protoactinium, is formed with proton number 91.

3. γ-EMISSION

This does not affect the number of particles in the nucleus. The γ-ray carries away energy from a nucleus which is left with an excess of energy after α- or β-particles are emitted. So A and Z **do not change** in γ-emission.

WORKED EXAMPLE

The nucleus of $^{238}_{92}\text{U}$ emits an α-particle. The resulting nucleus is itself radioactive and emits a β-particle. The next series of nuclei are also radioactive giving, in succession, one β-particle, five α-particles, two β-particles, one α-particle, two β-particles and finally one α-particle. The final nucleus is not radioactive. Calculate its nucleon number and proton number.

There are a total of 8 α-emissions. Due to these A will decrease by $8 \times 4 = 32$. Z will decrease by $8 \times 2 = 16$.

There are a total of 6 β-emissions. These do not change A, but increase Z by 6.

So the net decrease of A is 32 (from the α-emissions). The change in Z is a decrease of 16 (from the α-emissions) and an increase of 6 (from the β-emissions). This is a net decrease of 10.

So $^{238}_{92}\text{U}$ becomes $^{238-32}_{92-10}\text{X} = ^{206}_{82}\text{X}$. The new element formed, X, is actually an isotope of lead with nucleon number 206, and proton number 82.

9.16 HALF-LIFE

When the nucleus of a radioactive isotope emits its α- or β-particle it is said to **decay**. The time taken for half the atoms initially present to decay into their new element is called the **half-life**. For example the half-life of $^{234}_{91}\text{Pr}$ is 72 seconds. It decays by emitting β-particles into $^{234}_{92}\text{U}$. If a pure specimen of protoactinium is taken, then after 72 seconds the specimen will contain half protoactinium and half uranium atoms. After a further 72 seconds half of the remaining protoactinium will decay leaving one quarter protoactinium and three-quarters uranium, and so on.

A graph of the count rate plotted against time for a radioactive source is shown in Fig 9.6. The half-life, T, can be found from the graph as indicated. It is the time for the initial count rate to fall to $\frac{1}{2}$; or for the count rate to fall from $\frac{1}{2}$ to $\frac{1}{4}$; or from $\frac{1}{4}$ to $\frac{1}{8}$ and so on.

Fig 9.6 Half-life

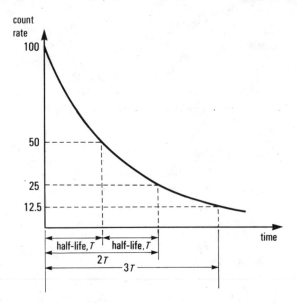

The graph obtained in any experiment is unlikely to have all the points falling on a smooth curve since radioactive decay is a **random** process. For this reason the count rate shows small random variations from the average value.

WORKED EXAMPLE

A sample of protoactinium with a half-life of 72 seconds decays by α-emission into uranium. What fraction of the protoactinium remains after 6 minutes?

6 minutes is 360 seconds. This is $\frac{360}{72}$, or 5 half-lives. After each half-life the amount remaining is halved. So after 5 half-lives the amount remaining is

$$\tfrac{1}{2}\times\tfrac{1}{2}\times\tfrac{1}{2}\times\tfrac{1}{2}\times\tfrac{1}{2}=\tfrac{1}{32}$$

of the original amount.

CHECK LIST ▶   Make sure you can answer the following questions.

1.   What two experimental facts most clearly support the nuclear model of the atom?
2.   In the decay of bismuth, $^{214}_{83}\text{Bi}$ into polonium $^{214}_{84}\text{Po}$, what type of particle is emitted?
3.   In the decay of polonium $^{214}_{84}\text{Po}$, into lead $^{210}_{82}\text{Pb}$, what type of particle is emitted?
4.   A radioactive isotope decays so that $\frac{1}{8}$ of it remains after 60 s. What is its half-life?

9.17 USES OF RADIOACTIVE ISOTOPES

1. TRACER TECHNIQUES

Radioactive isotopes are used as tracers in medicine, industry and research. In medicine some weakly radioactive isotopes can be swallowed or injected into the human body. The amounts of radioactivity are too small to cause any ill effects. An example is the use of an isotope of iodine, $^{131}_{53}I$. Chemically this behaves in the same way as normal non-radioactive iodine which is absorbed by the thyroid gland. Radioactive detectors can be used to see if the radioactive iodine is absorbed correctly by the gland.

Radioactive isotopes can be introduced into pipes to detect leaks. Radioactivity found outside the pipe will indicate the whereabouts of the leak. Short half-life isotopes are used for this purpose.

In marine research radioactive isotopes can be introduced into the sea-bed. The movement of this material can then be traced by studying the movement of the radioactivity.

2. STERILIZATION

Medical instruments such as scalpels or syringes are sterilized using radioactive isotopes. The instruments are wrapped in sealed containers. These are then subjected to an intense beam of γ-rays from an isotope cobalt-60, $^{60}_{27}Co$. The γ-rays destroy any bacteria or micro-organisms in the sealed containers.

3. THICKNESS MEASUREMENT

Sheet materials will absorb β-particles. The thicker the material the greater will be the absorption. The intensity of β-particles received one side of a sheet material from a source placed on the other side can therefore be used to indicate the thickness of the sheet. This can be used to control the thickness of materials during their manufacture. If the count rate is too low, then the sheet is too thick. An electric signal can be used to control the machinery to decrease the thickness. If the count rate is too high the control signal to the machine would increase the thickness.

The thickness of plating on tins can also be checked by measuring the amount of β-particles reflected back along their own path by the plating.

CHECK LIST ▶ Make sure you can answer the following question.

1　List six different uses of radioactive isotopes.

9.18 NUCLEAR FISSION – CHAIN REACTION

When a nucleus of an atom of uranium-235 ($^{235}_{92}U$) is bombarded by a neutron, the nucleus splits into two roughly equal parts. This process is called **nuclear fission**. A great deal of energy is released – the two smaller nuclei produced (called the fission-fragments) move with very high speed, and electromagnetic energy is radiated. In addition two or three further neutrons are produced. If these neutrons strike nuclei they may each cause fission. This can continue and produce a **chain reaction**, as shown in Fig 9.7.

Fig 9.6 Chain reaction

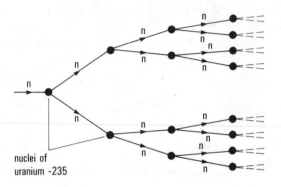

nuclei of
uranium -235

In an atomic bomb a chain reaction of this sort occurs. The energy released is enormous and extremely rapid. The source of the energy lies in the conversion of matter into energy. The mass of the uranium-235 nucleus is **slightly greater** than the combined masses of the fission fragments and extra neutrons. The mass lost is converted into energy – for each kilogram of mass lost nearly 10^{17}J of energy are produced.

9.19 NUCLEAR POWER REACTORS

In a nuclear reactor a controlled chain reaction occurs. To achieve this three essential components are needed.

1 **The nuclear fuel.** The uranium is sealed into rods. Groups of these rods are held together to form a fuel element.

2 **Control rods.** These are rods of boron- or cadmium-steel which asbsorb neutrons.

3 **The moderator.** This is a large core, often of graphite, which contains the fuel elements and the control rods.

The moderator slows down (or 'moderates') the speed of the neutrons. They are then more likely to cause fission before they escape from the core. Notice that the moderator reduces the speed of the neutrons. It does not moderate the reaction – on the contrary it allows it to happen. The control rods can be lowered into the core to absorb neutrons if the chain reaction is proceeding too quickly. They can be raised out of the core to increase the reaction rate.

The energy released in the form of heat is removed from the reactor by a coolant which passes through a heat exchanger. The coolant may be carbon dioxide gas at high pressure (in Advanced Gas-cooled Reactors – AGRs), or it may be high pressure water (in Pressurized Water Reactors – PWRs). The heat removed from the reactor is used to produce steam which then drives a turbine, as in conventional power stations.

A diagram of an Advanced Gas-cooled Reactor is shown in Fig 9.8.

Fig 9.8 Advanced gas-cooled reactor

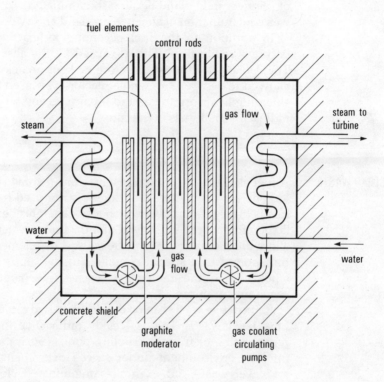

CHECK LIST ▶

Make sure you can answer the following questions.

1 What is a chain reaction?
2 What is the source of energy in nuclear fission?
3 What are the three main parts of a nuclear reactor?
4 Which part of the reactor slows the neutrons?
5 Which part of the reactor absorbs neutrons?

9.20 PROBLEMS OF NUCLEAR POWER GENERATION

The fuel used for nuclear power station fuel elements does not contain pure uranium-235. There is therefore no danger of a power station exploding like an atomic bomb. The dangers from nuclear power arise mainly from the fact that the fission fragments are radioactive. They must not be released into the air, and require careful processing when removed from the reactor.

At Chernobyl (in the USSR) in 1986 a series of operator errors led to the core overheating. There was a chemical explosion of the graphite which released a considerable amount of radioactivity into the air. Among the fission fragments carried with the radioactive cloud was Strontium-90. This radioactive isotope of strontium has a half-life of about 30 years. It is absorbed by grass, and so finds its way into animals which feed from grass. Following Chernobyl large numbers of reindeer in Lapland became contaminated. To a lesser extent there was contamination of sheep in Scotland and Wales.

In addition to the fuel becoming radioactive, the coolant also becomes radioactive. This is caused by the absorption of neutrons. The coolant itself must therefore be kept in a closed system and not allowed to escape. The whole reactor is encased in massive concrete shielding to absorp the α- and β-particles and γ-rays produced by the radioactive materials in the core.

9.21 NUCLEAR WASTE

A fuel element can remain in a reactor for some years before it ceases to generate heat. After that time it is removed from the reactor. The fuel is highly radioactive which also generates heat. The fuel element is therefore stored for several months under water in a special pool to allow the radioactivity to decrease and the element to cool. It is then transported in a special container to the reprocessing plant at Sellafield. Here the radioactive waste is separated out, as is the remaining uranium.

Radioactive waste can be divided into two categories:

1 **Low level waste.** This is weakly radioactive material produced in reprocessing or from the cooling ponds. Such materials are released into the environment under strict Government control. Any solid low-level waste, for example contaminated clothing, is buried at special sites.

2 **High level waste.** This is the highly radioactive fission fragments and the cladding of the fuel elements. All high level waste is stored. In liquid form the waste is stored in special tanks. Since the high level of radioactivity generates heat, these tanks must be cooled. The waste can also be turned into a glass like material and stored in stainless steel containers, also cooled. After about 100 years the radioactivity will decrease sufficiently to allow the disposal of the waste permanently, for example on the ocean bed.

9.22 NUCLEAR FUSION

In nuclear fission a heavy nucleus splits into two. There is a small decrease in mass and a resulting release of energy. It is also possible to turn matter into energy by fusing two light nuclei together. For example when two nuclei of deuterium (heavy hydrogen) fuse together there is a decrease in mass and a release of energy. This is called **nuclear fusion**.

To make nuclear fusion occur, the nuclei must get very close together. Since the nuclei are both positively charged they repel one another, and it is only when the particles are moving very fast indeed that they can get near enough to fuse. To achieve this, very high temperature, about 1 000 000 K are needed. To produce temperatures of this sort in the laboratory requires the passage of electric currents through the gas to heat it. Research is currently going on to attempt to harness the energy from nuclear fusion – the JET (Joint European Torus) project is one example.

Nuclear fusion is the source of energy from the sun, where light elements fuse together and so release energy. It is also the source of energy from a hydrogen atomic weapon. Here the high temperatures are reached by the explosion of a fission weapon.

CHECK LIST ▶

Make sure you can answer the following questions.

1 How are radioactive emissions prevented from escaping from the core of a reactor?
2 Why must the coolant be kept in a closed system?
2 What is low-level waste?
4 How is low-level waste disposed of?
5 What is high-level waste?
6 Why must high-level waste be stored a long time before it can be permanently disposed of?

SUMMARY

A. YOU SHOULD KNOW

1 Atoms are made up of protons, neutrons and electrons.
2 The relative charges on the proton, neutron and electron.
3 The approximate relative masses of the proton, neutron and electron.
4 The meaning of the terms proton number and nucleon number.
5 Radioactive decay is produced in the nucleus.
6 The names of the three types of radiation.
7 Radioactivity is unaffected by changes in temperature, pressure or chemical composition.
8 There is an ever-present background radiation.
9 The precautions needed in using radioactive sources in school laboratories.
10 The relative ionizing powers of α-, β- and γ-radiations.
11 The relative penetrating powers of the radiations.
12 The effects on A and Z of α- and β-decay.
13 The meaning of the term 'half-life'.
14 The uses of radioactive isotopes in tracers, sterilization, and thickness control.
15 The meaning of the term 'nuclear fission'.

16   The energy in fission comes from the conversion of a small amount of matter into energy.
17   The basic structure of a nuclear reactor.
18   The problems which accompany the generation of electricity by a nuclear reactor.
19   The meaning of the terms 'high- and low-level nuclear waste'.
20   The meaning of the term 'nuclear fusion'.

B. YOU SHOULD UNDERSTAND

1   How to calculate the number of neutrons in the nucleus from the nucleon and proton numbers.
2   That radioactivity produces ionization and that this is used in its detection.
3   The operation of a cloud chamber.
4   How to find the count rate from measurements of total count and time.
5   Why α- and β-particles are deflected in opposite directions in a magnetic field, and why β-particles are deflected most.
6   How to take account of the background count in radioactivity experiments.
7   The evidence from Geiger's and Marsden's experiment which leads to the nuclear model of the atom.
8   The mechanism of a chain reaction.
9   The function of the fuel element, moderator and control rods in a nuclear reactor.

C. APPLICATIONS.

You should be able to:
1   describe the structure of the atom.
2   explain what is meant by positive and negative ions.
3   explain what is meant by an isotope.
4   describe the health hazards of radioactivity.
5   summarize the properties of α- and β-particles and γ-rays in the form of a table.
6   determine the half-life from information about the count-rate at various times.
7   describe the disposal of high- and low-level waste.

QUESTIONS 9. ATOMIC STRUCTURE AND RADIOACTIVITY

MULTIPLE CHOICE QUESTIONS

The following are types of particle:

A neutron   B proton   C electron   D helium nucleus

1   Which particle is identical with an α-particle?

2   Which particle is identical with a β-particle?
3   Which particle causes the fission of a uranium-235 nucleus?

$^{235}_{92}U$ is an isotope of uranium. Which of the following is equal to
4   the number of neutrons in the nucleus?
5   the number of protons in the nucleus?

   A   327   B   235   C   143   D   92

The following terms are concerned with a nuclear reactor.
   A   moderator   B   fuel element   C   heat exchanger
     D   control rod
Which of these
6   enables the operator to change the rate at which the reactor produces heat?
7   slows down neutrons to enable fission to take place?
8   is stored in a water pool after removal from the reactor?

The following are uses of radioactive isotopes.

   A   Leak detection
   B   Thickness testing
   C   Sterilization of medical equipment
   D   Medical diagnosis

Which of these
9   MUST use β-particles?
10   MUST use a radioactive source with a short half-life.

The following are experiments concerned with radioactivity.

   A   Scattering of α-particles by gold foil
   B   Measurement of count rate at various times
   C   Deflection of radioactivity in a magnetic field
   D   Observation of radioactive particles in a cloud chamber

Which of these
11   shows that β-particles are negatively charged?
12   supports the nuclear model of the atom?

SHORT ANSWER QUESTIONS

13   Complete the following table:

	α	β	γ
Mass (electron = 1)	about 8000		
Charge		−e	
Absorption by 1 mm of aluminium		Some but not all absorbed	
Nature of radiation	Helium nucleus		

14   An experiment with a radioactive source is set up as shown in Fig 9A.

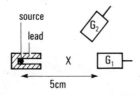

Fig 9A

The following observations are made:

(i) A piece of lead placed at X causes the count rate at detectors G_1 and G_2 to become zero.

(ii) A piece of paper placed at X significantly reduces the count rate at G_1

(iii) When a magnet is positioned so there is a magnetic field at X at right angles to the plane of the diagram, there is a large increase in count rate at G_2.

(a)   Explain which observation shows that the source produces no γ-radiation.

(b)   Explain which observation shows that β-particles are present.

(c)   Explain which observation shows that α-particles MAY be present.

(d)   Describe how you would try to decide for certain whether α-particles were emitted by the source or not.

(e)   Why are radioactive sources used in school laboratories replaced WITH TONGS in a LEAD CONTAINER as soon as the experiment is finished?

15   In measuring the thickness of cardboard using a radioactive source explain

(a)   why β-particles are more suitable than α-particles.

(*b*)   why β-particles are more suitable than γ-rays.
A graph of count rate against time is shown in Fig 9B.

Fig 9B

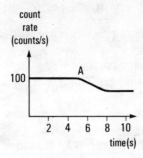

(*c*)   Describe what is happening to the thickness of the cardboard during this time.
(*d*)   In an automatic system to keep the thickness constant, what would happen at A if the count rate started to fall?

16   In an experiment to determine the half life of an isotope of protoactinium a graph of count rate against time is plotted, as shown in Fig 9C.

Fig 9C

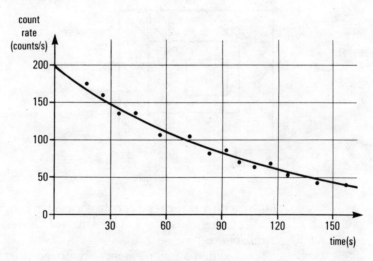

The graph shows a smooth curve with a scatter of points near to the curve.
(*a*)   Why do the points not lie exactly on the line?
(*b*)   Explain the meaning of the terms
        (i) isotope
        (ii) half-life.
(*c*)   Use the graph to determine the half-life of this isotope explaining your method.
(*d*)   Some radioactive isotopes produced in nuclear fission have long half-lives. Why is it particularly important that these are not allowed to escape into the environment?

17   The equation below indicates a possible reaction of uranium-235 in a nuclear reactor.

$$^{234}_{92}U + ^{1}_{0}n \rightarrow ^{148}_{57}La + ^{Y}_{X}Br + ^{1}_{0}n + ^{1}_{0}n + ^{1}_{0}n$$

The two fission fragments produced are isotopes of Lanthanum and Bromine.

(a)   What are the values of X and Y?

(b)   What do the numbers X and Y tell you about the nucleus of the isotope of bromine?

(c)   What is the name of the process represented by this equation?

(d)   Explain how the reactions of this kind can produce a 'chain reaction'.

(e)   The reaction is most likely to occur if the neutrons are moving slowly. Name the device in the reactor which slows the neutrons, and give an example of a material used for this purpose.

(f)   What are control rods in a reactor? Explain their purpose.

18   Fig 9D shows a simplified diagram of a nuclear reactor.

Fig 9D

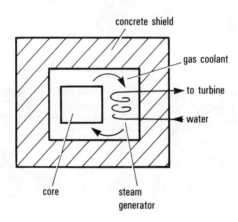

(a)   Why is the reactor core encased in concrete?

(b)   Why must the gas coolant not be allowed to escape into the atmosphere?

(c)   When a fuel element is removed from a reactor it is kept for some months in a pool of water. Why is this necessary?

(d)   Explain the difference between high- and low-level nuclear waste.

(e)   How is each form of waste disposed of?

ANSWERS

Answers are given below to multiple choice questions and those with a numerical answer.

QUESTIONS 1A. MOTION (PAGE 35)

1	C							
2	D							
3	B							
4	C							
5	C							
6	C							
7	(a)	20 m/s	(b)	20 m				
8	10 m/s, 40 m/s, 7.5 m/s^2							
9	2 m/s^2, ⅔ m/s^2, 800 m							
10	100 m, 10 m/s, 15 s, 16.7 m/s							
11	(a)	10 m/s	(b)	3 s	(c)	45 m	(d)	6 s
12	(a)	9.9 m/s^2	(b)	3.8 m/s				

QUESTIONS 1B. FORCE AND ACCELERATION (PAGE 44)

1	D						
2	C						
3	B						
4	D						
5	B						
6	A						
7	(a)	4 kg					
8	(a)	500 N	(b)	2 m/s^2			
9	(a)	1100 kg	(b)	500 N	(c)	0.9 m/s^2	
10	(b)	190 N	(c)	200 N			

QUESTIONS 1C. WORK ENERGY AND POWER (PAGE 58)

1	D					
2	C					
3	C					
4	A					
5	B					
6	(a)	1500 J	(c)	7.7 m/s		
7	(a)	600 W				
8	(a)	37 500 J	(b)	75 000 J	(c)	7500 W

9	(a)	50 J	(b)	10 J, 40 J	(c)	12.6 m/s
10	(a)	0.12 J				
11	(a)	2 J	(b)	1.6 J	(c)	1.2 J

QUESTIONS 2A.
MOMENTS, CENTRE OF
GRAVITY, PARALLEL
FORCES (PAGE 76)

1	C			
2	D			
3	B			
4	C			
5	A			
6	A			
7	(a)	50 N	(b)	80 N
8	(a)	20 N	(b)	160 N
9	(b)	20 N	(c)	30 N
11	1.3 m			
12	1700 N			
13	(b)	15 N		
14	Approx by drawing (a) 19 N (b) 90°			
15	(a)	(i) SPF (ii) Q (iii) R (b)	(i) 500 N	

QUESTIONS 2B.
PRESSURE OF LIQUIDS
AND GASES (PAGE 91)

1	D			
2	A			
3	C			
4	B			
5	D			
6	D			
7	$20 \, N/cm^2$			
8	(a)	$25 \, N/m^2$	(b)	$100 \, N/m^2$
9	60 000 N			
10	101 500 Pa			
11	2000 N			
13	(a)	13 600 Pa	(b)	1 360 m
14	150 kPa			
15	20 m			

QUESTIONS 2C.
MATTER AND
STRUCTURE.
MOLECULAR THEORY
(PAGE 100)

1	B			
2	D			
3	A			
4	C			
5	D			
6	B			
7	(a)	$1.3 \, g/cm^3$	(b)	43 g

QUESTIONS 3A.	1	D
THERMOMETRY.	2	B
EXPANSION OF SOLIDS	3	C
AND LIQUIDS (PAGE 112)	4	B
	5	A
	6	B
	7	44 divisions
	9	(a) X

QUESTIONS 3B. GASES.	1	C
MOLECULAR THEORY	2	D
(PAGE 119)	3	A
	4	44.4 kPa
	6	(a) 192 kPa (b) 27°C
	7	301 litres, 57 g
	8	A
	9	C
	10	B

QUESTIONS 3C.	1	C
CONDUCTION,	2	D
CONVECTION,	3	A
RADIATION (PAGE 127)	4	B
	5	D

QUESTIONS 3D. HEAT	1	A
CAPACITY. LATENT HEAT	2	D
EVAPORATION (PAGE	3	A
140)	4	C
	5	A
	6	(a) 6 000 J (b) 45°C
	7	67 200 J
	8	(a) (i) 46 000 J (ii) 47 680 J (b) 230 g
	9	(a) 0.84 kg
	10	(a) 600 J/kgK

QUESTIONS 4. WAVES	1	B
(PAGE 161)	2	A
	3	A

4	C	
5	D	
6	C	
7	C	
8	B	
9	D	
10	B	
11	C	
12	D	
13	(a)	10 cm/s
17	(b)	140 m

QUESTIONS 5. OPTICS (PAGE 194)

1	C			
2	B			
3	C			
4	D			
5	C			
6	C			
7	80°			
10	(b)	10 cm		
11	(a)	60 cm	(b)	12 cm

QUESTIONS 6. ELECTRICITY (PAGE 224)

1	B							
2	B							
3	B							
4	D							
5	A							
6	D							
7	C							
8	A							
9	D							
10	D							
11	B							
12	C							
16	(a)	300 Ω	(b)	0.02 A = 20 mA	(c)	2 V		
	(d)	200 Ω						
18	(a)	5 A	(b)	100 W	(c)	2.5 A	(d)	50 W
	(e)	25 W						
19	(d)	13 A	(e)	£3.60				

QUESTIONS 7. MAGNETISM AND ELECTROMAGNETISM (PAGE 253)		
1	C	
2	A	
3	A	
4	C	
5	C	
6	A	
7	C	
8	A	
9	A	
10	D	
11	A	
12	B	

18 (b) 400 (c) 48 W (d) 48 W

QUESTIONS 8. ELECTRONICS (PAGE 280)		
1	B	
2	A	
3	D	
4	C	
5	D	
6	B	
7	C	
8	B	
9	C	
10	B	
11	C	
12	C	

14 (a) 4 V (b) 50 Hz

19 (a)

A	B	C	D	E
0	0	1	1	1
1	0	0	1	0
0	1	1	0	0
1	1	0	0	0

(b)

A	B	C
0	0	0
1	0	1
0	1	1
1	1	1

20 (a)

	R	O	G
1	0	0	1
2	0	1	0
3	1	0	0
4	1	1	0

(b) (i) 3 (ii) 4 (iii) 1

QUESTIONS 9. ATOMIC STRUCTURE AND RADIOACTIVITY (PAGE 306)		
1	D	
2	C	
3	A	
4	C	
5	D	

6	D	
7	A	
8	B	
9	B	
10	A	
11	C	
12	A	
16	(c)	70 s
17	(a)	X = 85, Y = 35

INDEX